Sincerely,

Marcus Bach

REPORT TO PROTESTANTS

REPORT TO PROTESTANTS

A Personal Investigation of the Weakness,
Need, Vision, and Great Potential of
Protestants Today

BY

MARCUS BACH

Author of

THEY HAVE FOUND A FAITH

THE BOBBS-MERRILL COMPANY

PUBLISHERS

INDIANAPOLIS · NEW YORK

First Edition

To my colleague,
M. Willard Lampe,
Administrative Director of
the School of Religion at the
State University of Iowa,
and
to the many men and women of good faith
who befriended me during my journey
over Church Street, U.S.A.

CONTENTS

REPORT TO PROTESTANTS

CHAPTER ONE

Fairfield

A MINISTER is a hero in a community twice: the day he comes and the day he goes. I was going. The clammy basement of Fairfield's Evangelical Church was crowded with nearly all of my hundred and forty parishioners. Farmers had hurried through their chores and townsfolk had closed shop early to stage the best and biggest church supper of my two-year pastorate.

The families who never failed to fill their pews on Sunday morning lined the tables near the platform where I sat with the nine members of the church council. Less-familiar faces, those rarely seen at a regular church service, smiled warmly from seats of lesser honor across the crowded room. Emphasizing the high importance of the occasion, old Doctor Reynolds, who never came to the worship services, was there, ready with his usual criticism of all religious activities. Though his personal faith was obscured by skepticism, his was a rich religious heritage, steeped in the memory of a circuit-riding preacher father. Old Doc sat slouched in a high-back chair near the door, disconsolately yielding his nearly eighty years to another community proceeding. With a sickbed expression of solemn judgment, he rubbed his pince-nez against his pock-marked cheek and squinted ruefully in my direction. With sharp thrusts of his mawkish eyes, he queried: "Who's the patient? You or the congregation?"

The meal had been liberally seasoned with final expressions of praise and regret:

"You don't really want to go, do you? Who'll we ever get to take your place?"

"If you'd only stay, we'd show you how regular we could be at the services!"

"That's the trouble with a town of four hundred. It's only a steppingstone to something better."

When the last coffee cup had been drained, and the dishes were stacked in baskets on the long plank tables—family by family—the members of the church council formally spoke their pieces. One after another, the men pried into the past with five-minute talks on the state of the church and the will of the Lord for this Kansas community. The honor of making the final speech was conferred upon the president of the board, a prosperous cattleman whose extensive holdings gave him priority in congregational affairs. After lazily uncoiling his long, gangling figure from his chair, he suddenly became a gifted master of ceremonies.

"Young man," he began, smiling benignly, "this is for you." He held up in his toil-beaten hands a dingy salt sack, heavy with coins. Then he motioned for me to rise and handed me the moneybag with as much pride as if it were a blue ribbon for one of his own grand champions.

"You've been with us for two years," he continued. "We've tried to keep you here and treat you right. But you say there's more of an opportunity in Omaha, so I guess it's good-by. That sack, if the committee counted right, holds exactly eighty-six dollars and forty-three cents. If it wasn't for this depression we've just run into, it would be double that and then some. Far as I'm concerned, if you should want to change your mind and stay with us, we'll double it anyhow. I'm just a cattleman, but it looks to me as if you're leaving at a time when Fairfield needs you most. The Baptists over there—" he said this with a condescending toss of his head in the direction of the church across the corner—"get their new man next Sunday. Maybe if you two fellows got together, you could do great things for this town."

Then, with a shrug of finality, he turned grimly to his audience. "Well, folks, we've done our best. Now I guess we'll just have to leave him in the hands of the Lord!"

Hours later I sat alone with my moneybag and shipping crates in the squatty, cupolaed manse where I had lived for the past two years. The last car had churned homeward through the heavy gravel of the highway that ran past my door. The janitor had turned off the churchyard light. Wearily the hot Kansas wind blew the brown scent of scorched corn in through the open windows, and the parsonage suddenly seemed heavy with emptiness. My "library" was securely nailed down inside four orange crates; my Big Ben ticked off the long minutes from within a sturdy box marked FRAGILE; the rest of my earthly luggage was packed for moving in a set of traveling bags and a new wardrobe trunk. But the words of the cattleman haunted the deserted rooms—"Maybe you two fellows could do great things."

He had voiced a challenge for the future, but to me it was a judgment against the past. I did not measure my success by the fervent congregational farewell. The maternal sobbing and the sentimental singing of "Blest Be the Tie That Binds" had left me unmoved. These were obligatory scenes in the passing drama of any young man's first pastorate. Neither was my people's co-operation in the church's program an adequate yardstick. As a matter of principle, they had always met their denominational apportionment and, despite the depression, they had just re-decorated the church. The well-organized women's societies could have towed the church along without me at the helm. Attendance at services was a wind-and-weather matter, not a question of my personal success. The Sunday-school record was a source of pride for the superintendent, not me: Enrollment, 137; Attendance Today, 82; Attendance Last Sunday, 83; Attendance a Year Ago, 80. The catechetical classes which memorized the Heidelberg Catechism, short version, owed their existence not to my persuasion, but to incessant parental battering. The membership of the church had increased during the past two years because, in keeping with tradition, I had thrown out the denominational net for the annual draft of teen-agers each Eastertime.

To rouse a drowsy audience I needed only to apply the parables of Jesus in the easy idiom of Kansas farm experiences. The majority of my people worked with the land and the land, like God, blessed and chastized them. They had accepted my theology as they accepted the hot winds, and in return the faithful ladies of the congregation had looked after my personal well-being. The past two years had been spun on a series of dinners in which one hostess outdid the next. I was sure that I had eaten more fried chicken to the glory of God than any preacher in the Sunflower State.

But failure haunted me as I walked through the empty parsonage rooms: I evaluated my Fairfield career by the spiritual distance between the Baptist and the Evangelical churches. Though I had tried, I had been unable to cut that distance down. It was a geographical fact and a social reality. The Baptists had their corner and we had ours, and there was no need thinking that I could work both sides of the street. I had come to town imaginative and eager, well aware, but unwilling to believe, that for seventy years two Protestant congregations had been struggling along in a town of four hundred, refusing to work together. Into this divided world I had brought big ideas of church union, born of rebellion against the denominational bigotry which I had witnessed as a boy in the unholy wars between small-town congregations.

In my home town there were eight Protestant churches within a two-mile radius. But union services had always been impossible. Whenever the suggestion was made, my ministerial uncle and cousins and great-uncles and great-cousins of the German Reformed Church reiterated their objections: the Presbyterians and the Unitarians were too liberal; the Mennonites and the Lutherans and the Baptists were too conservative; the Methodists and Congregationalists had a questionable theology. About the only thing upon which these non-Roman Catholic churches could agree was that they should all be against the Roman Catholics. And they were. The big stone church-with-the-cross-on-the-top was taboo. A strict and clear-cut denominationalism was part of my heritage, a strong and stolid factor in my early Christian life.

Gradually I was caught between my mother's saintly devotion to the family church and my father's shrewd and canny questioning of Protestantism's many churches. His religious loyalty was vested in my mother's name, but he had his own ideas about the place where God could best be found: For her, it was in the third pew front, center section; for someone else, in a revival tent or in a Quaker meetinghouse; and, he sometimes hinted, for others it might be inside the big black doors of the church-with-the-cross-on-the-top.

But whenever I peered through the nursery windows of the family faith, I was confronted by the stern and bearded visage of Uncle August, pastor and patriarch, judge supreme at the bar of the Lord, fearless inquisitor of the Reformed faith. Often I wondered how other churches in the area could resist his unyielding doctrine. They were unyielding, too, and I came to accept this situation as the inevitable symbol of Protestant life.

This youthful condition dogged me through high-school years, but I inclined more and more to my father's views: "Let a man find God wherever he can and then take his place in the universal fellowship of believers." And during early seminary years I took my stand as a religious cosmopolite, always on the defensive against the denominationalists. I had neither the heart nor the head for theological calculus, nor the aptitude for sectarian chemistry. Ever-changing contemporary life and thought sailed by outside the study halls, while inside, unchanging creeds and symbols were perpetuated. I passed my days in jousts of verbal fencing with men whose ancient weapons scorned and shattered my modern fabrics of defense. I always lost, particularly on the question of church union. The only way I could possibly win was to flee. So at the end of three years, I fled—free, fearless and confused.

Then came the good omen. While wondering what I should do, I received a call from my preacher brother, inviting me to serve as interim pastor of a Fairfield, Kansas, congregation. This church was not affiliated with my denomination, the Reformed Church in the United States, but was a distant relative of the Evangelical Synod of North America. If the people of the Fairfield congregation were willing to risk their souls with a preacher of another denomination, they, too, must have realized the uselessness of hanging onto outmoded bigotries. My brother's explanation of the situation made my dreams for a united Protestantism suddenly seem real. My denomination and the Evangelical Synod were discussing merger. Inflamed with hope for an easy miracle, I had driven into dusty Main Street of Fairfield. When the church board invited me to stay, my denominational stock went up and interdenominationalism became a passion. Then came the growing eagerness for a local union; I would bring together the Baptist and the Evangelical churches of Fairfield. But gradually I learned that there are some mountains which simple faith cannot remove.

Throughout my first year I attributed my failure to the scholarly obstinacy of the Baptist minister. He was a remarkably tall, elderly man whose inordinate stature and whose knowledge of Fairfield after a ten-year pastorate effected a lasting diminution of my body and spirit. Never would I forget his sovereign reminder: "My boy, my boy, after you have been in the ministry as long as I——" And though he had left town six months ago, his resolute presence still guarded the enemy encampment. It was he who had gently assured me that ever since religion came to Fairfield, the Baptist Church and the Evangelical had defied each other from opposite corners across the dusty road. For nearly three-quarters of a century they had sent the same songs and prayers across the Kansas prairies on the indesinent Kansas winds, but never had they felt the power which a common heritage held for them. Families had been divided. Bitter factions had arisen. During the early years of the "tall preacher's ministry," an Evangelical broke a window in the Baptist Church, and someone retaliated by scrawling "Den of Thieves" with chalk on the black door of the Evangelical Church. He well remembered those days of open warfare and the certain afternoon, a decade ago, when he and the Evangelical minister had very nearly come to blows over the annual question of which church should get the schoolteachers.

Against the dead weight of this turbulent past and the complacent acceptance that conditions could never be improved, I had been forced into the conventional pattern of disunion. My formative plans had exhausted themselves under the duress of the town. All I had to show for my efforts was the casual admission of my church council that I got along better with the Baptists than any man the Evangelicals had ever had. Once I even spoke in the Baptist pulpit—at a funeral. Folks said I preached the best funeral sermons in the county.

"You two fellows could do great things" was a cattle call luring me to stay in these well-remembered meadows, parched though they were. I could not forget the determination which had come with me to Fairfield: to make my first pastorate a proving ground for an experiment; to persuade the Evangelicals here to become one with the Baptists. So far I had failed. Fairfield churches, had been so occupied recounting their differences that they had not had time to examine the features on which they might possibly agree. And yet there had been no broken windows during my pastorate. Conditions had improved with the years. Fleeting evidences of friendliness could be noted: a few of the Baptists had expressed regret at my decision to leave; Baptist farmers and Evangelical farmers had formed the habit of exchanging warmer greetings as the Sundays of my ministry had passed. Maybe the new Baptist man and I would be able to work the miracle. With the spade work I had done, we might grow the sturdy plant of a happy merger that would furnish seed for other communities throughout the nation.

Should I read a hint of prophecy and promise into the cattle-man's words? This was the question I wrestled with through the long night of my Fairfield farewell, and when morning came, I groggily folded up the sheets and laid them on the parsonage bed. A moving van was backing up to the spindled railing of the old front porch. The truckers tossed a thick green tarp to the dried-out lawn.

A farmer's car raced into town and came to a screeching halt before my door. The secretary of my church council hopped out.

"I telephoned the district superintendent," he called cheerfully.

"He said he'd get somebody for the Omaha church if you decided to stay!"

Providence, I was sure, had come to intervene in Fairfield's fate and mine!

The cattleman's big car drove up. "Really going?" he greeted, strolling to the porch where we stood.

It was my sign that heaven was fully concerned!

The neighbors came. The truckers were impatient. They had loaded the orange crates and asked whether the piano was to go. A woman reminded me that I had promised to have breakfast at her home. Church members gathered. A congregational meeting was rapidly forming on the parsonage lawn. The Baptist Church looked over beckoningly.

"By God!" said the truck driver. "Do we load the rest of the stuff or don't we?"

They didn't. I decided to stay. At least, somebody decided, and I stayed. The news raced through town with the speed of scandal. The women of the Ladies' Aid swarmed into the parsonage and unpacked the shipping crates, scrubbed the floors, put the pictures back on the hooks, made the bed, and brought me two pies for lunch. The following night the congregation staged a reception in the church basement and presented me with exactly double the eighty-six dollars and forty-three cents! Everybody who had been at the farewell was present—even Doctor Reynolds. Again his flaccid body was slouched in the high-back chair near the door. Again he sat patiently tapping his spectacles against his cheek, calmly counting the varying pulse beat of the community, stubbornly making his critical diagnosis.

A week later the Baptists welcomed the Reverend Larry S. Tyler, whom I accepted on sight as a likely partner for my great adventure. He was twenty-five, married, and anxious for success in his first charge. Supply preaching in small-town pastorates, together with what he had heard about the Fairfield situation, made him cautious when I presented my plans for Protestant unity. Though I assured him that his geniality and courage would thaw out any opposition we might encounter, he was wary.

"We may run into some drifts of opposition that we'll have to shovel through," he predicted knowingly. "Sentiments go deep. I know people who can talk in friendly terms about anything—except religion. They will co-operate on everything—except religion. It's strange, but true. One church for Fairfield? Well, I'm willing to sound out the prospect and see what might possibly be done."

During the weeks which followed, Larry Tyler and I were frequently seen together on Fairfield streets. The surprise of the townsfolk changed from sudden shock to silent wonder. The Baptist and Evangelical ministers had never appeared on the stage of the high-school auditorium together except for commencement exercises. Tyler and I officiated together at an Armistice Day observance and a Thanksgiving service. The non-sectarian *Clarion* weekly thought this was worthy of editorial mention. And when we served as judges at the Farmers' Institute, we made the headlines. But when the women of the Kensington Club talked of starting a community library and Tyler and I said we would take it on as an interdenominational project, a strange new faith had come to town and most of Fairfield was puzzled.

Then came the Advent season and with it the announcement of a cantata "to be presented jointly by the choirs of Fairfield's two Protestant churches." This courageous and cautiously worded publicity made clear that we were at least not attempting to include in our plans for union the small but redoubtable

Catholic Church just north of town! But it was an imprimatur on the report that two rival churches had, at long last, nonrival pastors. And for a pre-Christmas sermon I had the courage to choose the text, "Can two walk together, except they be agreed?"

I had always known that the choir was the battleground of the congregation, but never had I realized how much strategy was needed when two armies took to the field together. The Baptist soprano could sing "O Holy Night" just as effectively as the Evangelical soprano; and the daughter of the Evangelical banker could sing "The Birthday of the King" no better than the daughter of the Baptist banker. And who should play the accompaniment? Who should direct? Who should be doomed to execute the few short bars of recitative?

These were the great problems of a momentary Protestant unification. They would never have been solved without my zeal for victory and Tyler's steady hand. And also a happy coincidence. I played the violin, and Larry Tyler was an exceptionally fine choir director. By giving our respective choir leaders important solo roles, by assigning the first half of the cantata to the Baptist pianist and the last half to the Evangelical pianist, by inserting violin accompaniment in the parts that could stand an obbligato, and by leaving the directorial problems to Tyler's baton, we successfully steered the rehearsal course of *The Guiding Star*.

When the hushed and bated darkness of Christmas Eve crept over Fairfield, five hundred Christmas Christians gathered at the high school to make it a significant Holy Night and to celebrate the biggest local musicale that Fairfield had ever known. As I listened to the sectarian voices blend harmoniously in the universal music of the Christian faith, I was suddenly hopeful that music would solve the disputes that denominationalism had raised. Beyond personalities lay the thing, the spirit, the union toward which we were striving. Here was the principle which we would need to capture for any lasting unification of our people.

When the production was over and "Peace on earth, good will to men" still echoed in our hearts, some optimistic prophets predicted that this was the beginning of an era of real co-operation between the two congregations. The leader of my Ladies' Aid and a group of her intimate friends assured me I had their support "a hundred per cent." A few others expressed themselves warmly during the afterglow of enthusiasm.

But Doctor Reynolds, holding up the departing crowd as he paused at the auditorium door to shake my hand, said, "Don't get too foxy now, young fellow. It's all right to blend voices, but don't try to bring *minds* together into one chorus. That would make for as sad a night as this one has been pleasant."

Unperturbed by the old satyr's criticisms, Tyler and I forged ahead with our plans. At a party for the choirs, held in the city hall because of dissension over which church basement should be used, we secured the almost unanimous consent of the singers to present monthly union vespers. These were immediately scheduled to be held alternately in Fairfield's Protestant churches and presided over by Fairfield's two Protestant ministers. Once more, Tyler's baton, my violin, and the improving art and enthusiasm of the singers combined to produce several successful worship hours.

Once more, Old Doc was critical. One Monday morning when I met him at the bedside of an elderly parishioner, he demanded, "How far do you aim to carry this church federation business, young man?"

"Who knows?" I parried. "Our people are Protestant before they are Baptist or Evangelical."

"Untangling that thread won't get you anywhere," he calculated with an angry growl. "That doesn't even show good judgment. You can't change religions by changing names, and you can't change religious habits without knocking religion itself into a cocked hat. You can't change a man's churchgoing any more than you can change any other habit he's had all his life. My wife was Episcopalian. I guess that's Protestant of some sort, isn't it? But would you have got her to go anywhere but to the Episcopalians? You bet you wouldn't. Oh, she did try the Methodists when we were kids back home, but the Methodists shouted once in a while in those days. She couldn't get used to that. And I couldn't get used to kneeling when I went to church with her. You may get folks to sit together in a union vesper service—though I'm told even there the Baptists sit in one section and your folks in another—but that's as far as you can go. And even if you should bring the two churches together, what are you going to do with all the things the folks are used to and aren't used to? Do you think Tyler's Baptists would let you sprinkle them? And how would you feel about getting your people immersed?"

"But none of those things are essential," I argued. "What Protestantism must get used to first of all is a sense of brotherhood. If that can be accomplished, the things on which we disagree will no longer seem important."

Lugging his worn medicine case, Old Doc led me from the sickroom while he laid down his denominational law. "Churches aren't built on a sense of brotherhood, young man. They're built on things to be believed, and these things tie the people to God or whatever they're supposed to tie them to. Men aren't alike. Men don't believe alike. Things would be in a hell of a state in this world if they did. If they were all like you, all we'd have is ministers. If they were all like me, all we'd have would be broken-down practitioners. It'll never happen, thank God. And it'll never happen that everybody'll be Evangelical or

Baptist or Episcopal or even Methodist as the Old Gent was. And if you try to make one denomination out of two, you end up with a new denomination, and there you are. Anyhow the point is, you can go just so far with Fairfield folks and no farther. Maybe you've gone far enough already."

Though I was determined not to take Old Doc's criticism too seriously, his constant needling annoyed me. Perhaps because very often, throughout the long precarious process toward union, I had to admit he was right. There was no escaping the traditional adherence to churchology. It was not something that could be laid aside like an old coat or kicked off like an old shoe. Through long years our people had been taught that it was spiritual garb and heavenly footgear.

We ministers had ourselves to blame. For generations our clergy had made denominationalism synonymous with Christianity and, though we might subdue church rivalry for a while, the deep-seated alien sectarianism was left champing at the denominational bit. Somewhere along the way the leaders had taught the people that partisanship was their most precious heritage and a vital and indispenable part of their faith. This teaching intruded into our union services until neither music nor preaching could compete with it. And though Tyler and I co-operated in civic projects, though we organized an interchurch orchestra and built up the community library, the likelihood of a recusant clash always hung over us in desperate suspension.

My church board was always cool toward co-operation, and the cattleman spoke freely of his suspicion that it would lead to nothing constructive or permanent. The congregation was divided. Some said that there was merit in interchurch fellowship, particularly for the young people. Others felt that the plans were awkward and took too much time from "our own pro-

gram." Only a few showed genuine sympathy and understanding for our holy experiment. And Old Doc frequently called
me into his office for a lengthy consultation. He was the oracle
which the denominational gods had planted on Main Street.

"If you're really thinking of getting these two churches to be
one church, it's a lot of damn foolishness!" he would say emphatically.

"You think so?"

"Never thought otherwise," he growled. "Unite the churches
and you'll kill what religion there's left. Kill it deader than a
mackerel!"

Then, glowering at me over the top of his glasses, he always
added with a wail of despair, "You should be smart enough to
know that. One church? Might as well try to force all the rivers
into one ocean. Can't be done. Nature won't let you. There's
something pulls one stream this way and another that."

"Protestantism should be *one* stream, Doctor Reynolds! That's
what I'm trying to tell Fairfield!"

"What if you did have one church? Pretty soon somebody'd
get a new religious notion and go off to start some other kind of
denomination. I've told you before how preachers always end
up with three churches when they try to bring two Protestant
churches together."

Yet I had every reason to believe that the center of gravity
was shifting. At a union vesper on a rainy night the recognized
leaders of the two feuding factions of the respective boards took
up the offering jointly and walked down the aisle shoulder to
shoulder for the offertory prayer. Surely if this could take place
in Fairfield, it could happen anywhere in the Christian world!

And in early spring at an eventful conference in Kansas
City, Tyler and I concluded that interdenominational co-opera-

tion was happening somewhere, perhaps everywhere. A vigorous convention speaker fired us with a vision of the latest spiritual development of our times:

"Rumbling along our spiritual horizon like the glory train, gaining momentum, breaking down the dividing walls of denominationalism with conquering effect is a movement toward a united Protestantism. It is an awakened impulse, gentlemen, built upon the growing consciousness of the need for a world union of churches. Its aim is a global communion of Protestant faiths. This magnificent ideal has been a long time coming. During the last century international fellowship among Protestant leaders in world Christian associations, world Sunday-school movements, and world missionary endeavors blazed the way for complete Protestant co-operation. In 1910 the World Missionary Conference was established by Protestant representatives called to Edinburgh from all over the world. These courageous men were the harbingers of subsequent meetings which reflected the deepening spirit and longing for *one faith*. There were the Stockholm meeting in 1925 with its emphasis on Christian life and work, the Lausanne conference on faith and order in 1927, the International Missionary Council held at Jerusalem on the Mount of Olives in 1928. Today Protestantism is reverberating with the demand for a world-wide alliance of churches.

"And, gentlemen, America is giving the movement incalculable impetus. The increasing importance of the Federal Council of Churches cannot be overlooked. Then, too, let us consider the fact that some of our large denominations are talking about merging. Congregationalism and the Christian Church will soon come together as the Congregational-Christian Church. The historic German Reformed Church is considering a merger with the Evangelical Synod. These organic mergers are steadily leading us into a true and genuine Christian unity. The time of estrangement is rapidly passing. In our lifetime we shall see the result of what church statesmanship can do. You and I shall live to see Protestantism merged in its common heritage and united in its common cause. The renewal of Christian vitality, the massed and moving power of all Protestant forces shall be consolidated in a united front!"

Enthralled, I listened, wishing that every Baptist and every Evangelical in Fairfield were seated here with me.

"We are a marching army, gentlemen!" the speaker cried. "Sixty million strong here in the United States! Visualize our two hundred thousand churches moving solidly against the forces of evil and corruption. See our two hundred and fifty denominations united under one banner. Picture nearly two hundred thousand ministers spurred to action by One Lord, One Faith, One Baptism! Catch the vision, gentlemen, of a world population of two hundred million Protestants surging forward in an ecumenical spirit of truth! Rid yourself of disunity! Affirm unity in diversity! Recognize your faith as a transcendent world power rightly to be reckoned with!"

Protestantism, we were reminded, was not a negation. Although the term arose in the fog of the Reformation and was first applied to protesting princes in the German states in 1529, it could legally, logically, and with scholarly right be traced to the Latin word *protestore:* to proclaim! That is what it was: the proclamation of the distinguished principles of the Reformation, the priesthood of believers, the Bible as the authority in religion, the democracy of faith. I wondered what the Catholics in Fairfield would think of that. Had anyone ever told them that Protestantism also had a basis for union? What if they could hear our conference statesman say: "These vigorous tenets all Protestants hold, defend and cherish! Here is our common heritage! The dawn is breaking, gentlemen! The day is near when these basic beliefs will be forged into a world federation of churches."

Other platform speakers acknowledged the soundness of this prophecy and endorsed the formation of a Protestant *camaraderie;* a spiritual front, a church united in Christ.

In a final speech the conference chairman raised his hands over the gathering and cried: "Brothers in Christ, arise! Men of God, fall in line! Protestantism, awake! Find strength and power in an ecumenical spirit of truth!"

Above us in the crowded balcony a chorus broke forth with "Onward, Christian Soldiers!" It strode through the auditorium until it became a stormy recruiting hymn for the allied armies of a new Protestant faith. Tyler and I were among the first to rise to our feet. We were not only singing. We were marching past the reviewing stand of a world-wide alliance of Christian churches.

The apocalyptic power of the Kansas City meeting convinced me that what I was seeking to do in my little Kansas parish was a companion condition of what great men were seeking on a larger scale in that magical phrase "an ecumenical spirit of truth." The voice I had heard crying in the wilderness of Protestant disunity was my voice struggling for recognition in Fairfield. The conference speaker had seen and recorded from his Patmos Isle what I had glimpsed across the Kansas fields. His gospel of union and co-operation was merely my Fairfield evangel, preached and applied to the unbounded Protestant world. The glory train was rolling and the little gears of my hope and faith were turning its big wheels.

"This is the way to unite our churches!" I told Tyler impulsively as we rode home together. "From the high plateau straight down to sea level! When our people hear that this is a world movement with church leaders in command—wait and see what happens!"

Cautiously he said, "We have done well with church co-operation. But to come right out for church union or church merger, that's a big step. A tremendously big step. Even the speaker was not advocating actual unification——"

I interrupted him impatiently. "The entire movement for a world federation of churches means nothing," I insisted, "unless it goes farther than the easy-sounding phrase of 'unity in diversity.' We must get rid of denominationalism entirely and do away with the labels and tags that have divided us for four hundred years. My ideas may be more radical and revolutionary than those of the conference speaker, but that is what I think we need. Anything less won't get Protestantism anywhere."

Tyler's skepticism was deepening. "When we get our people in Fairfield together, I'll be more optimistic about uniting Protestants throughout the world."

But Fairfield was my world! Eagerly I returned to the fallow Kansas acres. I was the prophet of a global movement. I was Ezekiel feeling the hot breath of Jehovah and beholding the four winds of Jehovah stirring the dry bones of the whole house of faith: "Take a stick, O Son of man ... then take another stick ... join them ... and when thy people ask thee what thou meanest ... say to them, 'I am taking the children ... and gathering them ... and bringing them together, ... they shall no longer be divided ... they shall be my people ... and I will be their God!'"

It was easy scripture but a hard assignment, for I had ambitious plans. It was not only the Baptist Church and the Evangelical Church which I planned to sweep together with my new ecumenical broom: I also had my sights set on a little country church with which I had previously had as little fellowship as with the Catholics. This was Zion Lutheran, affiliated with the Missouri Synod and located only two miles southwest of town.

But throughout the county, as in Fairfield, spiritual paths ran parallel. Parochial territories were so well marked that I never crossed Lutheran boundaries and Lutheran never crossed mine.

I had often passed the gray stuccoed church and parsonage hidden by a windbreak of poplars and enclosed by a high gray picket fence. Insular and lonely was this Lutheran domain, and in three years I had met the young Lutheran pastor only twice. Long before he came, other Missouri Synod men had set an unbroken precedent: Lutherans did not co-operate in community affairs. But the Kansas City convention had given me courage to span the distance which separated all Protestants, so one day I drove through the gateway into the Lutheran stronghold. And when I sat with Pastor John Kurtz in his businesslike study, hemmed in by high shelves of books and many documents, he assured me he was glad I had come.

Conversation was extremely easy. His three young children slipped shyly in and out of the room. He spoke enthusiastically about his parish interests—his plans for a parochial school and his programs for religious education. But it was extremely difficult for me to come around to ecumenicalism. Finally, however, I was recounting with special ardor the Kansas City meeting and talking at length about the plans Tyler and I had for effecting a local Protestant unity.

"We want you to join us," I invited eagerly. "I've been thinking in terms of an Easter communion service. Think what it would mean: Lutheran, Baptist, Evangelical—coming from all over the country, standing together at the communion rail——"

"Which communion rail?" Kurtz smiled.

"Why, anyone's! Hold the service right here in your church, if you wish."

"Would your people come?"

"Well—I would imagine."

"Would the Baptists?"

"Nothing has been said as yet," I hastened to say. "I haven't even talked this over with Larry Tyler. I thought it would be best to see you first. He'll do everything he can."

John Kurtz looked at me and shook his head. "Even if your people and the Baptists would—which, of course, I doubt very much—we could not. You see, we observe close communion. That is, only for our members in good standing. But surely you knew that. And with your background in the Reformed Church you surely know that it was the interpretation of the Lord's Supper that divided Martin Luther, our founder, and Ulrich Zwingli, your Reformed Church leader."

Yes, of course. I was familiar with the teachings of Luther and Zwingli. I knew the details of the sixteenth-century Reformation in Europe. But this was Kansas. This was a local situation. We were young men, sitting together in a country parish, four hundred years from Wittenberg.

While I stared at him incredulously, he reeled off the theological details of Reformation disputes with amazing facility for every detail. I listened absorbed, mechanically registering the points which bore directly on our estrangement.

"Martin Luther," he was saying, "insisted that the Real Presence of Christ was in and under the bread and wine. Zwingli contended that the elements were merely symbolical and representative of Christ's presence. To us, communion is a source of divine power because Christ is present in the elements; to your church, it is still merely a memorial feast."

"Yes, yes," I acceded. "Christ in the believer, I think, is the way we explain it."

"Exactly." Kurtz nodded. "So you see what a distinction. To us, a mystical and redemptive act. To you, a memorial observance."

"But who knows exactly what happens in the Eucharist?" I appealed.

"Who knows?" said Kurtz in a stunned voice. "The Bible tells us. 'This *is* my body!' I should call that plain. I should say anything less than that is heretical. And surely you know there are other doctrinal differences which we would find irreconcilable. Original sin. Dr. Luther said that there was a special sin which went back to the sin of Adam. Your man Zwingli was a humanist. He said that sin is merely human weakness. Oh, no, my good friend, the more we search our faith the more removed from each other we become. I am sure you understand what I mean."

"I do!" I hastened to agree. "So let us say that the Eucharist is a means of bringing Christians together in a fellowship of mystical union with Christ."

"Ah, but how can you say that when your church does not believe in the ineffable mystery of the Real Presence?"

"Because I believe that every doctrine which divides Christians is a man-made doctrine and should be discarded."

"Discard communion?" he echoed in a tone of shocked incredulity.

"Never!" I said, amazed that he had read this idea into my words. "Discard interpretations that are keeping us apart."

Kurtz shook his head as if an open gate between us had been suddenly closed and bolted.

"Luther never took credit to himself for any doctrine he propounded," he said distantly. "He was always careful to say, 'It is not mine, not the product of my hand. But God's gift. I have not spun it out of my head; it did not grow in my garden. It is God's gift.' You see, our church is the church of rediscovered truth. Since it is that, we cannot tolerate doubt or indecision or every wild wind of doctrine that comes along. Truth is truth and on that a true Christian man must stand."

"But if we today could only bridge the schisms which our founders created," I pleaded. "Think what that would do for our people. Think how much more might have been accomplished if the Reformation had not been divided at its inception."

"It was not Luther's fault that it was divided," said Pastor Kurtz securely.

"But," I insisted, "I believe you will agree that Zwingli and Luther were working toward the same ultimate goal. Each rebelled against the corruption which had overtaken the Catholic Church and prepared and posted their theses pointing out those corruptions. Since both were priests of important parishes, their observations and conclusions were basically the same. Because they believed in the Bible as the final authority, each translated the Bible for his people—Luther for the Germans and Zwingli for the Swiss. Further to enlighten the people they each prepared a catechism. To invite them into corporate worship, they wrote hymns. But because they were skilled theologians, they started splitting hairs on doctrinal questions. These divisive elements I call nonessentials, and if we permit nonessentials to divide us, the partitions among Protestants will be perpetuated and increased in number."

"But I must insist," replied Pastor Kurtz, "that you are incorrect when you call doctrinal questions nonessential. We believe that the doctrines of our church are the same as those of apostolic times and of apostolic teaching. The heritage of truth is our greatest glory and therefore whatever we teach is essential, or it would not be taught."

"But you do not claim that your church is the only church in which men can be saved?"

Kurtz waved his hand impatiently, then paused to shoo his youngest daughter gently out of the room.

"We have never claimed that," he said. "The universal church with its priesthood of believers is to be founded on the universal Christ. But interpretations of doctrine came in as disruptive influences when every new reformer began tampering with the truth. Our church, being a continuation of the church of the apostles, has the marks of the true Christian Church. Ulrich Zwingli did not believe this. He thought he could improve on Martin Luther's inspired interpretations.

"So also did John Calvin, as you know. He, too, was a contemporary and a Catholic priest. A most excellent theologian, a reformer to be sure, and honestly converted to what he called 'the divine will of a sovereign God.' 'Where the glory of God is not made the end of government, it is not a legitimate sovereignty!' That's Calvin, and who is to say he has not made many other splendid statements?

"You might also find great likenesses between him and Dr. Luther. But doctrinally he stood somewhere between Luther and Zwingli, and he had his own plans for what the church should be like. You know the five points of Calvinism as well as I: predestination, unconditional election, irresistible grace, total depravity, and the familiar belief in 'once saved, always saved.' Calvin was, as we all know, the spiritual father of John Knox and between the two of them the world got a new denomination, Presbyterianism. Very well. Presbyterians have a right to follow Calvin just as I follow Martin Luther. But I believe that our interpretation of Scripture is correct. If I didn't, I wouldn't be here. Since I do, you must give me the right to follow what I believe to be God's truth."

John Kurtz would never know my feeling as I drove from his isolated Lutheran fortress. His words were no longer those of a Kansas pastor, bending himself to the problem of Fairfield, but a voice crying out of a sixteenth-century theological disputation, leaving me confused and at war with my ideals. My ride home might have been a return from the Wartburg, the castle hideout from which Luther's disturbing words shook and shattered the Christian world. And for this I feared and respected the modern follower of the mighty monk of Wittenberg. One moment I was saying, "Oh, for the security this man has found by following one resolute, unchanging doctrine of salvation!" The next I cried, "Always at a time when the Christian world desperately needs a united voice, the ceremonious phrasing of religious concepts arises like an explosive force!" And to clear my soul of this insoluble debate, I stopped at Old Doc's office before proceeding to my pastoral responsibilities at the Evangelical manse.

He was alone and I told him my story. And he laughed. With his hands stuffed inside his belt, he laughed heartily. But the outburst seemed only to precipitate a darker mood than was his usual nature.

"By God now!" he exclaimed angrily. "Are you figuring on being a Luther yourself and reforming the religion of Kansas? That's carrying things further than good sense allows. Do you think that is what your great Protestant leaders mean when they prate of world councils and church federations? Listen to me, boy! All they want is to bring about a psychological union. They're too smart to think they can or should go beyond that. An organic union? They know better than that. A united front? Sure, it might be done but watch out or you'll find yourself with an organizational union and spiritual disunion on your hands at the same time."

"I don't know what the leaders have in mind," I told him tersely. "But I do know that the entire plan for a world-wide Protestant union will mean nothing unless it recognizes itself as a revolutionary step to undo the evils engendered by the Reformation. It must constructively plan for more than a simple, expedient church co-operation or make-believe Christian fel-

lowship. It must realize that it is out to do away with denominationalism entirely and let the people know it. The divisions into
which denominations are broken are inherently wrong and sinful. They arose in the heat of revolt. The creeds which were
so generated won't fill the bill with my generation. We must
cut through them to arrive at the one creed the world needs:
unity!

"Now, of course, to bring that about will mean sacrifice. Many
men will have to admit that their jobs aren't as important as
they thought they were. They will have to confess that they
have been more interested in themselves than in Christian service. They have kept their churches going under the stimulus of
competition. The overlapping of denominational efforts in
areas of operation will have to be corrected. Sentiments must
make way for realistic and constructive work in social relations.
Preachers will have to give up their pulpits where, as here in our
town, the field is already overchurched. For once in the history
of the Christian church, leaders and people will have to say,
'Let's stop hiding behind doctrinal walls and sniping at one
another about petty differences. We haven't really found God
in this sectarian jungle and let's be honest and admit it.' Reac-
tionary prejudices, nonconviction about things preached, conse-
cration or a lack of it must all be brought out into the open.

"In short, the time has come for Protestantism to clean house,
and if we have the courage to do that, we will emerge as the
mightiest spiritual force in all the world!"

Old Doc just sat there. My impassioned *salut au monde* left
him completely indifferent. He rubbed his cheek with his
glasses, blinked at me a few times, then fumbled in his paper-
stuffed desk until he found the stub of a cigar. Dreamily he
lighted it and leaned back in his chair.

"I always had an idea," he said gravely, "that Protestantism was a great educating influence for Christianity. It goes along testing a truth here and a truth there, practicing one approach to God in this church and another in that. I always looked at it as a big research station. Here one investigator discovers that this theory works and there somebody else is experimenting with another approach. Here somebody comes up with a new discovery; over there is a religious clinic; yonder somebody is making his diagnosis; elsewhere somebody's finding out something in a post-mortem. Laboratories—that's what I thought it was like. I'd hate to think that all of these investigators were suddenly going to merge into one and restrict folks from a free search for truth. Truth has many faces. To make one school of thought out of two, one has to admit that one's belief doesn't matter. But all beliefs matter, my boy."

"I've made my own analysis," I said cryptically. "Something is wrong with Protestantism. Something is wrong with Fairfield's Protestantism. It's the sin of disunity and I'm still going to do something about it."

Old Doc chuckled dryly, unhearing. And when I reported this latest message from the oracle of Main Street to Tyler, he warned that Old Doc might be the sounding board for both congregations. But we had gone so far that we were determined to carry out our plans for going farther. In my scantily furnished study we spent long hours plotting with innocent intrigue and planning with wise design the uncertain prospectus for a united church of Fairfield.

A month went by. Two months. Six months. The liturgical calendar marked the coming of Advent, and we greeted this holy season by calling a joint meeting of our two church boards to meet in my parsonage. We announced that a matter of unusual importance would be up for discussion, and I confided to some of my key men that Tyler and I had formulated a plan for

closer church co-operation. How much closer I did not say. They
did not ask. They never dreamed that the plans might call for
more than union vesper services or a Christmas musicale. But
when the scheduled eight-o'clock hour found the front room
completely encircled by an interchurch legation composed of
farmers and businessmen, expectancy was tense. It was a stiff
and hedged-in setting. The odd assortment of parsonage chairs
had been augmented by some folding chairs from the church
basement. Here sat seventeen men, some clutching the lapels
of their work jackets, others clasping their knees, while the cattleman sat on his hands, blandly discussing noncontentious subjects of the day with the Baptist banker.

I asked Tyler to pray and we stood together under his well-
chosen words: "Behold how good and how pleasant it is for
brethren to dwell together in unity. . . . Thou knowest the spiritual needs of our community, O Lord. . . . Endow us with wisdom from on high! . . ." His fervent "Amen" hung suspended
for a moment as we sat down.

"Well," said the cattleman shrewdly, "what's the proposi-
tion?"

"Yes," drawled the spokesman for the Baptists, "as long as
we're here let's see what you two young fellows have figured
out."

Tyler gave me the nod and I took the floor.

"It goes back nearly two years," I began, "to a night when
this room wasn't so full of life as it is now. It was full of shipping crates and suitcases. That was the year of the drought.
Farther west they were getting sandstorms. We had wind that
burned out the corn. That night I said to myself, 'My people
have crop failures, but sometimes I feel as if I have had mine,
too.' I had been here two years then, and it seemed that religion

in Fairfield was just about what it was when I came. I was going on to a city church, but there was an idea I couldn't get out of my mind that night. It had been put there by one of the best men in my congregation. He said, 'You're leaving at a bad time. Maybe when the Baptists get their man, you two fellows could do great things for our town.'"

My eyes roved the circle; the cattleman watched me charily.

The growing feeling of intensity could not be ignored. I sought to modify it with "I don't know just what he meant or how far he thought we might go. But I know that his success both in the church and on his farm has been based largely on courage and taking a chance."

This drew all eyes over to where the cattleman sat.

Half pleased and half annoyed, he said, "Well, go on."

"When Brother Tyler prayed he spoke about the spiritual needs of our community. I believe the Lord has a will for us here. I believe Fairfield is just as important in the kingdom's work as any town or city anywhere in the world."

The men shifted uneasily. This was not Sunday morning.

"We think Fairfield is so important," I continued, "that it ought to be a proving ground for what can be done when Christian people really get together. Some months ago Brother Tyler and I stood together in an auditorium in Kansas City. Since then many of you have heard us talk about international Christian movements and Protestant federation. These are as important to you as Protestants as new methods of farming are to you as farmers. It means a better way of doing things. It means a religious co-operative. I've often been interested in the farmers' co-operatives in which most of you are members. Now we have an idea for a church co-operative. We want to tell you about it."

Larry Tyler told them with explicit analysis and cautious reserve. He assured them that he had investigated the movement and its ideas and was convinced that it was aimed directly at building up Christ's kingdom.

"The union of Protestantism has been under way ever since 1846 when a World Evangelical Alliance arranged prayer weeks throughout the Protestant world. It has developed in interdenominational movements such as the Young Men's Christian Association and the Young Women's Christian Association, in World Student Christian Federations and many world alliances. A workable union for all denominations is an ideal. A workable union for our two churches can be a reality."

"I hear a good many words," said a conservative member of the Baptist board, "but I don't know yet what anybody is driving at."

An uneasy shuffling and muffled comments convinced me that some of the other men did. I saw Tyler sit down and nod to me.

"Gentlemen," I said bluntly, "there are three ways in which our two churches can get together."

"Get together?" echoed an elderly member of my council. "What do you mean?"

"Co-operation! Union!" And though I spoke with as much restraint as possible, the essence of our long planning injected its passion into the words. The men stiffened with resistance. The cattleman's narrow blue eyes were electrical, a mixture of fire and light. The Baptist president sought confusedly to get Tyler's attention and to read his inscrutable expression. Rival board members exchanged hostile glances. I had expected that the announcement would introduce surprise, even confusion, and now I felt the startled rumbling of the denominational elements and saw the sectarian storm signals hoisted in the upraised faces.

Incredulously the leader of the Baptist faction said, "You don't mean you two men are suggesting one church? Or is that what you mean?"

"There are three plans," I repeated, but the notes I held seemed heavy with a deadening weight. I put them aside. "I will review them for you. They are not original. They have been tried—and successfully, too—in other communities."

"In how many?" asked the Baptist banker.

"In about four hundred," Tyler answered.

"Four hundred in the United States?" said one of my members. "That's not very many."

Amid somewhat noisy agreement and asides, the cattleman spoke up. "Well, let's have it," he said grimly, taking a note pad and the stub of a pencil from his loosely hung coat. "If there are new ways to get a ring in a bull's nose, I'm always ready to learn."

The laughter was awkward.

"I'm sure it will be easier than that." I smiled, but actually I wasn't sure. "In some localities where there were two churches, the smaller one simply gave up its denominational identity and united with the other."

"Oh, by heavens!" said a Baptist voice.

I stilled the comments with "I certainly know that isn't the plan for Fairfield! After all, our churches are fairly evenly matched in members and influence. We simply wanted to familiarize you with what is going on in plans for union. In some towns the congregations have agreed on what is called a community church. This is an arrangement whereby both denominations give up their denominational status and become an independent, autonomous religious unit serving the needs of the people."

These words, which had rung with so much power in my up-stairs study, seemed suddenly stripped of their meaning and shorn of their power.

The Evangelical banker spoke for everyone. "I can't for the life of me see where this sounds like Fairfield!"

His words set fire to their thoughts.

"What have our denominational headquarters ever done to us that we should cut them off?"

"You mean you want an orphan church with a minister with-out denominational standing?"

"Are you two fellows trying to find an excuse to work your-selves out of jobs?"

Tyler came to the rescue with a genial laugh.

"No, we're making the jobs bigger than before!" With a ges-ture from me, he rose to carry on. "The third plan we wanted to discuss with you was a program of close church federation. This has been tried and found successful and workable. Under its provision each congregation retains its connection with its denominational headquarters, but uses one common church building and unites with the other congregation in spiritual and civic activities as one united church. The advantages are rather obvious. Protestants in Fairfield should function as a single body of Christians. We could fill one church every Sunday morn-ing——"

A voice interrupted, "We could fill both churches if every-body came!"

"We would deepen the spiritual fellowship," Tyler continued. "Think of worshiping in a congregation of three hundred in-stead of about sixty! There's a challenge here, gentlemen, a real challenge!"

I had never heard him raise his voice in such enthusiasm. It was thrilling, but from then on the scene became confused.

The cattleman started with "Which church are you saying we should burn down first?"

A Baptist said, "My grandfather was one of the first to be baptized in that church across the street——"

An Evangelical: "Many was the time my father risked his neck to shingle the steeple on our church!"

The Baptist banker: "Competition is as necessary in religion as it is in business!"

A storekeeper: "Maybe it seems funny that we do business together, go to the same town affairs together, send our children to the same school, but can't get together on one church. But religion is different."

A farmer: "It is. Its roots go deep."

An Evangelical: "Church union won't work any miracles!"

"Church union," I said, "being a miracle of Christian faith, will have a tremendous and far-reaching effect! Think about the young people——"

"Where are they?" someone interrupted.

Tyler said good-naturedly, "Some do not go to church because they do not know which church to attend. But, gentlemen, if we can unite among ourselves without uniting the churches, let us do that!"

Impetuously I said, "We have tried that and we've gone as far as we can. What we need is not a First Baptist or a First Evangelical Church, but a First Church of Fairfield! It ought to be equipped to meet every need. Think of one church choir, one Sunday school, one great congregation, as Brother Tyler has said. Think of one church board, meeting as we are tonight to direct the spiritual forces of a united Protestantism toward community problems!"

One of my members admitted, "It all sounds good, but we aren't ready for it!"

"We must get ready for it! We can make no spiritual progress unless we move forward together!"

My words were swallowed up in:

"What about sacraments?"

"What about baptism?"

"You can't bring people together against their will!"

"We're satisfied with the way things are going!"

The Baptist banker was on his feet. "I don't get the drift of this," he was saying for members of both boards, it seemed. "Why shouldn't there be denominations? Lots of them. All kinds of them. One person wants this and one wants that. Why not? Some folks want candles burning in the church. Others don't. Some like one song. Others like another kind. We believe in immersion. You Evangelicals believe in sprinkling. Practice what you believe. We'll do the same. There's no more reason for doing away with denominations than there is for doing away with the forty-eight states. Some like California. Some like New York. I like Kansas. That's the way it is with denominations. I don't see that it's any mystery and I don't think it's any sin. Good fences make good neighbors, as every farmer knows. Far as I'm concerned, I'll say to our minister right now, 'Young man, build up our church! That's all we ask of you.' When a farmer gets a hired man, he doesn't pay him for working on his neighbor's farm. Not by a long shot. There's plenty of work to be done right on the old home place!"

Hardly had my heart gone out to Larry Tyler, bashed by this discipline, when I realized that I should save some sympathy for myself. The long, lean figure of the cattleman suddenly dominated the room, solid as the windmill on his grazing range.

"For once I agree with a banker," he said in a voice that molded his dry humor into solid fact. "Even with a Baptist banker! I'll speak my mind like he spoke his. You just build up *our* church, young man! That's a big enough job for you. Maybe when we are the best Evangelicals we can be and the Baptists are the best Baptists they can be, when every man is the best Christian he can be according to the light he has, union will come about automatically."

We kept our sympathy—Larry Tyler and I—each for himself —each for the other. We sat together for a long while that night admitting that the deepest aspect of our people's religion lay in its denominational particulars. This they felt with an intensity out of all proportion to the leveling power of the gospel or the familiar phrases of our pleas that "all should be one." What they wanted and what they felt they needed was not appeasement, compromise, or tolerance, but a new and vivid sense of denominational supremacy and sectarian imperialism. Union—perish the thought—would be the final milestone on the road to ruin!

And when I stood alone among the disarranged chairs, which had the appearance of having been kicked about, I tried again to think through Protestantism's dilemma. At the Kansas City conference many speakers had blamed ministers for church disunity. Clerical bigotry and unyielding dogmatism, personal self-seeking, institutionalism, intolerance, and stupidity had been accounted instruments of disunion. What was it in Fairfield?

Eventually I concluded that it must be something more than a local situation that made me feel so thoroughly threshed out. It was something deeper than building a church. It was a Protestant *Weltschmerz,* a sense of injury and pain at being a member of a divided kingdom. I felt there should be something which would cut across denominational frontiers. Something powerful. A consciousness of God. A sense of union in the Spirit of God. A fellowship of the soul. The brotherhood of man. Something. I could not express it adequately nor make it understood. But when I pursued it far, it always brought me back to Fairfield and straight up against the invincible walls of indoctrination behind which Baptist and Evangelical stood barricaded. Why had I ever hoped I could find a way through it or around it or over it into the open fields of the now nebulous world union of churches? Suddenly "One Lord, One Faith, One Baptism" sounded ridiculous. Disunion was destroying Protestantism, and I was incompetent to save it. I had no magic word for its redemption. The only thing of which I was dead sure in the urgency of the moment was that, though the two church boards had appeared to be friendly enemies, the rift between the churches was widening. I had widened it considerably.

The following day the meeting was the talk of the town. Through a mixture of crass contradictions about what had happened, a few remarks filtered in to me that there were a number of people who "wished they might have been there." They thought Tyler and I had shown remarkable courage. But few of these sympathizers were church members and their enthusiasm was hardly shared by any appreciable number of Baptist or Evangelical parishioners. Sadly some of my neighbors said, "I wouldn't have done it. . . . Don't try to do the impossible. . . . This has been going on a long time. . . . Don't start a church war!"

Old Doc met me in the post office. Growling under his breath, he said, "The fact that people don't agree is not a sign they're bad people. Just because men don't see eye to eye doesn't mean they're not good men. Not by a long shot. It's a sign they're free to think for themselves. Protestantism is religious democracy. Preach a sermon on that one of these times and I'll be in the front pew."

And the cattleman, coming to the parsonage early on Sunday morning, put his hand gently on my shoulder and with fatherly affection said, "A man rides best in his own saddle. I never saw anybody get along on two horses, outside of a circus performer."

Bitterly I walked across the familiar ground to the morning service. I felt as consigned to despair as the hard earth that waited another Kansas winter. For this Sabbath I had written out every word of my sermon, cautiously avoiding any reference to the board meeting or its aims. I would "preach the faith" according to good Evangelical doctrine and slowly edge out of the Fairfield parish. Already the familiar scene of cars pulling up in the churchyard and the sight of well-known figures climbing the steps with the aid of the iron handrail seemed like a reel spun out of a past with which I had only an attenuated connection.

But the setting was strangely altered on this morning. There were many cars. There were more people than I had seen since the last funeral service. The Baptist corner also was crowded and a record attendance seemed to be in store for Tyler. I quickened my steps and walked into the anteroom where the choir was waiting. I could not hide my surprise at the attendance. Eighteen singers instead of eight! They could not hide their pleasure at my expression of delight. But it was an enigmatical pleasure, I thought, into which I could read whatever I wished: loyalty, defiance, the new birth, or "We'll show the Baptists!" Whatever it was, here they were. And out in the auditorium were the crowded pews. And I stood in the pulpit with a congregation big as on Easter Sunday.

Tremblingly I wondered whether this might be the way to build up the kingdom. Pit one church against the other? Rid a congregation of inertia by threatening to have it absorbed by its neighbor? My thoughts swung like a pendulum: it's spite—it's a great awakening; it's defiance—it's penance; it's a big show-off to let me know the strength of the Evangelical battalion—it's the voice of my people saying, "First make us good Christians and when we're good enough and the Baptists are good enough, maybe we'll get together automatically!"

Into my remarks that morning crept what I thought to be a new power and a vital emphasis on the Christian life. Tyler told me that he felt this, too, in his experience with a crowded auditorium. It prompted us to find a new initiative in the old texts and an increasing stability to weather the formidable aftermath of our unhappy conference on unification. We hewed to our respective denominational lines while putting a healthy emphasis on the "social gospel." What we wanted was an evidence of a deepening spiritual life among our people while Protestant union waited. So, with each man guarding the sheep of his own flock and faithfully providing a good denominational sermon each Sunday morning, we fixed our eyes on that distant day of the "automatic get-together."

How distant? Who could tell? After less than a month, as if realizing that the sides were too evenly matched for either church to outdo the other, attendance on both corners began falling off. Then it dropped below normal, like the drop in theater attendance at Fairfield's Pastime when a movie outstayed its time. Everyone had seen it. And everyone had seen Larry Tyler and me in our epilogue to merger. The cycle had passed. The two church buildings sighed and settled back on their haunches to get set for another seventy years.

Dubiously and with a sense of having spent my energies and my ideas, I was again confronted by empty pews and pews occupied by the traditionally faithful. My few ardent supporters for union considered it to be for my best interest that their interest be withdrawn. Once more I condemned myself for my ineptitude, then accused Fairfield anew for its unpardonable sin of sectarianism. Above the faithful faces loomed the frightening masks of denominational self-conceit. I saw my people sitting where their fathers had worshiped, hearing as their fathers had heard, remembering as their fathers had remembered that the privilege of being an Evangelical was the first privilege claimed by the first Fairfield citizen and would be the last that he would relinquish. Across the corner the Baptists were very likely arguing out just such a priority for themselves. There had always been two sticks in Fairfield, and it would take a mightier Ezekiel than I to make them one.

Perhaps I did not know enough about my people's needs. Their sophistry mingled with some profound and mystical local wisdom; their stubborn convictions had in them a frightening profundity. After four years my congregation was more of a mystery than it was the day I came. Religion attracted and repelled them, but I felt that sectarianism was the prince of devils which had made them what they were today.

And yet, sometimes at the services, sometimes during the congregational singing, I solemnly admitted that they were seeking something while they sang: a reason and a motive which in an earlier day had inspired men to write the stirring hymns of the Christian faith. Where had that spirit gone? How could I recapture it for them and for me? Between the music of their hearts and the clangor of their petty pharisaical denominational feuds, I was plunged into a dilemma from which neither honest contrition nor revolt could set me free.

But I always came back to a single stifling thought: if I failed in Fairfield I was failing everywhere in the Protestant world.

CHAPTER TWO

The Doctor Called It Mitosis

WHILE I was being blown about by the winds of my uncertainties, Larry Tyler received a call from a church in Central City and announced that he was leaving Fairfield.

"Keeping things going here has been like walking on a rolling barrel," he told me, and I thought I sensed a note of accusation in his voice. "I'm about ready to get my feet back on the solid ground."

There was no procrastination and no delay. Sadly I saw the moving van pull up to the Baptist parsonage. Gloomily I watched Larry's parishioners gather to say farewell. A few members of my congregation also sauntered over in an unusual display of interdenominational good will. Baptist women wept, and there was no doubt about the sincerity of their emotions. Nor mine. But secretly I wished that I were packed inside one of the shipping barrels.

"I admire you for staying," Larry said. "Fairfield folks are all right."

They were. There was no doubt about it. Only the laws and habits and customs of sectarianism kept me from taking them all to my heart! Only their deep, grubbing roots kept them from accepting me. Each of us was planted in his own soil and only now, in the very human scene of parting, were religious differences momentarily forgotten.

"How will things be in Central City?" I asked.

Tyler laughed. "What do you think? A town of six thousand? Thirteen Protestant churches!"

"Heavens!"

"Three Presbyterian," he said with enthusiasm, as if he suddenly had more affection for a multiplicity of faiths than for another attempt at merger. "There's a Presbyterian in the U. S. A., a United Presbyterian, and an Associate Presbyterian. A Methodist. Two Lutheran of different synods. A Congregational-Christian. A Church of the Open Bible. A Church of the Nazarene. An Adventist group. A Church of Christ. A fundamentalist Baptist. And mine."

"Protestantism!"

Lifting a warning finger, he ironically repeated the words of the Baptist banker, "Competition is as necessary in religion as it is in business."

The statement was put to a final test when Larry's successor appeared in Fairfield in early spring. I heard him before I saw him. As I neared the drugstore corner on my way to the post office one morning, a strident voice broke out across the quietness of the town: "We Baptists don't take our name from John the Baptist, but I could see no objection if we did! We're a church as old as the apostolic age and as modern as today!"

Rounding the corner I caught sight of a long arm, swinging a big black hat in a sweeping gesture. Then I was confronted by the tall and patriarchal figure of Brother Langley, standing on Main Street as if he had been planted there for a generation. His shock of wiry, white hair bristled in the wind, and his black bow tie stood out sharply and severely beneath a face fired red with zealous spirituality. His congregation at the moment was Arnold Lembke, one of my parishioners, Fairfield's rural mail carrier. Lembke was completely overawed by the new pastor's metallic barrage and stood hypnotized under the effulgent blue eyes, blazing out their volleys of faith from beneath shaggy white brows. Immediately I tagged Langley as a Samson, and the ass's jawbone which he swung with deadly aim was conviction.

"Yes, yes!" he exclaimed when Lembke introduced me as his pastor, the minister from the church across the street. "I was looking forward to meeting you! But Mr. Lembke just put a question to me, 'Where do the Baptists come from?' I was saying that we *are* Anabaptists and we *aren't* Anabaptists! The Anabaptists, Mr. Lembke, were rebaptizers, a group of believers going back to Luther and before Luther, some scholars say. They believed that all those who were baptized as infants should be baptized again. And that's what I believe, though there are many Baptist ministers who do not, understand."

"That's right," Lembke agreed. "Reverend Tyler told me he'd take a man into his church on the baptism he had had some other place. He said he'd sprinkle a man, too, instead of ducking him under if the man wanted it done that way."

"Yes, yes, my friend!" Langley hastened to say. "But some of us are a bit more orthodox than Brother Tyler. Some Anabaptists sprinkled, too. Some poured. But a few immersed. Only a few, but the connection between Baptist and Anabaptist is through those few who immersed and who were the custodians of truth. That is my belief. God has a way of guarding the truth and weaving it like a silver cord through the lives of his trustful servants. Just because the church is tending toward laxity in some matters is all the more reason for some of us old stalwarts to keep the foundation from crumbling. Second Corinthians, chapter four, verses one and two: 'Seeing we have this ministry . . . we faint not . . . not walking in craftiness, nor handling the word of God deceitfully; but by manifestation of the truth commending ourselves to every man's conscience in the sight of God.'"

This he recited from memory but, while Arnold Lembke questioningly searched my face for my reaction to Fairfield's new contender for truth, Tyler's dynamic successor whipped a New Testament from inside his coat. Lightning-fast he found a text.

"Romans 6:3!" he announced. "'Know ye not, that so many of us as were baptized *into* Jesus Christ were baptized *into* his death?' Baptized *into,* gentlemen! *Baptizo,* says the original. That means to plunge or to dip. There you have it. I was once a Methodist. I was once a Congregationalist. But, thank the Lord, for the last twenty years I've been in knowledge of truth. *Baptizo!* Now, I say, if a man is going to baptize at all, or be baptized at all, let him do so in accordance with sound doctrine. *Baptizo!* Any Fairfield convert to my church, gentlemen, is going *under* the water. Three times. In the name of the Father, Son, and Holy Ghost!"

So saying, Samson caught hold of my hand, shook it vigorously, and said it was time we had a good long visit. Still swinging the big black hat, exuberant in body and mind, he accompanied me to the post office, and everyone we met garnered some sheaf of wisdom which Langley tossed out unstintingly from the rich harvest of his sixty-five years. For his incessant words were loud and clear and seemed to cut a swath along the old familiar street that led back home.

"I have heard of the attempt at amalgamation which you and Brother Tyler initiated! Yes, yes! I suppose that is why he is in Central City and I am here today. You see, it is the duty of civic and temporal organizations to bring people together in literary, musical, and cultural organizations. That is not religion at all.

Religion is adherence to the deep concepts of the spiritual life guided and nourished by the great beliefs and practices of the church. As you grow in your ministry you will see how the concept of union can never be effected by compulsion. That brings us immediately into politics, and there is nothing more disgraceful than politics in religion. Naturally the text, 'One Lord, One Faith, One Baptism,' has provided many young men with an excuse for a fling at union. But which faith? And which baptism?"

His hand shot into his pocket and came out with the New Testament. He opened it automatically.

"Colossians 2:6," he proclaimed. " 'As ye have therefore received Christ Jesus the Lord, so walk ye in Him: rooted and built up in him, and stablished in the faith, as ye have been taught, abounding therein with thanksgiving.' That's the marching order I'll be giving my congregation every Sunday morning. You may depend on it!"

And on the black wings of his words I saw my hopes for union drift off across the Kansas plains.

"I believe in the Baptist faith with the same fervor that you believe in the faith of your denomination," he vowed. "More so, no doubt, because of my conviction that my search for truth has ended. The New Testament church was founded on the believers' baptism and it consisted only of those who had been baptized upon a confession of faith. Infants, naturally, were excluded and infant baptism was unknown. That body of believers which held to the supremacy of the Scriptures and a church of regenerated, adult baptized Christians have throughout all the ages been the custodians of our faith. Naturally these custodians at the time of the Reformation had a break with Luther. They welcomed him as a reformer of Catholic domination, but they could

not follow him because we follow no *man*. Some of the unin-
formed think that Roger Williams, the apostle of religious liberty
in America, marks the beginning of our particular faith, but he
was only God's custodian for a brief period in the seventeenth
century. That is the way faith is perpetuated: through the custodianship of truth. It is truly wonderful!"

Everything about Baptist history and religion inspired this
untiring prophet with wonder. During this first peripatetic
visit with him I was being refreshed in how denominationalism
came into being and by what varying shades of doctrine the
crazy quilt of Protestantism had been composed. I was reminded how Anabaptism gave rise to the Mennonite movement
and how the Mennonites took their name from Menno Simons,
a Catholic priest, who, deserting the Church of Rome and
by-passing Luther, embraced the Anabaptist doctrines of nonresistance, refusal to take oaths, enforcement of church discipline over the individual life, adult baptism, and foot washing.
Always the Mennonites remained distinct from the Baptists,
though they had much in common. I was sure that if I were to
walk with a good Mennonite, he would have argued just as
strongly for his belief as Langley did for his convictions, and as
John Kurtz did for those to which he so tenaciously adhered.

Around me swirled the battles of truth against truth and doctrine against doctrine, wounding and slaying my ideas for union
while claiming to rescue them. Yet, to my partisan colleagues,
no man's faith was truly real unless it reflected the particular
traditions of the Reformation which each considered the glorious truth.

As I stood with Langley on the pavement outside my parsonage door, he drove the final great nail into his theses with a departing flourish of his black hat. "There is nothing greater," he

cried, "than to feel onself in the apostolic succession of the pos-
sessors of truth! When a man recognizes himself as such a
one, he cannot be moved!"

Distraught and discredited, I watched him go with swinging
stride to his own church lot. And when he slammed his parsonage door behind him, he shut me out with my insecure and
impractical ideas. I was standing alone, trying to make usable
the plans for the consolidation of Protestant forces which were
being discussed and fostered by the energy and sacrifice of great
religious leaders in conferences for church union on the other
side of the world. Their promises and reports were now remote
and indefinable. The dramatic presentation of the Kansas City
speaker, the proposals I read in *Literary Digest,* the vague results
locked in the minds of the active promoters of the cause no
longer seemed heroic; Samson had dispersed them like the Phil-
istines, and their death cries haunted me as I opened the parsonage door.

I closed it firmly without entering. My idea for a united Fairfield Protestantism *was* real. I had given four years of my life
to it. I needed to talk as impellingly about what I believed as my
companion talked about the convictions he defended from his
fenced-off corner. Next time we met I would point out our likenesses while he recounted our differences, and I would quote
Scripture to justify my contention for the elimination of sectarian
tags. The fateful design of the ecumenical dream was a light
worth following.

But how long would I be able to pursue it? How could I pursue it when I was ambushed on all sides by the opposition?
These questions went with me as I resolutely climbed into my
car and headed out of town. Driving aimlessly over familiar
township roads, I weighed the value of dogma and argumenta-
tion against the reality of life in the Fairfield countryside.

The steady Kansas wind breathed spring into the earth. The farmers in their fields, the women in the yards, the chickens and pigs and cattle, the lonely windmills turning in the pastures, the distant cluster of buildings in the village—all this was real, while Anabaptist and Baptist and Menno Simons and Roger Williams were only historic milestones fading against the ancient years of religious confusion.

In the distance loomed the Lutheran church grounds, recalling my visit with Pastor Kurtz. How much alike Langley and he actually were, though they would never be able to agree. They had been set in their respective molds and there they had hardened. They had found their denominational grooves and in them they operated with a slow, stubborn pace. But I could not dismiss them with an invective. Though each lived in his stuffy little sectarian cell, I envied him: Kurtz because he was the incontestable champion of spiritual authority for his people; Langley because he would be able to do for Fairfield's Baptists exactly what he wanted to do for them. This Scripture-quoting, Bible-packing son of the morning was the man to in-doctrinate them with their own doctrine. The young minister and the old. Each knew what he believed and neither ever wavered, while I rode restlessly on the receding crest of a hazy ideal, wondering if there was any power mighty enough to break through the massive denominational walls which had been in the building since the birthday of the Reformation—October 31, 1517—when Martin Luther, out of his distress and agony over the corruption of the faith in which he was ordained a priest, nailed his ninety-five theses to the door of his church in Witten-berg.

The bookish phrase was enfeebled by the intransient space that spread out around me as I drove along the open road. But the words that returned to me from the seminary classroom echoed and re-echoed until they became the ultimate cry of an indisputable truth, emerging as my conclusion on Protestantism's dilemma. More than four hundred years of division and debate had gone into Fairfield's religious pattern. Our bigotries and estrangements were by no means local. They were as wide as the Protestant world and as old as the first reformers.

The conventional thing for me, as a loyal Protestant, was to perpetuate these differences. Wherever Protestantism had established itself, it had done so in hostile battalions. Protestantism was Kurtz preaching Lutheranism, Langley preaching the Baptist plan, Mennonites going back to Menno Simons, Presbyterians to Calvin, and each calling his fenced-off landscape glorious. Should I conform to the pattern and go back to Zwingli? Or should I prepare a good sound series of sermons for Fairfield, a new history of the Reformation, showing that every founder of every denomination had made Christian unity more difficult because of his intransigence?

I would devote one sermon to Luther and show how uncompromising he was with the Anabaptists and how once he called them "Heretics!" Then another to the Anabaptists to prove that they felt that Luther had not gone far enough in extricating himself from Catholic doctrine and Catholic influence. A third to the Reformed faith with the comment that before 1560 there were already two conflicting camps: the German Reformed and the Dutch Reformed which, until this very day, had never got together because the first insisted on being Zwinglian and the second Calvinistic. Then I would show how Calvin, being extremely anti-Roman, would have nothing to do with Luther who retained Roman customs which, he said, were in keeping with Scripture. And while all these eminent reformers were carrying on their lamentable disputations, another group was rising. The Moravian Church, following the pre-Reformation reformer, John Huss, had its own Luther in the leadership of San Augusta. He was Luther's friend and they had much in common, but not enough to make possible a united church. Never did the many leaders of the Reformation sit down together and try to work out a plan for a single organic Protestant church.

Wherever Protestantism went, it continued to divide without conquering. England's reformer was a king. Henry VIII had the courage to oppose Rome and to renounce papal jurisdiction over his empire just as the priests had been doing. England did not become Lutheran or Presbyterian or Reformed, though these faiths were established in Europe and their influence was extended to the British Isles during Henry's time. England's religion became Anglicanism and the first Protestant archbishop was Thomas Cranmer. Anglicanism was a continuation of Catholicism with Reformation influences. So it could not unite with the movements on the Continent even though the original reformers still lived.

More tragic still was the fact that Anglicanism, though it was the faith of kings and the royal religion of Queen Elizabeth, was fated to be humiliated by division within itself at an early period of its eager life. Schism erupted the high hope of a united spiritual empire. Certain Anglican ministers revolted against the Act of Uniformity which ordered them to use *The Book of Common Prayer* and no other liturgical form. They were also annoyed that Elizabeth had been named Governor Supreme over the church.

John Robinson was one of the objectors who arose to wound the inflexible Anglican pride. Robert Browne was another and, with their congregations, these men left the Church of England and became Separatists—those seeking to reform the church from without. The Puritans, English Protestants who wanted to further reform and "purify" Anglicanism from within, agreed with the principle but opposed the practice of the Separatists and in the confusion there were atrocities worse than broken windowpanes or scribbling on church doors. And these groups never got together in England, no more than Baptists and Evangelicals and Lutherans in Fairfield. Separatists Browne and Robinson went to Holland with their people and gave them the well-known formula of Protestant reform: God intended that the individual should exercise freedom and responsibility of private judgment in matters of the spiritual life. Anglicanism they rejected, but thought in terms of a state church for themselves. With Presbyterianism they had no fellowship, but they were Calvinistic. They professed no claim to Lutheran doctrine or Reformed doctrine, but they considered the Bible the final expression of God's absolute will. Had they fashioned a creed it would probably have been "The just shall live by faith." And when the world wanted to identify them, they were called Congregationalists. But never once in all this growing multiplicity of religious movements did these early groups ever attempt to create one church indivisible. Though they had so much in common, they saw only their little differences.

Who was to say that this was not happening in Fairfield today? In the very moment that the early Protestant cavalcade rumbled through my mind, I was forced to confess that the differences which divided Langley and me went back that far. And the things that kept Kurtz and me apart went back that far. And we were narrow-minded and blind because we refused to admit that there were bigger things which brought us together. The people. Life. The land. Suffering and joy. Our brief mortal lives and the eternalness of God. But even the roads over which I was driving were section roads which had always been construed as parish lines. This was Lutheran territory.

This Baptist. This Evangelical. This was the Catholic section. Even the cemeteries had their staked-off areas and the town had its stores and banks which depended on church affiliation for patronage. Fairfield's sectarianism was hemming me in!

Sermons and a new history of the Reformation would only aggravate a bad situation. Protestantism's history was immense and intricate. Once in Fenny Drayton, Leicestershire, George Fox, a weaver's son, walked among the creeds of seventeenth-century England, pondering on problems which were confronting me: What is the essence of faith? What is basic and inviolable in all religions? It was revealed to him that the true religion was based on the "will of man in harmony with the will of God." What more was needed than this? Could a thought at once so simple and profound be stylized into denominationalism? Placing more and more emphasis on an indwelling spirit rather than on external forms, he was soon surrounded by followers from many churches and from among the unchurched. With extraordinary success, they demonstrated that as life is well lived, God is near; and as a man inclines his soul to the inner voice he is guided aright. Fox urged men to tremble at the word of the Lord and for this the world called him and his congregations "Quakers," though they referred to themselves as the Children of Light or the Society of Friends. And whatever Fox's motives in the beginning, here was another new name in Christendom and another new church.

Still they came—new names and new denominations. In Germany, out of the ever-rocking cradle of Protestantism, a school of Pietists appeared. Pledged to the mysticism of the Christian life, they searched the Bible and their hearts, and saw God wherever they found devotion and human need. Like the Quakers, like the Mennonites, the Pietists advocated and conformed to nonresistance, dressed simply, spoke plainly, refused to take oaths, and righteously despised the bedazzlement of the sinful world. Alexander Mack, one of their chief exponents, tramped through the Palatinate and Switzerland preaching the gospel and proclaiming the features in which the Pietists were distinctive. Unlike the Quakers, they observed certain churchly rites. Unlike the Mennonites, they baptized by immersing their kneeling confirmants three times face forward in the water. Pietism was a leaven that spread through eighteenth-century Protestantism with a purifying power, but out of it came another group, the Church of the Brethren.

There was no escape. Perhaps Old Doc was right when he said, "Try to unite two rival churches and you start a third." Old Doc, recalling the romance of his circuit-riding father, knew that it was John Wesley's nonsectarian effort that produced Methodism. Though Wesley was an Anglican, the Moravian Brethren stirred his religious quest. The Oxford Holy Club tempted him with its monastic severity, and he fasted and meditated and rose before daybreak to partake of the Sacrament. What was it he wanted? What was it he sought that was not offered in the shopwindows on Protestant Avenue in the days of his seeking?

Whatever it was, he said he found it one evening, May 24, 1738, at a quarter to nine. He, an Anglican, found it when he heard a Moravian reading the writings of Luther. But it was not Lutheranism or Moravianism or Anglicanism to which he devoted himself. It was to a new movement, Methodism, and it meant another star in the overcrowded Protestant heaven! What if he did hold to his early ordination and consider himself an Anglican until his dying day? What if he did urge all Methodists who had been Anglicans to remain Anglicans? What merit was there in his saying, "We do not propose to start another church but wish only that men might through our mind and method enrich the faith they now possess"? Despite his contribution toward the strict enforcement of the rules and manner of the Christian life, Wesley, like all the other reformers, had weakened the central core of Protestant unity.

I returned to Fairfield struggling with the realization that there was no solution of the dilemma. There was no remedy for disunity. Under the scourge of denominational labels, every religious movement that had arisen out of the Reformation had disrupted the Christian ideal of the undivided brotherhood of man. But this belated conclusion did not rescue me from the swirling waters of Protestantism. The familiar Fairfield streets brought back all the old feelings of insecurity, and as if by habit I found myself turning into the alley behind the long, boxcarlike building which was the office of my tyrannical councilor, Old Doc Reynolds. Though this was an unlikely harbor for any man adrift in a religious fog, I parked my car in the sunlit, graveled alley, climbed the three rickety wooden steps, and opened the back door to Doc's sanctum.

The air in this cramped and cluttered private office was heavy with the scent of cigar smoke and iodoform. The door leading to the examining room was closed. There was no sign of life anywhere in the building. Outside, Main Street was wrapped in its noon-hour lethargy. The turgid silence was broken only by the dripping faucet near Old Doc's desk, incessantly spitting into the sink. Wearily I dropped into the worn leather Morris chair. Before me on the colorless wall hung the musty black saddlebag which Reynolds kept as the proud memento of his father, the "Old Gent." Near by a fading American flag was tacked up as if to symbolize Old Doc's demands for a democratic faith.

The faucet dripped, recounting days and years. My gaze roved to it idly, and in the monotonous sound I remembered hearing

Old Doc curse it and complain that the place was going to hell. I sat motionless, caught by the ceaseless, rhythmic spatter, hearing in the drip, drip, drip, the interminable march of the Protestant parade: Lutheranism, Anabaptist and Baptist, the Reformed faith, the Presbyterian faith, Anglicanism, Congregationalism, the Quakers, the Church of the Brethren, the Moravians, the Methodists . . . It was an endless procession. And when European division was transported to the free soil of America, Protestantism became ten times more multitudinous.

Lutherans held their first service on Hudson Bay in 1619. They brought an awakened sense of personal religion as their offering to the altar of democracy. Their Bible was Luther's translation; their book of instruction, Luther's catechism; their canon law, the Augsburg Confession. But, despite this common code, there were soon separate and distinctive groups within groups. Pastor Kurtz was one kind of Lutheran. There were many others: Slovakian, Icelandic, Finnish, and Evangelical Lutherans; Free Lutherans and Apostolic Lutherans; German, English, and Scandinavian Lutherans; Independent, Protestant, and Evangelical Lutherans, and synods which claimed their special provinces—Buffalo, Texas, Iowa, Ohio, Missouri.

The Mennonites settled in Germantown, Pennsylvania, in 1683. They came from Germany, Switzerland, Holland, and Moravia. Great were their contributions to agriculture and the frontier life. But with all their sincerity and in all their adherence to Anabaptist doctrine and the articles of their Christian faith, they split into Mennonite Brethren in Christ and Reformed Mennonites and Stauffer Mennonites and Old Order Mennonites and Krimmer Mennonites *Brüder Gemeinde,* and Old Order Amish, Hutterian Brethren, Mennonite Brethren Church of North America, Central Conference of Mennonites, Unaffiliated Mennonite Congregations, the Mennonite Church, the General

Conference of the Mennonite Church of North America, the Church of God in Christ Mennonite, and the Conservative Amish Mennonite Church.

The word "divisive," alien to America, was native to American Protestantism. Let Brother Langley glorify Baptist history; did it not stand as the most divided among divided faiths? Some Baptists believed in the observance of Saturday as the Sabbath. These banded together. Some formed a clique around Calvinistic doctrines. The slavery question divided the church into two parallel tiers. Some groups introduced foot washing. Others insisted that baptism should be performed only in running streams. And so there were Northern Baptists and Southern, Negro, General, Separate, Primitive, General Six-Principle, Seventh Day Regular, Duck River, United, Two-Seed-in-the-Spirit Predestinarian Baptists, Independent, Freewill, and Colored Freewill!

My Reformed Church in the United States held its first communion near Philadelphia in 1725. It was essentially a layman's movement for twenty years. Then a minister came from Holland, sent by the Dutch synod as a missionary to Dutch and German-speaking families in Pennsylvania. They learned one another's thoughts, and slowly doctrines were disseminated, the doctrines contained in the Bible and interpreted for the people in the Heidelberg Catechism. The Evangelical Synod, with which the Reformed Church was discussing merger, was organized in 1840 near St. Louis, Missouri. It also considered the Heidelberg Catechism authoritative, but supplemented it with Luther's and with the Augsburg Confession. These many authorities would need to be resolved into an essential truth or into the liberty of conscience before the merger could be effected.

Presbyterianism established itself in 1610 with a church and a pastor in Virginia. Presbyterians came from England and

Scotland and Wales. They came devoted to Calvinistic beliefs and to the Westminster Catechism and to the cardinal principle of the sovereign will of God. But their sovereign union was marred by division: the Presbyterian Church in the U.S.A., the Presbyterian Church in the U. S., the United Presbyterian, the Reformed Presbyterian Old School, the Reformed Presbyterian New School, Associate Presbyterian, Associate Reformed Presbyterian, Cumberland Presbyterian, Colored Cumberland Presbyterian, and Orthodox Presbyterian.

And as I wondered whether one might find an example of the security of union anywhere, I thought of Congregationalism, brought by the Pilgrims to historic Cape Cod and Plymouth in 1620. Early in its American endeavor it united Pilgrim and Puritan. Great men were among them—Brewster, Bradford, Winslow—heroically determined to impart to the individual freedom of private judgment and to the church the fellowship of all who could be trusted with this inspired privilege. Harvard and Yale, forty-two colleges and eighteen seminaries were among Congregationalism's contributions to American faith. Spiritualized academic bands carried religion and culture into the frontiers. Rarely had a denomination demonstrated such a genius for remaining intact! But in 1819 a hundred and more churches broke away in the great defection that gave rise to Unitarianism. The question, "Is God one God or one God in three?" made for another broken home in the struggling Christian family.

A united church? It was too much to ask. Protestantism, having been born in schisms, would always be schismatic. The dangerous liberty of putting into man's hands the right to find God in his own way had defeated its own purpose. All denominations had always insisted and always would insist that their way of life was based on truth, just as Langley insisted on it, and

Kurtz. All the while divisions increased, and the gulfs between men widened until they could no longer be bridged.

Suddenly I looked up and clutched the arms of the chair. Old Doc stood in the doorway, glowering at me over his glasses.

"Sick?" he demanded.

"No. I didn't hear you come in."

"What brings you here in the heat of the day?"

"The books," I said gropingly.

"Books?"

"Didn't you say once you had some books to donate to our community library?"

"That was back in the Tyler regime," he grunted. "You still want them?"

He was pleased that I said I did, debated for a moment whether he should begin with the old bookcase or with a stack of volumes piled above his desk. Then he shuffled over to the sink and turned and twisted the leaky faucet.

"Drip, dammit!" he concluded, giving it up as a bad job and dropping his aged body into his high-backed swivel chair.

"Arnold Lembke tells me you had quite a talk with the new Baptist man. How do you think you two'll make out?"

"Each on his own corner," I confessed hopelessly.

"Still playing around with that high-fangled church union idea? How's it coming?"

"You mean locally?" I asked feebly.

"Anywhere!" growled Reynolds, lighting the stub of a cigar.

"Well," I said, pulling myself out of the depths into which the morning had plunged me, "we're just now beginning to see the significance of the conference held at Lausanne."

"Lausanne? Where's that? Down near Topeka?"

"Lausanne, Switzerland."

"Switzerland! What the devil has that got to do with Fairfield?"

"Christian leaders got together to see how they could get their people together."

"Do the people know it?"

"Well, they should. I've been trying to tell mine."

"What happened over there—in Switzerland?"

"Progress was made," I said dubiously, irked at Old Doc's skeptical probing. Would it mean anything to him to tell him it was a Conference on Faith and Order and that there were five hundred delegates representing ninety denominations? Would he be well advised to know that this was Christendom's "disarmament conference," intent on rising above the differences which dissipate spiritual energy and insult the Founder of our faith? Old Doc would very likely force me into the admission that Lausanne suggested no surrender or compromise of any doctrine or creed and that it carried no authority to committing denominations to "union." I confined my commentary to saying, "It is simply another great forward step to invite Christian and non-Christian alike to enter into the joy of the Lord."

"What's that mean?" Reynolds wanted to know.

"Exactly what it says," I replied, equally irritable, then added with little faith in my own words, "I think it means that some day Protestant churches will be united ecumenically just as all of you doctors are united under the A.M.A."

Arguing with Old Doc had become a habit, and I could almost anticipate his reply.

"Oh, my God!" he said. "There are all kinds of doctors and they aren't all under the A.M.A. There are osteopaths and homeopaths and naturopaths and a hundred other paths! But many of them lead to health just the same!"

"But there *is* a medical authority," I insisted impatiently, "and the reason for it is clear. The patient believes that doctors believe alike and diagnose alike and prescribe alike. Now, if we Protestants could present such an authority——"

"Authority, authority!" Reynolds moaned, screwing his pock-marked face into an expression of distaste. "Another church had that idea once and it didn't pan out. A fellow called Luther had something to say about that."

"Luther," I said with a wave of my hand. "At this point I don't know what to think about Luther. Maybe he should simply have confined himself to reforming the Catholic Church and let it go at that."

"He *did* reform the Catholic Church," Doc argued, eying the musty bookcase as if he could put his hands on the evidence. "Without him it would have gone from bad to worse. But he didn't reform it from the inside. He started up some competition. That's my trouble here. No competition and I'm getting stale."

He glanced ruefully at his disheveled office. His gaze roved to an ancient wooden spool case in which pills were stored. He sighed at the sight of his cluttered desk. He shook his head dismally at the leaky faucet. "I've had my way too long. A young fellow ought to come to town. A two-party system is a darn sight better than one any day."

"Religion's different," I said boldly. "I've decided that when Luther made every man a priest, denominational hell broke loose."

Old Doc champed on his cigar.

"Maybe the Catholic was right," I went on. "In Luther's day he said, 'Break down the walls of Mother Church and you'll soon have so many sects you won't be able to count them.' That's certainly happening and it's still happening right here in Fairfield."

"Well, dammit!" shouted Old Doc. "Let it happen! That's Protestantism!"

"At its worst!" I defied. "Though Protestantism was born in schism and has always been schismatic, there are enough convictions on which all Protestants agree to wipe out our differences."

"For instance?"

"All Protestants can get together on the belief that the basis of spiritual authority is the Bible. All agree that the individual is more important than an ecclesiastical system. The heart of Protestantism is a direct personal relation between man and God. All of these existed from the time of Luther. We've had them for centuries, but there are still two churches here in Fairfield fighting for their lives. Three, with the Lutherans."

"But if they all agree on the points you've mentioned, there must be stronger points that keep them apart."

"There aren't. We're divided because of nonessentials."

"What's a nonessential? Baptism?"

"The mode and manner, yes."

"Ah, but not to Brother Langley!"

The words were accompanied by a mischievous chuckle, and with triumphant flourish Old Doc scratched a match on the bottom of his chair.

In spite of the blighting effect which my sojourn into Protestantism's past had produced on me and my ideal, I was still willing to take up Reynolds' challenge, not only on the question of baptism, but on every argumentative belief that caused men and churches to transgress the divine law of Christian unity. As long as religion was characterized by distinguishing denominational marks it would be a weak, ineffectual force. It could not be rebuilt until there was spiritual teamwork among believers. A brotherhood of faith. Divisive elements, like the mode of baptism, would have to go. But when I contemplated that, the vitally prophetic figure of Brother Langley loomed threateningly, and Samson romped through my renewed crusade for ecumenicalism, swinging his convictions with a holy passion.

"It *is* an essential to Langley, isn't it?" queried Old Doc through a puff of cigar smoke.

"That's the trouble," I snapped. "Every leader is always anxious to sell his ideas and his interpretations to the Protestant world."

"Yes," drawled my oracle in a strangely tender voice, "seems to me the Old Gent used to tell us that when Luther came on the scene there were immediately others just as ambitious as he was."

"The Old Gent was exactly right!" I agreed. "But think what all those reformers might have done co-operatively: Luther, the theologian; Menno Simons, the mystic; Zwingli, the humanist; Calvin, the legalist; Cranmer, the sacramentalist. And all the rest. How the people would have rallied to them! How I would rally to them if they had given us one church, pure and strong. But because they were divided among themselves, they divided the people."

"By heavens!" exclaimed Old Doc. "What about a man's convictions?"

"There is no greater conviction than a united church. That is really the great ideal of the Christian faith, but division has got into the way and the ideal must fight for its life. Whatever makes Christians small and bigoted is a sin which destroys the meaning of Christianity. Men know a lot about churches, but they know very little about God.

"What would the reformers find if they came back today? Luther would discover some twenty different Lutheran synods and conferences. Zwingli would be faced by a variety of Reformed churches. Menno Simons would be welcomed by eighteen Mennonite groups holding to various hair-splitting interpretations. Calvin would run into thirteen Presbyterian bodies. Cranmer would find high-church and low-church Episcopalians. Most of the reformers would have to look twice to recognize their denominations at all."

"Well, now, I tell you," mused Old Doc, "if the churches are really kept apart more by downright stubbornness than by what they profess to believe, that's a different story. If that's the situation, it's a bad state of affairs. But if they're kept apart because they have convictions which to them are right and without which their religion won't have meaning, you'll never get them together. If you did, I'd probably start another denomination myself just to break up your religious monopoly. That is, if I *had* any convictions. The only honest-to-God conviction I have is that a man ought to be allowed to find God honestly. But folks have lost their will to think and their passion to act. The world is headed straight into a hell of indifference and that's a hell of a condition. That's something I'd like to see the churches do something about!"

Heavily he lifted himself from his squeaking chair and went to the dusty bookcase. He pulled out a few books. Handing me a copy of *The Book of Common Prayer,* he said, "I suppose you wouldn't want to put this in your community library, but you can take it for yourself. It was my wife's."

On the inside cover I read: "To Helen, in remembrance of her confirmation. From Father and Mother."

Reynolds stood with a book in each hand, gazing solemnly from one title to the other. "These two," he said, "used to ride in the Old Gent's saddlebag. Wesley's *Sermons* and the *Methodist Discipline.*"

He chuckled resignedly and laid them on the desk. Then he cocked his ears. The Main Street door was opening and there was heavy stamping in the waiting room. "Anybody with a step like that can't have much wrong with him," he figured slyly. "Look the books over and take what you want. Someday this office and the whole shebang will be gone anyhow."

He went out, closing the door behind his shuffling form. The office was stifling. Through the tiny, tightly closed north window I saw the wall of the Farmers' and Merchants' Bank (Baptist). Through the south window I saw the State Bank (Evangelical). Again Fairfield's sectarianism was hemming me in. The office with its smells and its dripping faucet drove despair into my heart and told me that my struggle had been completely futile. I was squandering my years. For what? For church business. I opened the back door and closed my eyes in pain against the sharp sunlight.

From the examining room came a grumpy voice catechizing a patient. Farmer Charley Hasick came around to a statement of his complaints. He needed eight hundred dollars for repairs on his farm machinery and the banks had turned him down.

"Both of them?" asked Reynolds.

"Both of them."

Old Doc swore and said he would help.

Sometimes something seemed bigger even than church union. Sometimes something returned like the remembered experiences of bits of obscure ministry among the Fairfield people. A death, a wedding, a visit to a farm where lived forgotten people, a church service on a sunlit day, a hint of spiritual unification with other men and all men with God. The feeling came like a breath of life, quickly, and then passed. It was too great to despise church boundaries. It was too mighty to be conscious of denominational walls. Whoever had experienced it did not care to analyze it or explain. Who had never felt it could not understand.

Absently I opened *The Book of Common Prayer*. I paged through the sections on Holy Communion, Holy Baptism, Visitation of the Sick, The Psalter, The Ordering of Priests, The Catechism, The Litany. . . . It was essentially like the book of worship which I used. It had its sections on Collects and Prayers and, standing in the open doorway, I read, "Grant, we beseech thee, merciful God, that thy Church, being gathered together in unity by thy Holy Spirit, may manifest thy power among all people——"

We had a prayer like that. Every church very likely had a prayer like that. Every church very likely prayed for Christian unity. What did it mean? Protestant men and Protestant groups had a habit of following their own pursuit of glory, following it wherever it led them, regardless of church tradition or church prayers. I thought of Presbyterianism and Anglicanism and Congregationalism all praying for unity in their early days in England and all going their own way. All the multifarious groups in America were praying for it and had been praying for it ever since the first ship brought the first Protestant to American shores, but they all meant unity according to their particular brand of belief. Surely any reasonable person would see the bitter incongruity of God's people pitched in segregated camps, armed to the teeth with homemade doctrines.

Heavily I laid *The Book of Common Prayer* on the stack of books on Old Doc's desk; under it was *The Life of John Wesley, the Man*. Wesley, surely, must also have prayed, "Grant, we beseech thee, that thy Church, being gathered together in unity by thy Holy Spirit——"

In all of the many groups operative in America I was sure I

would never be able to find a place. I was a homeless Protestant and, feeling sorry for myself and for all I believed and hoped, I turned to go.

Old Doc stopped me at the door. "Not taking the books?" he wanted to know.

"Yes, I'll take them," I said.

"I know they're old," he admitted. "And religion does change, I suppose."

"It does and it doesn't," I replied.

I went to the desk. He moved to the door and tossed his cigar stub into the alley. He stood in the doorway as if he too could use a deep breath of the warm spring air. But he gazed off into the neighborhood yard where Mrs. Mueller, down on her hands and knees, puttered around in the fresh soil of her garden.

"Protestantism," mused Old Doc, "ought to remind a man of spring. Or spring of Protestantism. New life beginning to move. New cells splitting up. I've watched it many years from this door. It's as you say, things change and things don't change. Did you ever think of Protestantism like that? What I mean is that it's like the process we call mitosis—cell division—cell growth." Then he added to himself as if recalling a long-forgotten line from some early medical text, "The multiplication of cells is one of the manifestations of an inherent vital force."

Then he went on in the same thoughtful, droning tone: "A manifestation of vital force in any organization or organism is change of form. And there is the development of nerve force from the cells themselves." He turned to me stolidly, hunching forward with interest. "That's what I mean when I say you can't unite Protestantism without destroying it. There's no such thing as growth without change. Do you follow me?"

"I follow you," I said. "But I still see two churches across the street from each other and I still know that when you come right down to it, you cannot persuade Protestants to forget their differences."

"If you could, you'd kill Protestantism dead in its tracks! Stop growth and you invite death!" Old Doc shouted as he strode over and expended a moment of fury on the faucet. But it resisted him, too. Breathing heavily, he dropped into his chair.

"To be correct," he said quietly, "Protestantism is heterotype mitosis. It is more than producing *like* cells; it's a process in which there is separation and subdivision and growth. Always growth. Eventually cells are created that are different from the parent cell. Like the growth in denominations, with the gametes seeing to it that hereditary characteristics are transmitted and yet allowing for change and newborn features just the same. Mitosis is life. . . . Spring. . . . Nature putting on her own show of mitotic division. Try to stop it. You can't. But you want to stop it in Protestantism. You want to be one to put an end to the process. You can't do that any more than you can stop nature. My advice to you, young man, is to let the cells multiply. Let them?" He snorted. "They will anyhow, no matter what you do or how you may feel about it!"

"But, Doctor Reynolds," I said, "let's admit that Protestantism is weakened by the fact that it can't speak with an authoritarian voice in Fairfield's politics, nor in its educational system, nor in its plan for the salvation of men. Let's admit that the leaders of a world union of churches have only a plan of mild co-operation in mind. The fact remains that the only way real religious power can be attained is by putting complete union ahead of denominationalism and by forgetting about differences which should no longer divide. Langley, Kurtz, and I all will have to give up something in order to gain a greater good."

"In cell life," Old Doc was saying while the words were still in my throat, "there is a period of augmentation, another of perfection, another of decline, and, finally, one of cessation. As long as vitality can use chemical and physical agencies for building up the system, these agencies tend to preservation, but, when life ceases, they tend to destruction. Not because the vital principle has not the power of resisting these agencies, but because it can no longer turn them into the channel for preserving the system. If that's not a case for Protestantism . . ."

His words trailed off and his eyes studied the tilting stack of books.

"The Old Gent," he said, "didn't know anything about the life history of cells or the work of gametes. But he knew about Methodism and he preached it until I was so damn proud of it I wore a blue button that said, 'Another Methodist!' He used to say, 'Never criticize another faith because chances are the Methodists started it.' That warning was called up when somebody said something insulting about the Church of the Nazarene. The Old Gent was ready to fight. He let it be known that the Nazarenes had excellent blood. You bet they did! Didn't they grow out of the Wesleyan revival 'long about 1880? He told us about the Christian Church and how it was started because of the revivalistic zeal of James O'Kelley, of Virginia, a Methodist, and how Baptist Abner Jones, of Vermont, also came into that picture. He had the whole story of how the Evangelical Church, like yours right here in Fairfield, was started by Jacob Albright, who was baptized a Lutheran——"

"Converted in the Reformed!" I supplied.

"—and licensed to preach by the Methodists!" shouted Old Doc with a conquering cry. "He told us about the Congregational-Methodists and the Zion Apostolic Methodists and the Salvation Army and God knows how many more that came out of Methodism, until whenever I looked at a map of the world I thought sure there couldn't be a spot where Methodism hadn't been planted! Would you say it shouldn't have happened that way? Would you say Methodism could have overrun the world by being just *one* brand of Methodism? Or could any other denomination have done what it's done if it had stayed intact? Well, it doesn't matter whether we think it could have been done or not. The cells of vital Protestantism break, grow, multiply! They always have, they always must, they always will! That's the only sign of life and growth I know of! That's the way mitosis works!"

So I was asked to justify the incompatibility of Protestant Christians with an easy phrase. With a metaphor. And the old ogre sat in his chair blowing his infernal smoke, defying me to name a single Protestant group which could not be included in his short course on religious histology.

"What about the Campbellite movement?" he gloated.

And I had to admit that this group also fit his analogy. Thomas Campbell, a minister of the Associate branch of Presbyterianism, tried in the early nineteenth century to establish a church which would embrace all churches in a church without a creed. Barton W. Stone, another Presbyterian, came with his congregation. Other groups caught the idea, and finally they settled on a name as nondenominational as possible, Disciples of Christ.

"Well," I countered, "it was a great idea and a holy cause."

"But the Disciples of Christ is a typical denomination," Doc argued. "They never did get all denominations together. Nobody ever will! By the way—" he chuckled wisely—"did the Campbellites stay united among themselves?"

"No," I sighed. "Today there are Northern Disciples and

Southern Disciples and I suppose Progressive Disciples and Conservative Disciples."

"Wonderful!" cried Old Doc gleefully. "Mitotic division all over the place!"

Protestantism's perplexing past made it impossible not to agree, for out of the Campbellites came Sidney Rigdon, leading my attention to another group. Rigdon was one of the first to spread the news that a Vermont farm boy, Joseph Smith, had discovered a buried manuscript with "pages like unto gold." Rigdon became a missionary. Joseph Smith became a prophet. The Book of Mormon proclaimed a new religion to the world. And yet the Mormon faith, organized as a church in 1830, designed to end all seeking after sects and creeds, quickly divided into factions which were as intolerant of one another as the world had been of its martyred prophet, seer, and revelator, Joseph. Mormonism was spread across America as the Church of Jesus Christ of Latter-day Saints, the Reorganized Church of Jesus Christ of Latter-day Saints, the Church of Christ Temple Lot, the Church of Jesus Christ Bickertonites, the Church of Jesus Christ Cutlerites, and the Church of Jesus Christ Strangites.

What Doctor Reynolds called an evidence of vitality and life I construed as the unholy act of separation. No group had escaped; none had been spared—not even the Quakers, or the Moravians, or the Church of the Brethren. All were victims of Protestantism's besetting sin.

"You can excuse the multiplicity of Protestant denominations with your analogy," I said, "but the fact remains that we are weak and ineffectual because there are more than two hundred different groups operative in America today."

"Remarkable!" Old Doc blurted out with a reckless laugh.

"There are also more than two hundred chromosomes in primitive germ cells! So that's good! It's not unity that makes life move. It's diversity. It's not somebody sitting on a throne and saying, 'I'm speaking for a hundred million Christians!' It's you and Langley and Kurtz and Tyler and all the rest of you telling us what religion has done for you and letting us decide whether it can do the same for us. And that, young man, is what religion is, whether you like it or not. And that is exactly why and how Protestantism came into the world."

CHAPTER THREE

Fairfield Invaded

WHILE Fairfield was still fighting the battles of the Reformation, a new reformation began in a meadow near the edge of town. No one had been impressed when the itinerant Pentecostal evangelist arrived by truck and trailer and announced at the Farmers' Service Station that he had come "to take the town for Jesus." Brother A. E. Saunders, a tanned, two-fisted Kentuckian from the Cumberland country, pitched his gospel tent, rented planks from the lumberyard and improvised benches, sprinkled sawdust in the aisles, and strung up his gospel banner: JESUS SAVES! Then with the technique of a publicity agent for a dog-and-pony show, he directed a group of Fairfield youngsters up one street and down another, door to door. By sundown the town was thoroughly circularized. Luther nailed his theses to the portals of Castle Church; Saunders pushed his through every front door. I found three broadsides stuffed under the door of the Evangelical manse: HAVE YOU BEEN BORN AGAIN? . . . THE HOLY GHOST BAPTISM IS THE POWER YOU NEED! . . . GOD CALLING—ARE YOU LISTENING?

Nightly services and three on Sunday was the schedule announced for a two-week stay. To me such ambition was ample proof that Brother Saunders knew nothing about our community. Fairfield was not a revival town. And it was harvesttime;

81

the farmers would be working late in the fields. I was sure that both Baptists and Evangelicals would shy away from these services as they did from an apportionment Sunday. Did Brother Saunders think he could break through this apathy with his sensational advertising? Pictorial handbills featured a special attraction: HEAR SOUL-STIRRING SONGS OF THE OLD-TIME RELIGION. . . . SISTER AUDEY SAUNDERS & SISTER MARIE DONALDSON, SPIRIT-FILLED SINGERS & MARIMBA EXPERTS.

On their first evening I heard them through the open window of my study. The anvil-like tones of the marimba resounded against the high-pitched, rollicking voices of Brother Saunders' gospel team. They were singing "Revive Us Again" with a jazzy swing-time rhythm. I leaned back in my swivel chair and listened. Suddenly a raucous voice broke in upon the singing: "Come on folks!" the evangelist bellowed. "Let's join in!"

During the next few lines Brother Saunders' discordant tenor startled the slumbering winds of the Kansas earth. Feeble, reluctant voices joined in. Again the music was interrupted: "Say! You folks *need* reviving! It's good we came! Praise the Lord! Sing!" he cried, calling for dear life. "That's why the Lord gave you vocal chords! Use 'em! Let's hear it again!"

Perhaps I should inform this arduous newcomer that it would take more than a duet and his rabble-rousing to stir Fairfield from its autumn inertia and lure the farmers from their harvest chores.

The singing ended, a peal of ribald laughter broke across the field and into my parsonage. "Yes, Lord! Revive 'em! Again! And again!" Saunders' prayerful aside to the Almighty was as wanton as his laughter.

Shock followed upon shock. I heard praying that night—coming across two Fairfield city blocks: Saunders and the sisters praying at the same time. Each praying a different impromptu prayer. Each praying his heart out to high heaven and interspersing the words with a loud clapping of hands and hilarious shouts of "O Glory!" and "Hallelujah!" I heard Brother Saunders preaching that night in a manner even more unorthodox than the praying. His sermon thundered into town like the Lord's last offer to Sodom. In vain I tried to make out what he was saying. His voice would reach frenzied cries, then drop to a whisper; rise to a sharp falsetto, then stop as if sliced off with a knife. This pattern was repeated over and over on an ever higher and more emotional scale.

A neighbor came excitedly to the parsonage. She said I ought to do something. "A good rousing sermon against this trash is what I'd be in favor of!" she vowed. Another neighbor strolled over with a better plan. He said, "Ignore the whole thing. I'll give these Holy Rollers till Sunday. Then the tent will fold up quicker than all get out!"

But all of the townspeople were not of the same opinion. As the days passed, Fairfield was split into Saunders and anti-Saunders factions pitted against each other and against the neutrals. Some said it was the Lord's will that the evangelist had moved in; others proposed that he should be arrested for disturbing the peace. They thought the tumult and shouting sacrilegious. Brother Langley took the affair courageously in stride and knocked boldly at the trailer door. I stood at his side as an unwilling accomplice, towed along by his insistence that we make Fairfield's official religious objection unanimous.

Saunders swung open the door with a hearty, "Praise the Lord!"

"Brother," said Langley, "I represent the Baptist faith in this community and my friend here represents the Evangelicals."

"God bless you, Brothers!"

Saunders stepped into the sunlight with outstretched hand and invited us to sit down on the grass.

Langley declined for both of us.

"I've been wondering, Brother," my spokesman began tersely, "whether you Pentecostals consider it ethical to move into a community lock, stock and barrel without consulting the town's established ministry?"

"Praise the Lord, Brother!" laughed Saunders. "We came here so of a sudden we were set up miracle-fast, like as the Lord Himself was pitching the tent! Come and join us! The Lord is ever wanting helpers, you know!"

"And I suppose you will come and help me on Sunday?" Langley asked shrewdly.

Saunders' blue eyes narrowed in a fearless and omniscient searching of his inquisitor. Bluntly he asked, "Have you received the Holy Ghost since you believed?"

Langley straightened with a shock. "According to your primitive conception, no! According to Scripture, a thousand times, yes! 'By their fruits ye shall know them!' "

"What fruits, Brother?"

"Not tongues!" said Langley cryptically. "Tongues are of the Devil!"

"How can you say that, Brother, when the New Testament is right full of tongues and plain as can be on the matter? Why, on the very first Pentecost, you remember, Acts 2:4: 'They were all filled with the Holy Ghost, and began to speak with unknown tongues, as the Spirit gave them utterance!' "

"Read it right!" warned Langley. "The true reading is that they began to speak in *other* tongues, not *unknown* tongues, and Acts 2:6 says: 'Every man heard them speak in his *own* language!' We don't need such a miracle here in Fairfield. We all understand English."

"Praise the Lord, Brother!" Saunders laughed. "But you don't all understand the language of the Lord. That's what the unknown really is, for sure."

"It's nonsensical jabber!" said Langley. "It's self-hypnotism!"

"Praise the Lord, Brother!" corrected Saunders. "I've heard men speak German, French, and even Chinese under the Spirit's power. Indeed I have. You see, at Pentecost the Comforter came which Jesus had promised He would most surely send. Now what the world needs right now is——"

"I know my Scripture!" Langley warned. "And I and every other Bible scholar know that Paul warned against speaking in tongues in First Corinthians 14. Read it!" And he whipped his worn and trusty Testament from his pocket. Even before he deftly found the passage, he was quoting, " 'I had rather speak five words with my understanding ... than ten thousand words in an unknown tongue!' "

"But, Brother," cried Saunders victoriously, "that's the very chapter in which Paul commends the gift of tongues! Read the second verse: 'He that speaketh in an unknown tongue speaketh not unto men, but unto God!' Read the fifth verse: 'I would that ye all spake with tongues!' And the eighteenth: 'I thank my God that I speak with tongues more than ye all.' "

Scripture and counter-Scripture flew furiously in Farmer Barben's field while I listened and marveled and finally departed wondering which side had won.

All of this was excellent publicity for Brother Saunders and his attendance grew. He built up his crowds from fifty to ninety in four days, and on Friday night, under the aegis of a "specially inspired" Holy Ghost meeting, he called out over a hundred and fifty curious and interested children of iniquity, including me.

Under the strong electric glare the grimy sawdust made an ugly path to glory. On the springy, makeshift platform, the huge marimba sparkled. Behind the instrument the two sisters danced a sprightly little step while they played and wildly sang the pep songs of Pentecost. Brother Saunders moved back and forth across the sagging planks, clapping his hands, singing, calling for emotion. A small chorus of local singers stood on the sawdust patch before him. They were Fairfield people, three of them members of my church. I counted about thirty of my parishioners in the audience and they counted me. There was an awkward moment of exchanging nods, then we were caught up in the uncouth grandeur of the meeting.

Regardless of what I might say about the propriety of things, the incontrovertible fact remained that the evangelist was getting some of my people "revived." When his sermonettes between the songs rose from intimate whispers to enraptured shouts, the audience responded with fervent, impulsive amens. He was working every moment, giving unstintingly of all the boundless energy he had. The singers were doing the same. Saunders always seemed to have one more exciting pronouncement up his sleeve. He insisted that the Lord had special blessings in store for Fairfield if men would only believe. He wept, he prayed, he sang, he blessed, he challenged, and chastised.

Then in a voice which seemed to rock the light bulbs hanging loosely on their twisted cords, he demanded, "Who's thankful tonight? Who's not ashamed to praise the Lord? Who's ready?"

A woman rose to her feet. She was a farmer's wife from a near-by town. In a trembling tone, she said, "I'm so thankful that the Lord lets us gather here and praise His holy name. I'm so thankful. It has helped me just when I needed it."

"God bless you, Sister, God bless you!" Saunders exclaimed. "Who's next?"

A Baptist townsman got up to say, "I want to praise the Lord for hearing my prayer last night. He heard my prayer last night. Yes, He did, and I want to thank Him."

"Of course you do!" Saunders agreed. "And He certainly did hear your prayer. He always does. Yes, sir! Thank you, Jesus!"

Two other testimonials were evoked by the urgently persuasive voice and never-wearying enthusiasm of the evangelist. He testified about the numberless personal blessings he had derived from the old-time religion. The sisters testified to their countless rewards until the chorus of fervent amens indicated that the audience was being convinced that a religious experience was by all odds the greatest adventure in life. Harrowingly I told myself that Saunders had done in four days what I had been unable to do in four years. He was getting requests for public prayers. Hands were being raised all around me.

"Let's everybody pray!" Saunders shouted. "God can hear and understand no matter if the whole world prays at once!"

A loud cacophony of prayers mounted steadily while the musicians and several of the worshipers excitedly clapped their hands and talked things out with the Lord.

At the final "Amen and amen!" a spontaneous song careened through the tent, only to be broken off sharply by the jumping, shouting, ecstatical Saunders, speaking in an unintelligible gibberish and finally crying out, "Jesus is waiting! The Holy Ghost is here!"

This exhibition was followed by an intense silence, reverent as that which often pervaded my service at communiontime. But this was quickly broken by a stir in the audience. A blue-shirted figure rose from his place. Clutching a shapeless hat in his hand, he worked his way to the sawdust sanctuary near the two-by-four altar rail. Stiffly and awkwardly he approached while people hunched forward with a sudden thrill and "Arnold Lembke!" was whispered through the congregation. Saunders, vigorously proclaiming that the Lord was loosing tremendous power in this "canvas-covered upper room," seized Lembke's hat and laid his strong hands on Lembke's shock of rusty hair.

"God bless you, Brother!" Saunders cried. "Last night you were saved and sanctified! Tonight the baptism!"

The singers broke instantly into "There Is Power in the Blood," bringing the mallets down joyously on the marimba. Firmly, forcibly, Saunders compelled Lembke to his knees. The singers sang and praised the Lord. The evangelist prayed with a rhythmical, curtsying movement, "Right now, O Lord, right now!"

Lembke collapsed on the sawdust-covered earth. "God! God!" he wailed, his cry convulsed with weeping. Saunders laughed and cried, "Yes, yes, Brother, it's all right! It's *all* right!"

Lembke lifted up his face. He half rose, then dropped to his knees, his body quivering as if under an electrical force. He made a fluttering, flying motion with his hands and arms. In a jumbled jargon of nonsensical words, he gave vent to the rapture reflected on his tanned and tear-stained face. He was "speaking in tongues" and Brother Saunders, shaking his clenched hands above his shoulders, assured us all it was "the language of the Lord."

Lembke's wife came up front while the singers led the amazed audience in "What Shall Save Us from Our Sins?" She threw her arms around her husband and they stood together weeping while Saunders blessed them both and called for others to start their happy journey up the glory road. Behind me I heard weeping and turned to see Lembke's mother happily shedding tears over the "salvation" of her son. From various parts of the tent I heard half-whispered, tremulous expressions, "Praise the Lord" and "O Jesus," ballots cast for Brother Saunders and the Church of God!

Even more impressive was the response he was getting to his altar call. A dozen people huddled on the ground with heads buried in their arms. Some were sobbing penitently. And Saunders, having made a final plea to sinners in the congregation who were "stubbornly rejecting the voice of God," moved along the altar rail laying his hands on the heads of the prodigals. The singers joined him, praying loud, audacious prayers and whispering words of advice and courage, silently humming snatches of songs and fervently crying, "Glory, glory!" and "O Lord, it's wonderful, it's wonderful, it's something you don't get anywhere in the world!"

I stayed to see two other conversions and one more demonstration of the "baptism of the Holy Spirit with the evidence of speaking in tongues."

My part in all this was mental anguish, pity for the victims who were induced to place themselves on such a spiritual rack. But as I walked the shadowy Fairfield streets that night, I did a lot of thinking about Protestantism and about a mail carrier whose name had for years been on my church roll. Against my own lack of a spiritual dynamic, I weighed the cold fact that the gospel tent was crowded on a week night to hear the old story of evangelistic religion. I pondered the absence of evocative achievements in my ministry. In a short week a stranger had won the confidence of one of my members and probably changed his life. It had needed changing. An outsider with a loud and confident voice had become the instrument for a charismatic demonstration. But what I had seen was uncomfortably reminiscent of what I had expected my ministry to do when I left the seminary. Religion was supposed to save the lost and raise the fallen. And Fairfield would very likely agree that if it did nothing else under God's high heaven, it should, at least, keep a man from getting drunk. That was basic and elemental! Yet I had "talked religion" many times to Arnold Lembke. So had the Reverend Mr. Langley. But his dogma and doctrine had proved as ineffectual as my mild persuasion and earnest prayers.

Though "Holy Roller" emotionalism was offensive to most of my members, I feared that Lembke's name would not be the only one that would be crossed off the Evangelical roster at the next council meeting. The "old-time religion" which Saunders had brought to town was what a cross section of Fairfield Christians had looked for in vain in the Evangelical and Baptist churches. His preaching and revival tactics had also awakened a spiritual consciousness among a number of unchurched families. What had stood in the way of these people before? Why was it necessary for them to "find God" in the sawdust chapel in Barben's meadow?

My first answer was cast in the mold of all my thinking about Protestantism's weakness: rival churches and doctrinal bigotry had so wearied our people that they welcomed a spiritual force from outside their tradition and were willing to accept it as their revolt against denominational confusion. But even while I contemplated this, I heard again the chorus of accusing voices from my congregation: "We lost Arnold Lembke because we never heard any sound denominational preaching." This part of my flock would never be lured from their traditional fold, but they, too, would ask why "conversions" were not happening in our church. That night was the beginning of my reluctant acceptance of Old Doc's theories about Protestantism. Though still holding tenaciously to my original pronouncement against the evil inherent in the formative elements of our faith, I saw religious mitosis taking place in Fairfield.

The revival tent stayed up four weeks instead of two. After that nine families from my church and five from the Baptist rented an empty feed-store building and started a local Church of God. Brother Saunders consented to stay on as their minister, claiming that it was clearly the will of the Lord. Neither the fulminations of Langley nor my resentment against another denomination in the town could stop things. Samson and Ezekiel were helpless, and opposition only added fuel to the Pentecostal fire. Bible classes were begun. Wednesday prayer meetings were introduced. The "full gospel" was promised and preached. The baptism of the Holy Ghost was earnestly sought and the meetings were charged with many a lusty "Hallelujah" and a hearty "Praise the Lord!" Arnold Lembke, together with his "brothers and sisters in the Lord," was carrying the heavenly mail.

The bankers said, "It's a dramatic interlude. Fairfield's not a holiness town. Our people aren't Church of God caliber."

My neighbors predicted, "They won't make a go of it. As long as the revival was on, folks were putting something into the offering. It'll be a different story from here on."

The cattleman committed himself beyond doubt: "You've given folks around here the idea that one church is about as good or as bad as the next, so I suppose the Lembkes and the rest think it doesn't make much difference where they go. If you'd let people know that there's a right road and a wrong road and make it clear that ours is the right road, we wouldn't have things like this happening."

His was not an isolated opinion. I caught it in the glances of my parishioners. A council member came around to endorse the cattleman's views. "You've got to let our people know what our church believes and what we demand of folks. And we want to know where you stand in building up our denomination in this town. Seems to me if you did that, we wouldn't have lost these families."

"But what about the Baptists? Certainly people know where Brother Langley stands, but he has lost members, too, and, I hear, is ready to lose a few more," I countered without effect.

Old Doc was the only outsider who was happy about the Pentecostal invasion. With the magniloquence of a major prophet, he voiced his irreducible views: "There's more down-right interest and big talk about religion in this town right now than there's been for years! Arnold Lembke's ma, who used to go on about her pains, hasn't been in to see me for two months. She's got something else on her mind besides herself for a change. She's all het up about Arnold turning the old feed store into a gospel hall. Long as religion's been on earth some folks have been watching other folks get converted, have been getting converted themselves, or have been getting hold of some newfangled idea about how God is supposed to work." Stamping a seal on my fearful deductions, he added with a laugh, "Halle-lujah, boy, this is what I meant when I called it mitosis!"

But I clung stubbornly to my chosen polemic: Protestantism by reason of its division drives people into spiritual detours. The fences which denominationalism has built are more important than the God denominationalism proclaims. Clearer than ever, I felt that my church considered it more admirable to be a good Evangelical than to be a good Christian. It was more necessary to be loyal to an organization than to demonstrate the unity of the Christian life. Impatiently I argued that sectarianism spelled death for a vital faith and substituted for a living religion his-toric creeds, devotion to a dead past, homage to the tempera-mental impulses of forgotten leaders, custodianship of ancient rivalries, idolatrous affection for denominational acclaim, and a jealous selfishness for staked-off areas of operation in Fairfields all over the world. Every discriminatory division militated against the very end for which the Christian church was planned.

Was my indignation simply a reflection of what was happening in my parish, or was it registering the unhappy plight of a Protestant world unready and unfit to encounter a fellowship of Christians who acknowledge one Lord? That idea was certainly slow in the making. It was a vaporous cloud idly drifting in a far-off hemisphere.

The last report that had filtered in to me spoke vaguely of a proposed world conference to devote itself to questions of "faith and order." Dimly through this announcement came an acknowledgment of intercommunion between the Orthodox Church and the Anglican Church, and also between the Anglican Church and the Old Catholic Church. Once more, it was said, Christians were demonstrating union.

In the light of my Fairfield problem, these statements were spurious and overbearing. Who were these church leaders with a genius for effecting foreign unions but incompetent to suggest a plan for uniting two churches separated by a graveled country road? Of what use was a world conference on faith and order when the average Protestant had not yet learned to work cooperatively with his Christian neighbor?

Confused, I looked out of my aberrations and saw the Church of God take its place among us as another denomination, bringing to four the schismatic families represented by the children of God in our community. Five, actually, for across the high and half-forgotten Protestant-Catholic fence, a rumor screamed into my troubled ministry like an explosive projectile. A girl in my congregation announced that she was marrying a Catholic boy. Worse than that, she was "turning"!

The solid, vine-covered little red-brick church north of town suddenly took on the aspect of a witch house from which the thin and bony fingers of a dead past reached forth to snatch the best teacher I had in my Sunday school. Catherine Meyers, the only daughter of a deacon on my board of trustees, was a pleasant, attractive girl who had been valedictorian at the recent high-school graduation. She sang in the choir, and all of the congregation agreed that she was the most talented young woman in the church. But none of these facts had prevented her from being swooped up, body and soul, by her love for Catholic Donald Ryan.

Her father was philosophical. "Love is love," he said. "We don't like it either, but we've always made it a rule to let Catherine live her own life."

Other Evangelicals were not so docile. "What have the Catholics got that we haven't got?" they asked. And answered, "The Catholics have got a hold on their people. Did you see any of them hit the sawdust trail at the revival? They weren't even there. Was the priest there along with our minister? No. The Catholics know what they believe; they don't care how many religions come to town."

Catherine's grandmother came to the parsonage wringing her hands and tearfully voicing her despair: "How can she do it? Think of us—one of Fairfield's best Evangelical families! Think of her fitting herself into the Mass and the confession. Think of her praying to the saints and saying the Hail Marys. How can she ever bring herself to call the priest 'father?' All their awful ideas about purgatory! Paying the priest to get souls out of hell! Think of her children growing up Catholic! She has to promise that in writing! You must save her!"

I tried. I talked to Catherine, who had already begun taking instruction in the Catholic faith. Reminding her of Protestant-

ism's heritage and its cherished beliefs, I made a strong point
of the fact that the church should be not an end but rather a
means to the perfecting of the Christian life. I properly emphasized the merit of faith and the uselessness of empty good works
and mechanical acts. I told her about the Reformation—as
Kurtz or Langley would have—and pointed out at what great
cost Protestantism was born to replace the power of the papacy.
I stressed the fact that in Roman Catholicism she would have to
accept the infallibility of the Pope when he spoke on doctrines
pertaining to faith and morals and assured her that she would
be expected to comply with requests of the church in civic and
social affairs. I appealed to her respect for her parents' loyalty
to our denomination.

When I finished she said, "I don't think it makes much difference. We all believe in the same God, don't we? We're all
Christians, aren't we? I don't see much more difference between
the Catholics and the Evangelicals than I do between the Baptists and the Evangelicals. The churches really don't work
together or get along anyway."

"You're right," I told her, though I knew the town would
have risen against me as its worst heretic if it had been listening.
"There is little more real fellowship and reciprocity between us
and the church across the street than there is between us and
the church north of town. We have carried our freedom to dif-
fer so far that we have become enemies with our own people.
The very features that made Protestantism great—religious
idealism and a fellowship of faith—now also make it small. But
you and I, being Protestants, have the right to attempt to change
this situation. If you become a Catholic, though, you cannot
honestly disagree with the church's decisions. You can disagree
with me or with Brother Langley, and we will respect your personal convictions. The Protestant enjoys the authority of his

church because he is the church. You are the church, Catherine. That is one of Protestantism's great glories. A religion that sustains us is better than a religion which we must sustain."

But after a lengthy conference, I realized that Catherine's mind was made up. Her love for Donald Ryan and a lack of love for Fairfield's Protestantism laughed at my poor logic.

Brother Langley, waiting for me the next morning for a walk to the post office, swung his black hat in insatiable protest.

"If you really preach the faith, Brother," he repeated earnestly over and over, "if you really preach the faith, Catholicism can't stand up before it. It simply cannot. It's like throwing a light into a dark closet. The darkness must go. The light of truth is that light, Brother! I do wish you had called me in. I surely do!"

And Old Doc gravely told me: "I should think Catholicism ought to lose these rounds where the younger generation is concerned. I thought young folks wanted to think for themselves and take a chance on trying their own wings. How's come Catherine is suddenly willing to have hers clipped? As a Protestant she could attend Catholic services if she had a mind to, but it won't work the other way around. Say what you want to, Catholics tend to be exclusive. Now understand, I don't think the Lord gives a damn whether a man is Catholic or not. If He did, He'd see to it that all babies are born Protestant. All He knows is that we're *born*. Saying you belong to this church or that won't open any pearly gates anywhere, you can bet on that. But what gets me is that Protestantism doesn't have the punch to win these rounds even when all the odds are on our side."

The church council showed the same displeasure when we met that week in the church basement. As we sat huddled around the furnace on the bitter wintry night, the cattleman grimly observed, "If you let somebody steal a melon here and a melon there, pretty soon you have an empty patch!"

"Gentlemen," I said, "if I've been a poor watchman over the Evangelical interests——"

"No, now!" said an elder magnanimously. "You're doing all right. It's just a matter of holding things together a little more."

Catherine's father stirred uneasily in his chair. "I'm sorry about this whole business, men. But, you know, these things have happened before and they'll probably happen again."

We turned to him and the cattleman expressed our fears when he challenged, "You certainly aren't thinking of joining up somewhere else, are you, Robert?"

"I? Certainly not!"

I was never sure. The Evangelical chains that linked my people to one another—to me—to the church—to God—were fearfully tenuous. I greeted every Sabbath morning with an anxious glance at the churchyard, wondering whether the attendance would be good or bad, the congregation hostile or friendly. My insecurity warped my sense of the fitness of things. To whom was I, as a Protestant, responsible? Presumably to God. And God was the still small voice of conscience which told me time and again to beat the drums for union regardless of personal cost.

And that conviction moved me to heroic indiscretion at our annual congregational meeting on the first Sunday in January. After the church dinner while we sat around the tables and heard the reports read by the various superintendents and directors of organizations and finances, I asked permission to have a statement included in the congregational minutes. I said that I had brought mimeographed copies for every member. I wanted them to read it instead of hearing it read. Proudly I distributed copies of a philippic written in the heat of passion just the night before. In and out of the tables I made my way, putting a copy into the lifted hands of everyone. Brother Saunders could have felt no more righteous when he stuffed his broadsides into Fairfield homes. This was my true bill for Fairfield's dilemma, and I was ready to back it up until I came to the last table and discovered Old Doc, sitting like a half-forgotten ghost in his chair near the door.

"What the devil's this now?" he mumbled.

I faltered. For a moment I disregarded his extended hand. He was not a member of the congregation. He was a guest, invited only for the dinner. It was none of his affair. He was an outsider, a freethinker, my disreputable oracle! But he was also Doctor Reynolds, the custodian of Fairfield's life and death for more than half a century.

I handed him one of the poorly mimeographed sheets and with it went my courage and my heart. Dimly, almost contemptuously, I looked at the statement which everyone was now reading. It was by no means written in the idiom of the town. No one would understand. The cattleman, the banker, the council, the women, the farmers, the townsfolk—to them it would be only a torrent of words, carping at them, flailing them for not following the vague pattern of the unity I so earnestly felt and could not bring to pass. A funereal silence descended on our meeting and I tried with ever-growing anxiety to find the vanished glory in my thesis which began:

"Listen, Fairfield Protestants! This faith of ours is a good faith! It has ideals considerably higher than denominational walls! It has a vision of God which, if we will grasp it and believe it, will let us follow that vision in our own way! People of every nation under heaven, the greatest and the lowliest of mankind, have found Protestantism challenging, serviceable, redemptive. It has endowed the human race with the dignity of freedom, the allurement of the good life, the liberty of knowledge, the institutions of democracy, the oneness of mankind.

This faith of ours is a good faith! It holds the same secrets and powers and blessings inherent in religions more ancient and more modern, with some extra secrets and some greater revelations for those who have the strong will to believe. But God has never played Protestantism as His favorite. Nor will He so long as we stress separation instead of brotherhood. The inexorable laws of survival apply to us more fully and completely than to other religions because we have dared to pose as freedom's faith, permitting man to find God in his own way and without the imperialism of church or creed! Listen, Fairfield Protestants! This faith of ours——"

The president of the council was speaking. In his characteristically languid but confident way, he was saying, "Well, if this is all, do I hear the motion to adjourn?"

I looked up.

"I so move," someone said.

"Second the motion," said a voice.

Then the sound of chairs screaming on the concrete floor, the rattle of dishes, the din of voices, the clatter of feet as children broke pell-mell up to the auditorium to play hide-and-seek under the pews. The cold flashed in through the open door as the people departed. The janitor rattled the furnace grates, then noisily closed off the registers.

"Young people's meeting tonight same as always?" he called to me.

I nodded. He did not understand and called to me again. I told him, "Yes." But all seemed involuntary and without definite intention. The voices were unreal.

"It was a good meeting. . . . I'm taking the paper you wrote home with me. . . . It's getting mighty cold. . . . I'm leaving some pie for you in the kitchen. . . . When are you coming out to see us? . . . Well, another year. . . . Happy New Year again to you!"

Mimeographed sheets were taken and mimeographed sheets were left, and which filled me with least concern I did not quite know. I only knew that my efforts were as exhausted as the year upon which we had so dismally reported, and though I seemed to see deeply into my own mind, all I could find was resignation to a lost cause. My counterreformation was solving nothing and crushing no one but myself.

Old Doc, bundled in his fur coat, his round fur cap pressed down over his ears, gave me a bearlike grip of the hand.

"That's the best damn thing you've ever written," he growled, "and it's as good for the Baptists and the Lutherans as it is for the Evangelicals!"

"Sure," I agreed dully. "That's right."

"Keep it up," said Reynolds stubbornly and braced his body against the evening cold.

Puzzled, I wondered what he meant by this unexpected re-action. During the following week I heard that the corrupt old philosopher had twisted my message into a plain case for denominationalism! He was saying that if every Fairfield church would begin to live and appreciate its heritage, that was all the town needed and that was just about all there was to religion anyhow. But my church board and my church societies knew what I meant, and the suspicion that I was the moon-struck victim of an impractical dream took on unprecedented proportions. The rumor that Langley and Saunders and Kurtz had a better idea of what was expected of a parish preacher was almost unanimously accepted as fact.

The earth cringed stubborn and bare under the gray skies of winter and I went despairingly about my pastoral duties. But Lent came with its promise of spring. This was the rallying season for congregational efforts. On Easter Sunday new members would be received—by the Evangelicals, the Baptists, the

דוד

Lutherans and the Church of God. Seriously I catechized my-self. Did it really matter that it was impossible for us to have union services during Holy Week? Was it really unchristian for each church to campaign ardently for new members on its own behalf? Should it be cause for concern to see four church announcements spread across the *Clarion* like the competitive ads of four cut-rate stores? Did Fairfield have the right to change the Scripture, "Seek ye the Lord *while* He may be found," to *"where* He may be found?" I could not forget my ecumenical dream while Fairfield churches were struggling: for members, for money, for a well-defined program, and always *against one another.*

But about the time I was prepared to pick up my crusade once more, one of my most loyal members called at the parsonage. Mrs. Willard Duncan, a banker's widow, who had always faithfully supported all my efforts on my little acre in the king-dom, politely announced that she had found a new faith. She had come to explain why she would no longer attend my services and earnestly entreat me to understand her action. She had experienced a most remarkable healing through Christian Science and now, after much deliberation and prayer, had de-cided to drive to the city each Sunday morning to attend services at the First Church of Christ, Scientist.

"I have the very highest regard for you and your ministry," she assured. "You are doing a great deal for us and our com-munity. But what I have found and experienced in Science are things I have always felt should be part of one's religious life. The ministry of healing—healing of body and mind—is ob-viously what Jesus came to demonstrate."

"Well," I faltered, "if you had spoken to me . . . *I* believe in prayer for the sick. I believe in it very much—more, perhaps, than our denomination believes in it——"

She reached over with her jeweled hand.

"I'm sure you do," she comforted. "I'm sure you believe very much in prayer. But Science has made it more scientific. And there are other things. It will be a source of strength to know that no matter where I attend the Science services, they will always be uniform. Whether I go to Florida or New York or California, or whether I visit my sister Josephine in South Dakota, the services will always be the same. And wherever I meet Scientists, they seem always to think alike and reason alike."

"But that's deadening!" I exclaimed.

She lifted her eyebrows in surprise. "I thought you would understand." She smiled. "Since you have been trying to bring our church and the other churches together——"

"But not so everyone will think alike!" I hastened to explain. "No, that's something different. I'm only concerned because sectarianism contradicts Christian fellowship——"

She interrupted with a wave of her hand. "I have much respect for both churches," she said. "In fact, for all churches. They all fill a certain place for certain people. But, you see, as for me——"

Just then I spied Brother Langley passing by. Impulsively I went to the door and called him in, desperately rounding up Protestantism's strongest reserve. And as Mrs. Duncan voiced a distressed note of protest, Samson came in swinging. He grasped the situation at once and commandeered the big guns. A fusillade broke out over my poor apostate, and I could feel her going down ingloriously under this orthodox attack. Pleasing to me was the fact that Langley knew Christian Science history. He was well aware that Mary Baker Eddy once said that "the less we know or think about hygiene, the less we are predisposed to sickness." He referred to as "tommyrot," the tenet that, "Man is never sick, for mind is not sick and matter cannot be."

"You will discover the irrationality of the principles on which Christian Science operates if you will but study them, madam! You will realize the movement is nothing but a dictatorship, directed by the shrewd headquarters of the Mother Church in Boston. Is Christian Science a religion? Ridiculous, madam! It is a fraud-idea corresponding to the Isis cult of antiquity. Paul's plea is mine: 'I beseech you, brethren, by the name of our Lord Jesus Christ, that ye all speak the same thing, and that there be no divisions among you; but that ye be perfectly joined together in the same mind and in the same judgment.' Christian Science reduces God to a principle," he cried. "It makes Jesus Christ a phrase. It rejects the plan of salvation, denies the Trinity and opposes the holy sacraments, including baptism!"

A blaze of Scripture texts and a devastating denunciation of Christian Science as pagan, heretical, and satanic followed. But when he paused to reload, Mrs. Duncan rose from her chair with perfect poise and dignity; tucking her large leather purse under her arm and smiling at us patiently, she said, "I am very sorry, gentlemen, that I have made myself the object of so much concern. Do forgive me."

Then she left, while Brother Langley followed her out, crying, "Your soul, my good woman! Your salvation!"

Mrs. Duncan simply waved her hand. There was something about religion that made it a matter of the heart. It could not be made to obey or disobey just by giving commands or reciting the New Testament. One single spiritual experience meant more to Mrs. Duncan than my four years of sermonizing. The essential quality in religion was an adventure—an adventure of such great proportions that my seminary training might not fathom it, while one moment of probing the human heart made it suddenly real and inviolable. For me, in my parsonage room, there had been re-enacted the story of the man who was blind, but who now saw men walking like trees.

Mrs. Duncan had found something better than I had offered from my pulpit. Arnold Lembke found a better product, too. So did Catherine Meyers. This was a day of better products.

The church might go on without these members, but I couldn't. My congregation was disintegrating. The Pentecostals were undermining it at the bottom, the Catholics were digging in at the top, and the Christian Scientists were sneaking in between! To leave town seemed my only escape. Helpless and shamed, I told myself it was all caused by the weakness and sin of divided denominationalism.

Poor misguided Langley, quoting a text: "That there be no divisions among you." Who taught our people the art of dividing? Who started it? I would recommend that he read again the history of the Reformation, the history of Protestantism.

Mitosis? Nonsense! We were merely reaping the wild harvest of our opposing camps. Had we Fairfield Protestants been *one,* would Mrs. Duncan have left us, even if she had found a supplementary faith elsewhere? Religion in Fairfield had become a war of secession. And when I left town someone else would come in to divide further. This was the end of my attempt at spiritually humanizing the people whose minds and lives were sunk into the dead earth of spiritual partisanship. My first church. My first failure. Ezekiel throwing down the sticks in disgust. What did international church meetings across the ocean mean? What merit was there in such grandiose gestures of Protestant unity if the spirit did not filter down to the people in the pews? Did the world leaders actually care about the problems of local congregations?

There was a pounding at the front door and a familiar voice called, "Anybody home?"

It was the cattleman who, with his usual composure, but with the hint of a hard bargain in his voice, said, "I hear we've run into some more trouble. Reverend Langley was down at the post office telling quite a group what happened. Or is this just talk?"

"No. It's right. Langley was in on it, but I don't suppose it mattered much one way or the other. You know how it is when Mrs. Duncan makes up her mind about something."

"Yes. But what do you think about this business anyhow?" he asked with a note of far-reaching implication. "She was about the best member we've got."

Our eyes met. I knew what he wanted me to say, so I said it. "It's about time I left, isn't it? It's only right that you get someone who can hold the church together."

"First he'll have to build it up again," he said impatiently and with an almost scornful smile.

"I know," I told him.

"Personally, I hate to see you go," he apologized. "But if you would stay, what do you think you might be able to do in our situation?"

I looked at him quietly. His face became a study in fatherly pain and irritability.

"I know Fairfield hasn't been an easy job." He shrugged belatedly. "Not that I think you could have put us all into one herd lot and never expected any of us to kick over the bars. But Mrs. Duncan was kind of special."

"Well, I . . . I feel, of course, that if Mrs. Duncan didn't find what she needed in our church——"

"But that's just it! She always did find what she needed long as we were good Evangelicals. That's the point. Now I tell you what I think. All our trouble started when you got this every-body-get-together idea. Step by step you thought more about bringing the Baptists over to us or us over to the Baptists than you did about building up our own church. And the man we need is a man who is willing to do *that*."

"You mean, get *more* denominationally minded?"

"I don't know what you want to call it. But long as I can remember the ministers we've had were denominational minis-ters. You can go 'way back and you'll find that they always had something to say for what our denomination believed and what it taught. Well, that's the only way we know and I don't think it's such a bad way either. But now, since you've come along with this other idea—well, you see how things have gone. When my stock breaks through the fence, I fix the wires!"

I was the fence and the wires, and I was suddenly broken beyond repair.

The cattleman slapped his work gloves decisively and slowly into his open hand. I heard the sound and it was a parish clock counting off my lost years. The pain of disillusionment he would not have understood. He just stood there as if we were already in the midst of shipping crates and empty rooms. Perhaps he was right. At least I had neither faith nor energy with which to meet his arguments or defend the idea I had fought for so long. We were suddenly far apart, my cattleman-president and I—my congregation and I—the community and I—we had nothing in common for which to bargain, nothing on which we could agree.

Vaguely and half to myself I said, "I wonder if Fairfield is being polished off to mirror the world."

He held his gloves strongly in his hands, listening.

"I was wondering," I repeated, "if Fairfield is a picture of Protestantism everywhere. Sometimes I've thought of that.

Competition in world missions may be like Fairfield counting the cost of gain or loss in church attendance. The race for new churches—Fairfield battling for new members. The struggle for denominational influence around the globe—Fairfield's Baptist Church and Fairfield's Evangelical trying to control the village board. And meanwhile we're being preyed upon by renegade groups who are taking advantage of our weaknesses. Protestantism isn't a marching army at all; it's religious politics, a two-hundred-party system, reflected in empty pews and empty lives. Mine included."

He looked at me scornfully. "Fairfield is Fairfield and that's just the point. We who have lived here all our lives think we know pretty well what's best."

"Do you, Mr. Jordan? Do you really?"

"I think we do," he said. Then, after a brief pause, he added, "When would you suggest that we have a board meeting?"

"Tonight," I replied without feeling.

"Don't hurry," he said without malice. "It's not a bad town, you know."

I looked up quickly, but he was walking slowly toward the window and stood looking out on the gravel street. Did he also remember? For with those words he had greeted me when I first came to town. Once more I was driving with the cattleman for the first time down Main Street—the lonely, suspiciously intimate street where every day slowly, absorbingly, I had become more a part of the people. I was walking with him into the "Evangelical" bank, and past Old Doc's office, and to the post office and to the garage and the store. . . . "Thought you'd like to meet the fellow who's preaching his trial sermon tomorrow." . . . I was going with him through the manse. I was conducting my first congregational meeting. I was standing in the church behind locked doors rehearsing a baccalaureate address. I was calling for the first time on a family into which death had come. I was with the cattleman, and his expression never changed whether we walked through lush, wind-stirred fields or through fields of dust and burned-out grain. I was hauling crude oil for farmers during the chinch-bug years when they dug ditches to save their crops. I was answering the door to find a parishioner with vegetables and chickens and baskets of fruit. I was watching the attendance record and turning the out-of-date mimeograph machine. I was doing the thousand little things for which the good Lord had called me to Fairfield. I was His hired man.

But I was also the Lord's watchman on the Protestant ramparts in this town and I was signaling distress. Disunion strode my parish. Reporting: A struggling Baptist Church and a struggling Evangelical Church and a struggling Lutheran Church and a struggling Church of God! Reporting: If American Protestantism is like Fairfield Protestantism something must be done! If Fairfield is the Protestant world, sound the alarm!

The heavy steps of the president of my board broke in upon my reverie. He had turned away from the window and was saying, "I'll see if I can get the other men by tonight. Maybe it'd be best if you sort of write out what you told me awhile ago."

Then he stopped and pulled on his gloves thoughtfully. "I'm not saying that you're all wrong," he admitted gravely. "In fact, maybe you're right. Maybe all God's people ought to be one in one church arrangement. But in Fairfield it looks like we're not ready for that. We haven't come that far. Maybe the kingdom of God is really a bigger thing than we'd know what to do with."

I watched him walk slowly to his car. He got in and the motor started. The wheels turned slowly in the loose gravel.

He drove away reluctantly, and the sound of his departing closed around me as I stood alone at the open door.

Solemn and pleasant stood the Baptist Church on its corner. Sacred and tranquil stood the church of the Evangelicals. Whether they would ever be one seemed less important than it ever had before. The cattleman's admission that I might be right left me strangely aware that I might be wrong.

I thought of Langley and Kurtz who had found their religious views completely satisfying; they had invested their lives in them. So had Brother Saunders and Arnold Lembke. And Catherine Meyers. And Mrs. Duncan. Had not the core of my preaching been the quest of "finding God" and had not these people found Him? And perhaps the cattleman had, too, in his way, and even Old Doc in his.

Suddenly instead of my foolish agony I felt a sense of peace and security that transcended every barrier which religion had ever raised. Lutheranism, Anabaptist and Baptist, the Reformed faith, the Presbyterian faith, Anglicanism, Congregationalism, the Quakers, the Church of the Brethren, the Moravians, the Methodists—all rushed in to visit me as I wandered through the cupolaed, sectarian manse. At last I felt a oneness with the Christian world!

Why, when I was really a homeless Protestant? Why, when I knew that Protestantism's tendency toward disseverment was congenital? Old Doc could call it an indication of life, but it was really devotion to the tribal gods of many manufactured faiths. Perhaps my sense of release was due to the thought that I would soon emancipate myself from this unholy labor at Babel. Let others finish the tower and dedicate it. I walked the parsonage rooms saying, "Lack of co-operation is a vice. Suspicion and bigotry among faiths are ungodly."

I sought my study only to be met again by the dream of a united Protestantism. It swept over me, dissolved in my questioning, returned and fled again during these hours and during the ensuing days when the mingled feelings of the congregation combined in an awkward and unrealistic farewell. I was leaving, surer than ever that Protestantism, having been born in schisms, would always be schismatic, that the dangerous liberty of putting into man's hands his right to find God in his own way had defeated its own purpose. All the churches in Fairfield were arguing that their way of life was based on truth. And all the while the gulfs widened and the hope for brotherhood became more remote. Behind the symbolism of division, back of the denominational walls were hidden personal antagonisms, prejudices, intolerances, and hatreds. The deeper doctrinal aspects in every faith were things which the laity never fully understood. Yet, these were elements that divided. They filtered down, garbled and confuted the thinking of the people in the pews. Meanwhile men sat in conferences working out on paper plans for Protestant unity, an ideal that had to be lived, first of all, in the individual heart.

Oh, to turn back and try once more! To set up a pulpit halfway between my church and the Baptist Church! "See here, Mr. Cattleman! See here, Mr. Baptist Banker! The Galilean had no name or label for His religion. See here, Brother Langley and Pastor Kurtz and Brother Saunders, let's sit down together once more and talk this over!"

But instead the day came when the open windows of my car framed the Baptist Church on my right and the Evangelical on my left. I was hemmed in between boxes and bags. Beside me was a lunch basket which a thoughtful neighbor had brought over at the last moment. Tucked into the basket was a copy of the *Clarion,* looking up at me with the editor's reminder that I was leaving "with plans for the immediate future indefinite."

That was true. Driving away, gravel-deep in disillusion, my spirit heavy as the loaded car, I had no itinerary in mind except a momentary one that took me over to a stuccoed bungalow to say good-by to Old Doc, who had been too ill to attend the congregational farewell.

Bundled to his chin in a heavy lounging robe, he greeted me with an oath of disdain at his condition, then voiced an equally impressive outburst at the mess I'd made of things in his beloved town. "Dammit! Why can't you get it through your head that Protestantism is supposed to be the way it is? Why don't you believe me, boy? Why don't you take an old man's word for knowing something about these things? How can a man beat any sense and understanding into you youngsters these days? How many spring seasons do you have to see before you'll know that you can't stop nature and growth?"

Skeptically I listened to another homespun peroration, yet with misgivings of my own which made me almost ready to agree with him. But I was given no opportunity. Suddenly at the door appeared the tall, timeless figure of the cattleman, hat thrust back on his head, his blue work jacket flung over his shoulder like an invitation to spring. "Just saw the car," he drawled. "Going to get away or staying around for dinner?"

"No," I said quickly. "This is my last call."

"They come and they go, Jordan," Reynolds said with a hopeless shrug. "Long as I can remember, ministers have come and gone in and out of here. Some stayed longer than others, but none of them ever really became citizens of the community. Fairfield's just a steppingstone for a better job somewhere else."

"But this fellow isn't leaving for a better job," figured the cattleman. "He's just leaving!"

"Damn foolishness!" Old Doc complained.

I extended my hand. He blinked at me distrustfully, then put his hand in mine. "Dammit then, good luck," he said. "Let's hear from you sometime."

I thanked him and turned away. The cattleman stepped slowly aside, making way for me at the door. "Good-by again," he said. "Sure you don't want to come and have a bite of dinner first?"

I shook my head, walked to the street, and squeezed into the car, leaving the cattleman at the door and Old Doc framed in the tapestried window of his front room, stubbornly and sadly nodding at my final wave of farewell. Slowly and for the last time I was moving down the Fairfield street with its low, nondescript frame homes, moving toward the graveled highway between the rolling spaces covered by farms. Tractors droned over the earth, leaving the turned-up ground behind them much as I was leaving my pastoral acres. Farmers waved to me from their fields and from their wagons. Everyone always waved in the Fairfield farming country. Baptists and Evangelicals, Church of God or Catholics or Lutherans, churchmen and non-churchmen alike—they never let anyone drive by without a greeting. I was aware, too, that theirs was a security which I might well remember. Living had been good in Fairfield and much would be memorable. Even now, as the distance widened between me and the little white steepled church, events and faces came into mind with new meaning, and the words of the cattleman returned to me like a softly spoken benediction: "Maybe the kingdom of God is a bigger thing than we'd know what to do with."

CHAPTER FOUR

The Latter Rain Is Falling

THERE was no escaping religion. Defiant in my release from active church leadership and disillusioned about the ideal of church union, I drove from Fairfield ready to be absorbed into the disorganized ranks of the Protestant laity. I shed old sentiments courageously, and yet I could never quite disassociate myself from little white-steepled churches. The sudden feeling of security which came with my freedom from denominational toil waned when I caught sight of church activities. Inevitably I identified myself with the young man who was placing the subject of next Sunday's sermon in his bulletin board and with the old clergyman who was bestowing his final blessing upon a happy wedding party leaving the parsonage. But the evident reality of Protestantism's division made me dare the denominational gods to show me wherein I had erred.

Gradually I realized how ill-equipped a pulpit dodger is among the laity. Only an exaggerated idealism could have led a man from the friendly confines of a Kansas parish into the hostile and competitive America of the bankrupt thirties. And while the specter of depression haunted the nation and me, the timeless specter of Scriptural warning was also stalking at my side—the warning about a man having put his hand to the plow and looking back.

My dwindling resources were squandered on courses in music

and dramatic art in a New York conservatory. But always my limited talents involved me in heaven's affairs against my will: church choirs and church orchestras and church chancel dramas. After fleeing to Cleveland and cub reporting, I landed an assignment with the Federated Council of Churches, where I was given the job of finding out what young people were thinking about religion. Young people were confused and so was I, so my report was never finished. I joined the Civic Theatre, which should have been a sure escape but instead led me straight to the chancel of the Church of the Covenant and a collaboration with director Clancy Cooper on a series of religious plays. Through lean depression months I fled religious work only to learn that I was a poor book salesman and an incompetent music clerk and that no one would buy insurance from me. My violin became my only source of income.

In Chicago thirteen weeks in radio and two weeks as soloist at services conducted by a Jew converted to the Christian faith prepared the way for a flier with a musical troupe. After playing the "big churches" of the Midwest for a month, we disbanded because we could no longer trust the freewill offerings or our booking agent. Church conventions, young people's conferences, and church recitals—I was playing more hymns to the glory of God than I had ever done in Kansas, but they were not paying off in this world's goods. Not even in chicken dinners.

There was no escaping religion, and frequently I admitted to myself that I did not want to escape. Though the variegated activities of my first year after Fairfield had made my induction into the laity complete, I could never entirely forget the problems of Protestantism which had defeated me and my first pastorate. When Sunday morning bells brought country roads and city streets to life, I wished for every Protestant a few months as a religious itinerant, a cosmopolite, a sleuth on Church Street, U.S.A. I wished for every denominationalist the Sunday-morning experience of walking around church corners.

From a vine-covered Methodist Church came the voice of the Methodists joining in a timeless song, "Praise God from Whom All Blessings Flow." And that was exactly what the Baptists were singing in the Baptist Church. And in the Presbyterian Church and in the Reformed Church and in many other churches I heard the same song. I heard it again in the English Lutheran Church of the United Lutheran Church in America and in the Lutheran Church of the American Lutheran Conference. It was part of the Mennonite service, and I heard it in the Congregational-Christian Church and in the Church of the Nazarene. It was only a song, but it was a symbol of unity, and it transformed sectarian city and countryside into a metropolis of a united faith. All that was needed was a consciousness of union and suddenly "Praise God from Whom All Blessings Flow" would become a world-shaking, global hosanna.

Wherever I went, Protestantism had a creed that its people recited: "I believe in God the Father Almighty." I heard it in rural churches and in college chapels, in the Southern hills and in a busy harbor mission. It was the voice of Protestantism, molded in one essential belief, united in one basic aim, resounding across America and out against the far horizons of the Christian world.

But I always came back to reality: Protestantism does not recognize its likenesses; it remains hopelessly divided. The telltale marks of a Fairfield psychosis were everywhere. During my tour of the Midwest I met two ministers who lived less than a mile apart in a small town but who had not spoken to each other for eleven years. At a religious convention in New Jersey some of the delegates refused to participate in a communion service with ministers of another denomination. In town and city I found ministerial alliances sharply divided into two groups, and there was often bad blood between the liberals and the conservatives.

The Fairfield mural was extended. The ancient seeds of denominationalism, borne down upon the Reformation tide, were scattered at large throughout Protestantism. Time and circumstance had planted them, ministers had nurtured them, and now there was nothing to reap but the whirlwind. Though many ministers had probably become more tolerant between the sowing and the reaping, it was too late. Intolerances were as deep-seated as religion itself, and the man in the pew knew nothing about the term nor the spirit of ecumenicalism. And I, swallowed up by the laity, could do less about it than I had attempted in Fairfield a year before.

Worshiping in the pew instead of in the pulpit, I gained a new perspective. Seeking for spiritual guidance instead of guiding others, I gradually realized that the distance between pulpit and pew was a great distance—greater perhaps than that which had separated the two churches I had tried to unite. I began to wonder how many times my parishioners in Fairfield had come to church bogged down in personal problems which I had by-passed with big talk about religion's place in the international scene. How often had I disappointed them as I was now being disappointed by the cold unfriendliness of Protestant Christians?

Looking for an answer to my own questioning of spiritual values, I suddenly saw a weakness in the social gospel I had preached. A man caught in the conflicts of daily life did not want a dissertation on world affairs. Neither would he be satisfied by Langley's theological tirades. What he needed was a definable reality in the Christian life and a usable power to

meet his personal, everyday needs. During the agonizing, fruit-
less months following Fairfield, I decided that before churches
united, churches must be revitalized. Union would be meaningless unless Protestantism could be welded into a fellowship
and a brotherhood; the people in the pews must be reached by
the man in the pulpit. And though I habitually responded to
the bells on Sunday morning, I knew I was a homeless Protestant, puzzled and confused.

Weary and jobless, I invested my last dollar one night in
Milwaukee to hear Fritz Kreisler in the city auditorium. From
the moment his bow touched the strings I sat at his feet, as on
a mountainside, hearing the beatitudes of a universal faith. It
was the most beautiful music I had ever heard, so full of sweet-
ness and passion that I felt, somehow, I was entering a new
phase of my life. Yet, it was all related to the old phase, for as
the audience faded from my thoughts, I saw Baptists and Evangelicals, ministers and laity—all Protestants, whatever their
make or kind—sitting together and forgetting their differences
in the indescribable art and life of music and its maker. There
was nothing for them to say. They just sat there. And I sat
there. And God came down and walked among us. It seemed to
me that no one would dare boast that he belonged to this church
group or that church group or that he followed this reformer
or that founder of a faith, and that all should be ashamed that
there had ever been any creed or belief that had separated them
and kept them apart from the universal spirit of the Divine Presence.

Late that night in my rented sleeping quarters, a gaunt, high-
ceilinged room in an old house on Wisconsin Avenue, I packed
my fiddle in its case and snapped the locks. I was no Kreisler. I
could never be. After I had heard him, anything less seemed useless and futile. The next morning I went to a downtown em-

ployment agency which I had shunned ever since I arrived in Milwaukee. The courteous receptionist gave me the usual forms, and I shared a table where a grimy-faced man bent laboriously over his application material, swearing under his breath at "the damn things folks want to know about you when all you want is a job." I agreed with him. But all that was needed in his case was a telephone call and off he went to be a janitor's helper in an office building.

My qualifications did not rate that well. The gracious directress of the Steuben Society's Employment Bureau greeted me with modest hauteur. Her precise, businesslike voice matched her smooth, stylish coiffure and the trim tailored suit she wore; but there was kindness in the well-modulated tones. Sitting proudly behind her orderly desk, she tucked a lace kerchief into her sleeve, arched her brows over my application, and adjusted her ribboned spectacles.

After a moment of scanning my life history she exclaimed with gracious motherly wonder, "Well! What kind of an applicant do we have here! Not interested in church work any more?"

I shook my head.

"Your application says 'Protestant,' " she went on with sincere interest, her words touched by a soft German accent. "What kind of Protestant?"

"Of the Reformed Church."

"Is that the same as the Lutheran?"

"No," I said. "Ulrich Zwingli was our founder."

With a despairing wave of her hand, she sighed. "I thought I knew all of these religious groups. But I am still learning. It was different in Germany where I came from; there we did not have so many. But tell me, did you ever hear of the Assemblies of God?"

"I've heard of the Church of God."

"That is something like it. They are both Pentecostal."

"Well, I know about the Church of God," I repeated dubiously.

She looked at me searchingly, then laughed softly in a way that put a comfortable sensation in my heart. "You know," she said thoughtfully with great dignity, "it is really wonderful how things work out. When did you decide to place your application with us?"

"Last night," I answered, puzzled both by her words and manner.

"Last night," she mused. "And last night a position was suddenly left vacant—just for you it seems."

"Where?"

"With your training and experience I am sure you are well fitted to direct an orchestra, are you not?"

"Perhaps. Where?"

"In a church."

"I don't think so."

"My church on Eighteenth and Brown. Well," she hastened to add, "I say *my* church, but I am really quite a new member there. It has helped me very, very much, though. Wouldn't you like to go with me on Sunday and see what a real Pentecostal church is like?"

"You're a Pentecostal?" I asked incredulously.

"Yes," she replied her voice warm with holy pride. "I was a very good Evangelical in Germany, but here in Milwaukee I am Assembly of God. Bad times came in Germany and we lost our estate there and my husband died. I really had nothing when I came here. But in the Assembly of God, there I found everything I needed. Of course all I needed was faith. That is all anyone needs, is it not? Faith helped me get this position. It does not seem like much perhaps, as you see, but you have no idea the people who come here needing the same help I needed. Who knows? Maybe the good Lord just planned it all this way—for me to be here in this place, I mean, when there are so many people who need all kinds of help these days. So will you come to church with me and see what you think of the orchestra?"

On Sunday morning I waited for Mrs. Sorge at the corner of Eighteenth and Brown in front of a large, new brick building which was identified by a bold sign: BETHEL TABER-NACLE. The music jarring against the closed windows took me back to Fairfield and a tent revival. Vying with happy youthful voices, the orchestra blasted forth to shame the devil with "Bringing in the Sheaves." This was evidently the stirring benediction for the Sunday-school services. Cars were bringing worshipers to the curb while others crowded the narrow sidewalks along the streets. Everybody hurried, as if drawn by the joyful singing and the riotous music. There were well-dressed people and people in shabby clothes. The cars which lined the curb for several blocks in every direction included expensive new models, reliable second-hand bargains, and nondescript carriages stripped of their beauty and efficiency. Again and again a man or a woman rushed over to where I stood, extending a friendly, eager hand with a hearty "Praise the Lord, Brother! Coming in?"

Mrs. Sorge, with a mink fur piece around her shoulders, Bible and purse tucked under her arm, stepped from a cab, apologizing for her delay.

"We're not late," I said. "The children haven't come out of Sunday school."

She laughed. "That's just it," she said in her precise business voice: "they don't come out. Here we go right from Sunday school into the service. Sometimes it is hard to tell when one stops and the other begins."

As she talked, we entered the well-equipped building. The large auditorium was already crowded with five or six hundred people. On the spacious platform the group of young musicians were tuning up their instruments and readjusting their flimsy music stands. The pianist was unconcernedly running over bits of gospel hymns. In the pews, kneeling worshipers mumbled prayers and occasionally a voice broke out with a sudden "O glory!" Mrs. Sorge ushered me into her pew in the center of the auditorium. Behind us a row of older people knelt with their heads pillowed in their arms, praying softly in German.

"The noise and things may bother you," she whispered as we seated ourselves. "It did me at first. Still does, sometimes."

"I know about what to expect," I told her.

She smiled patiently and opened her German Bible to the second chapter of the Book of Acts: "And when the day of Pentecost was fully come, they were all with one accord in one place. . . . And they were all filled with the Holy Ghost, and began to speak with other tongues . . ."

The theological wall between Brother Saunders and Brother Langley rose before me. On the one side I stood alone, clinging to the ideologies of the historic churches, while on Brother Saunders' side were hundreds of the faithful, battering at the wall which shut them off from the lukewarm Christians of traditional Protestantism, praying that all might be led to the light.

The goodness and earnestness of these people were no less sincere than my own faithful churchgoing. The spirit of seeking which permeated this auditorium was one with my own secret, implacable confidence in religion as a great adventure in the lives and hopes of people everywhere. I did not begrudge this congregation its wanton enthusiasm. Recognizing it as a part of the eternal religious quest, I exiled myself for the moment from all denominations and accepted religion for religion's sake.

Mrs. Sorge glanced up, pleased at the constantly growing congregation which now tested the capacity of the auditorium. "Pastor Ulrich," she said, "started this church just twelve years ago with only two families."

"In a tent?" I asked.

"No, in an old store building."

Brother Saunders had done much better. Two is to fourteen as . . . Ulrich had built up a congregation of eight hundred in twelve years. There were not so many people in Fairfield, but by the same ratio of success, Arnold Lembke was probably spending his afternoons this year working on a new church building.

Unannounced, the orchestra suddenly burst into "When They Ring Those Golden Bells." Undirected, spontaneously, the audience began to sing. Mrs. Sorge nodded in the direction of the platform. "There's your job, if you want it." She smiled.

The thirty-piece ensemble was playing furiously. Did I want it? Could I ever imagine myself associated with the "Holy Rollers" even in the attenuated connection of concertmaster?

The door behind the platform opened and a gray-haired but youthful, athletic-built man strode to the plain pulpit and lifted his hands. The singing congregation got up and remained standing for the invocation at the end of the song. It was a holiness invocation that lost no time in beating at the gates of heaven and at the hearts of the worshipers. Lusty amens split the Sabbath air. Immediately someone in the audience started singing "Send Down the Rain." Without changing the music on the rickety stands, the orchestra joined in. People sang happily and

people laughed. The service was officially started up the gay and
glorious Pentecostal road, leaving behind those to whom religion should be solemn, tranquil, and sedate.

Pastor Ulrich spoke in a loud but conversational manner,
greeting the people, reminding them of the goodness of the
Lord, and asking them if they were thankful for their many
blessings. Then with sudden, happy intonation he began to
sing, "Oh, there's sunshine, blessed sunshine——" Instantly the
orchestra took its cue, and the people mingled their enthusiastic
voices in loud praises. There were, however, moments un-
profaned by interruption when Pastor Ulrich read Scripture
passages and extemporized on the sufferings of Jesus during His
last week on earth. Occasionally he included German words
and phrases and even added a few lines of a German classical
poem on the Lord's Passion. But then followed impromptu
prayers. Clasped hands were raised throughout the audience,
and shouts of praise resounded from almost every pew.

Mrs. Sorge remained remarkably silent, contributing only a
whispered "Thank you, dear Jesus" to the surging emotion of
the service. But her face registered no disapproval; instead she
smiled happily and often closed her eyes to drink in the intoxi-
cating wine of spiritual peace. While people were still praying
and shouting, Pastor Ulrich loudly proclaimed that it was time
to praise the Lord with testimonials. Instantly the noise was subdued.

With scholarly precision that surpassed Brother Langley's, he
established the thesis that "no real blood-bought, Holy Ghost-
filled Christian will ever miss an opportunity to witness for
Jesus." With his strong voice and well-chosen words, he controlled the sway of the service.

"I want to bless Him this morning," said a radiant voice, and
a young woman rose with upraised hand, eyes lifted to heaven.

"My family is here with me, sitting here beside me. They came from their own church to see what I had found here in the Assembly of God. I am so grateful. Thank you, Jesus!"

"Churches won't get anyone to heaven." Pastor Ulrich laughed. "This church won't get anyone to heaven, but I know there is no other way to get there but to get under the precious blood of Jesus Christ and be born again! Amen!"

Testimonials were impulsive and sincere, although many seemed laconic and far-fetched, particularly one which drifted over us from the rear of the auditorium. "I know that some-one must of been praying for me this week because I sure had a good week. I want to thank those folks for those prayers if they were praying. It sure is wonderful."

Quietly Mrs. Sorge rose and stood with her gloved fingers resting on the pew before her.

"Yes, yes!" encouraged Pastor Ulrich, pleased.

"I am very thankful," she said softly, "that God gives one so many opportunities for service and helps one to help others. My faith has meant much to me, and I hope and pray that it will help many others. I will always appreciate the prayers of every-one for me and for those whom the Lord sends my way."

Someone softly and dramatically started "For You I Am Praying," and the congregation sang it in subdued tones with muffled orchestra accompaniment. Suddenly I realized that Mrs. Sorge had not invited me to her church merely to consider the prospect of becoming director of the orchestra. I had not only been swallowed up in the ranks of the laity: I was now one of the lukewarm Christians to whom she and her colleagues offered the revitalizing power of the Holy Ghost.

As the testimonies continued I knew that Pastor Ulrich's congregation had grown by just this method. Ministers through-out the city had crossed names off their church rolls just as I had done in Fairfield. "Sometimes it is necessary to leave your family church to find God" was a part of the Pentecostal gospel which Pastor Ulrich preached that morning. He was not only out to rescue the perishing among the unchurched, but also from among Lutherans, Baptists, Presbyterians, Congregationalists, Methodists. Members had been fed into this new religion by the hundred and more tributaries and meandering streams that are the Protestant faith.

The fervor of my Fairfield crusade rushed over me again. For a moment I was far removed from the Pentecostal conflagration on Eighteenth and Brown. I was again the Lord's watchman on the ramparts of Protestantism signaling distress. Reporting: That the Assemblies of God and the Churches of God are making a strong bid for power! Reporting: That I have visited many churches and that this one is the most crowded! Reporting: That I have looked in vain for a traditional Protestant church where Sunday evening services are conducted—but here is the announcement of Sunday evening *and* Sunday afternoon services! Reporting: The outcome of Protestantism's major weaknesses. Old Doc's mitotic explanation was not sufficient. These new faiths arose because Protestantism was divided and because traditional churches had lost the awareness of the individual's need.

I was called from this fantasy when Mrs. Sorge tapped my hand and pointed to a young man who was walking slowly down the long center aisle toward the platform. The congregation watched in awed silence as he moved forward with humble, hesitant steps, an embarrassed and expectant light glowing in his dark eyes. As if to steady his thin, nervous body, he clasped his hands before him like an acolyte approaching the altar. Pastor Ulrich stood waiting, pleased and impressed, and when the young man reached the altar in front of the pulpit, the minister extended his hand and said in a soft whisper, "Come up on the platform, Joseph! Come on! God bless you!"

Joseph shook his head, smiling with an enigmatical expression as if some boundless wonder had overtaken him. He turned to the congregation and stood for a moment as if groping for words in his first public appearance. His eyes narrowed and with contagious fervor, he said, "My friends, many of you know me. You know what has happened to me." He paused, closed his eyes for a moment and rubbed his thin white hands together a number of times, as if to renounce his own strength deliberately and let the spirit speak.

"What more is there to say?" he went on quietly in a soft voice, his words marked by a Hungarian accent. "God, who is greater than any man, has touched me and healed me and brought me here today to tell you that I am healed. Fully healed. I want to say to you and to Him, I want to promise Him, that all that I have will from now on be used in His service and to His honor. But what have I to give? Nothing. Only perhaps my music." He laughed in a lonely, enravished way as though feeling transcended words. The audience responded with soft amens.

"Go ahead!" urged Pastor Ulrich. "Tell us everything! It's a time to be happy. Praise the Lord!"

"Well," said Joseph, absently brushing back his black hair as he looked up at the pastor, "you know what it was. Here in my hand, in my bow hand, and in my ankle—tuberculosis of the bone, they called it. Doctors here, doctors in Vienna said so. But now, look! Look at it! It is gone! But it is not only that. It is something here that has been healed." And he quietly beat his breast with his hand and his pallid face seemed transfigured. "Heal the soul, my friends, and the body is healed."

"Amen! Praise the Lord!"

"Thank you, Jesus!"

"Praise God forever!"

"Glory to God!"

These exclamations from the audience had no effect upon Joseph. He stood alone at the altar, lost in his own vision of the greatness of God.

"My dear friends, we have witnessed a miracle!" cried Pastor Ulrich. "But miracles are not unusual among people who are filled with the spirit of God. Yes, thank God! Miracles! As rewards to the faithful and as signs to unbelievers! Praise the Lord! Be happy, Joseph, and let me tell you how you can praise Him. Here, musician, give him your violin. Joseph has been healed. He told me he would never play his fiddle again except in the service of the Lord. Well, that is hard on the Alhambra Theatre where he was concertmaster for so long, but it is good for God!"

"Amen, amen!"

"Oh, glory, Jesus!"

"Let the devil take care of the theater music. We'll take care of the music of heaven. Amen! There, Joseph, there's a violin. Come now—don't hold back! Come!"

Reluctantly, apologetically, abdicating every right to such a privilege, Joseph took the instrument. I was sure that he would much rather have walked with God alone, apart, anywhere but here. He shook his head vigorously against being urged up to the platform. Remaining on the audience level, he stood with his thin body bent abjectly over the violin and touched the bow to the strings. Against a background of impulsive and thoughtless exclamations of praise, in the same service where rollicking Pentecostal songs had jolted my critical ear, he began *Ziegeunerweisen*. Having often struggled with its difficult beauty, I immediately recognized the touch of an artist who was transporting the Pentecostals from their humble pews to the luxury of a concert hall.

Yet, as I turned my gaze from Joseph to his audience, I realized that I alone had left the church on Eighteenth and Brown. The worshipers around me were not following with rapt pleasure the richly gifted tones of the violin; they were watching one of the redeemed as he returned to God the talent God had given. For this experience this audience had a complete capacity. It was their formula for happiness. Heaven had saved a poor lost sinner so that he might save others. His prayers had been answered in order that he now might answer prayers. The precious gift of music was being placed upon the altar as the offering which the Lord had demanded in payment for His grace. Joseph was giving up his music professionally in order to "play only in the service of the Lord," and the listening, worshiping hundreds who surrounded him were gaining from his experience inspiration and courage to serve as valiantly as he was serving.

A wandering and homeless Protestant, I sat among people who had attained oneness with God—the reward of faith which they had sought in their traditional denominations and had not found.

The rapid finale of *Ziegeunerweisen* swept across the spellbound audience. Forgetting for a moment the divine abasement of his miraculous healing and his blood-bought salvation, Joseph sent the bow flying across the strings with dramatic intensities, fleeing with gypsy freedom back to his professional sensuality. The orchestra leaned forward, Pastor Ulrich's face broke into radiance, the audience murmured. That God should so hold in majestic wildness the mad passion of the "devil's instrument" was thrilling, captivating. And when the music stopped and the bow was carried by its own impulse over the head of the performer, when the applause was a shout of praise and a chorus of hallelujahs, I broke through generations of German Protestant restraint and added my own enthusiastic and strangely liberating "Thank you, Lord!"

Mrs. Sorge smiled, pleased, and I told her that I was anxious to meet Joseph. But he walked quickly out the side door as soon as the service was over. Neither was it possible for me to meet Pastor Ulrich, for he had gone immediately on a sick call and would not be back until the afternoon service.

"But he wants to see you," Mrs. Sorge assured me, "for I spoke to him on the telephone. He says he would like it very much if you would consider the orchestra job."

"Why not Joseph?" I asked. "He is better qualified than I."

"Joseph has other plans," said my companion. "Anyhow he wants to spend all the time he can tarrying for the baptism of the Spirit."

I returned to Bethel Tabernacle that evening, crept into a pew near the door, and listened and wondered while all Pentecost broke loose in charismatic demonstrations which surpassed in orderly excitement anything I had heard or witnessed anywhere. Again the songs and music were spirited, and the sermon was a powerful plea for changed lives as "our best appreciation for all our good Lord suffered and endured for us." Pastor Ulrich always approached his congregation with complete self-confidence, sure he could give them exactly what they needed. There was no doubt in his mind about being on this church corner to stay. Time and the Lord would bring in the fallen, and he would keep the enthusiasm flowing through the channels of grace.

A special innovation at this Sunday-evening service was prayer for the sick, followed by testimonies from those who had "felt the healing power." There was also an altar call which resulted in Holy Ghost baptisms, accompanied by talking in tongues. Sometimes when a convert would speak in the "unknown language," Pastor Ulrich would interpret the lines in the rhythm and cadence of the original. Such a demonstration had a tremendous effect on the audience. The spirit of God had spoken, so theirs must be the right road to glory. The shouting reached frenzied peaks as fierce sobbing mingled with exultant laughter. The fervor was heightened by soul-harrying outbursts from people kneeling at the platform seeking the baptism. Frequently a piercing shriek rose out of the bedlam as some soul was "saved." From a corner of a pew up front came a mother's groveling cry praying for a daughter who had "fallen from grace." And always Pastor Ulrich controlled the service with commands shouted above the din of noisy worship.

As I listened, I could not imagine myself having any part in such a service. The disruptive congregational shouting and the mysterious speaking in tongues would be even more disturbing if I were sitting on the platform with the orchestra. But I needed a job. I wanted to meet Joseph. And I wanted to know more about the Pentecostals. I wanted to report to myself and to Protestantism.

So next morning I kept an appointment with Pastor Ulrich. His wife informed me that he was in the attic and directed me to the stairs. I started up. Loud voices in German came from the attic quarters. On the landing I heard the metallic clatter of a printing press mingled with exuberant praises to the Lord for having started the machine.

I rapped.

"Herein!" commanded the voice of the Pastor.

The attic room resembled a cramped steepled belfry, but it looked like a busy corner in a news plant at presstime. One man was running the motor-driven press, another was hand-setting type, two girls were folding and stacking bulletins. Pastor Ulrich, with shirt sleeves rolled up and pencil behind his ear, was meeting the deadline.

"Praise the Lord, Brother!" was the greeting accompanied by a broad smile and an extended hand. "You're the young man Sister Sorge found aren't you? Come into my office and watch out for your head."

His "office" was a desk in an alcove at the front of the attic, where a window looked out over neighborhood yards. He motioned me to a chair and seated himself on the desk dangling his legs.

"Well, you're a Christian?" he queried.

"I am."

"Have you had any religious experiences?"

"Many of them."

"Have you had the baptism? No, I can see you haven't. Well, praise the Lord just the same. God is good. Hallelujah! *Du kannst ja wohl Deutsch sprechen?*"

When I assured him I could, he swung around on the desk and in a victorious voice called, "Johannes! Here's your man!"

"Praise the Lord!" said Johannes lifting his eyes from the press and registering glory.

"Well," said Ulrich in a businesslike tone, "you have a job. In fact, you have two jobs. We need someone to translate our tracts and bulletins from German into English, and we need a director for our church orchestra. Now I want you to observe," he implored, "how the good Lord works. Think how you were led here. It helps you and it helps us. But it wasn't just an accident or a coincidence. The Lord sets things in motion and turns them over to His children for them to work out." He clasped his hands together fervently. "Hallelujah! When do you want to start?"

"Well, there's the matter of arrangements," I said hesitantly.

"I think I'd like to know a little more about details, such as the hours and—— What about the salary?"

Ulrich was crestfallen. "O ye of little faith!" he moaned, shaking his head in keen disappointment. "The Lord, Brother! He knows how to handle these affairs. Let's trust Him a bit. I've been here twelve years and have never asked for a salary. You saw how things are going at the church. Did you notice that we took no collection? Should I ask the good Lord for nickels and dimes? You come and live with us. We've always got an empty room. Come and try it once and see what happens."

He jumped from the desk and began picking up some German tracts which he wanted to show me. I was troubled and amused. But why not "try it and see what happens"? Where would one find a better listening post from which to hear and judge the Pentecostal winds? A week, two weeks—what could I lose? Fantastic and impractical though Ulrich's faith might be, there was tempting wonder in his philosophy: "The Lord sets things in motion and turns them over to His children to work out."

Next day I moved into this local Pentecostal headquarters as tenant and employee. I ate at the family table where family worship, Bible reading, and prayer were the infallible rule. I knelt with the workers in the printing shop whenever one of them got an inspiration to meditate or praise the Lord. And on the first Wednesday night of my new employment, I attended the weekly prayer service, which was devoted to supplications for the sick and the lost. Some two hundred people assembled in the church to wail and moan and shed compassionate tears for loved ones who desperately needed God.

"O Jesus, you know Sister Elsie Martin! You know she needs your help, Lord! She's tried doctors, she's tried medicine, she's tried everything she knows how to try, and she's coming to you! O Jesus, she's coming to you! Don't cast her out, dear Jesus, don't cast her out! She's pressing through the crowd to touch the hem of your garment, right now, O Lord! Praise you, O Jesus! Right now while she's lying at home and can't come to this meeting, though her heart is here. Touch her, O Jesus, and heal her, O Lord! Help Sister Elsie, help Sister Elsie, and heal her! Reach down that mighty hand and touch her with your mighty healing power, and we'll give you all the praise and all the glory in Jesus' name. Amen."

Old men and old women broke through the vicissitudes of mingled prayers with tears and earnest cries that a son or a daughter might "see the light." Young people entreated the Lord that their families might be guided to the one church where the Holy Ghost was waiting. And while the praying jarred the windows and the tempestuous wailing and shouting of the worshipers begged Jesus to bear the news of glory to the churches everywhere, Pastor Ulrich put in his plea to the Lord loud enough for all the people to hear: "Give us workers, O Lord! O Lord, workers for the reaping!"

Mrs. Sorge sat quietly in her pew, her face strangely lighted by a tender smile. There were others like her at the service, solemnly observing the enthusiasm of other worshipers, reverently whispering prayers. Joseph sat with his hands clasped fiercely together in his lap, his eyes sealed tightly against the encumbrances of an intruding world.

I met Joseph that night after the meeting, and as we walked the long distance to the parsonage together, he talked with intense feeling about his experience.

"A month ago," he said quietly, "I would never have believed this—had anyone told me I would be kneeling in a prayer meeting. Oh, no. That was farthest from my thoughts. All religion was far from my thoughts. I was thinking only about what to do with my life now that my career was ending. The doctors had talked, you know, about amputating my foot and my hand. I had consulted specialists. Many were the times I sat in a streetcar and pressed my face against the window looking out, envying everybody and feeling that no one was more hopeless than I. I saw my job going. Well, I was getting a hundred and fifty dollars a week. Money, though, didn't mean anything any more. Only my hand, that was what I was thinking about. What is a person to say? My mother was always praying for me at the prayer meetings. I didn't think anything about that. Oh, no, that was not for me! But, well, here I am. God is very real. Nothing else matters but that we serve Him."

"What do you plan to do now?" I asked.

"Well, I am praying and waiting," he said with a quiet laugh. "I want the baptism, you know."

"Then you believe there is something to the baptism of the Holy Spirit?"

"Oh, of course! Certainly! That is the only way to explain what happened to the disciples in the upper room! They were weak and cowardly and afraid to open their mouths. But they got the baptism and there they were, speaking boldly and praying on the streets, ready to die for what they believed. What happened to them? The baptism of the Holy Ghost. That was the difference. Now, I have seen that happen right here—right here in this church—and in other Pentecostal churches it happens, too. So, I tarry at Jerusalem, as they say."

On the following Sunday morning I took over the church orchestra. Or rather I became one of the anonymous first violinists in the thirty-piece aggregation. "Director" was a misnomer. The ambitious players, trying to keep up with five or six hundred ambitious singers, were too occupied to watch a baton.

Besides, to the Pentecostals music was not the reading and execution of a score; it was making a joyful noise unto the Lord; it was filling the earth with the praises of God; it was praising the Lord with the trumpet and the harp. And as the Sundays passed, I found much of my old restraint lost in the happy passion of the contagious song fests. I was "a fiddling Pentecostal," and when Joseph played his solo with a Kreislerlike touch, my orchestra and I stood condemned. But always my admiration for him absorbed my misgivings about staying too long in the work on Eighteenth and Brown.

"Why ever leave?" he would ask. Often during pleasant visits at the small apartment where he lived with his wife and three young children, it was difficult to give him an answer. Nothing was more satisfying than hours spent with Bach's *Concerto for Two Violins,* but always too soon for me we turned from music to Scripture, underlining every passage which referred to the Pentecostal experience.

"It is the only life, my friend," Joseph inevitably concluded. "You must never leave. Where is the challenge to work for God greater than right where you are? What more do you need in life than people you can trust and a job that you like?"

"Once I had a great idea, Joseph," I confided. "In fact, all my life I have dreamed of a united Protestantism."

"Yes?"

"One church in places where there are now many churches fighting against one another, struggling to keep going, arguing about their differences. Brother Ulrich is always preaching about how traditional Protestantism has failed and I agree with him. But it wouldn't fail if all Protestant churches could be united in common beliefs and in a common goal——"

"They could be," Joseph interrupted enthusiastically. "They

could be if all church members would seek the Holy Ghost! But on what else can the churches unite?"

"There are many other things," I insisted. "Despite all its faults, Protestantism is a universal religion and must accept the responsibility for a new world order. The early Christian Church was a protest against world corruption. So was the Reformation, and the church of today must also be motivated by that great aim. We cannot isolate ourselves from world affairs. The church must give to the world a spiritual law and moral order. But that is impossible as long as Protestantism is divided."

"Then let's seek the baptism and take the message to the churches!" Joseph exclaimed. "Only the power of the Holy Ghost can bring such a thing to pass!"

Joseph was always insistent that we end every visit with a tarrying service, but I found an excuse to evade these special prayers. As I left him, he would shake my hand warmly and say, *"Aufwiedersehen"* because it was more intimate and more meaningful than "good-by."

The mystical promise of the Holy Ghost had become a passion in the young Hungarian's life. He spent many hours seeking the blessing at home and always stayed for the tarrying services after the regular meetings at the church. So it was no surprise when the report circulated that Joseph had received the Holy Ghost. It was a genuine baptism. He had spoken in tongues. The story was on everyone's lips. In the printery the press stopped while prayers of gratitude were said. Everyone who came in that day put a special ring of triumph in his customary "Praise the Lord!" Joseph was the topic at the dinner table, on the telephone, and in the Pentecostal households throughout the city. A prayer service was announced for the evening.

Humbly that night Joseph stood up before the worshipers to testify. A sense of rapture possessed him, and the overpowering conviction in his voice held us enthralled. The usual amens, the Pentecostal applause, were hushed and awed. Joseph spoke with a boldness that defied my doubts about the efficacy of the Holy Ghost experience. Though he humbly acknowledged his unfitness to testify, he laughed confidently as he said, "The things I want to say come so thick and fast, I don't know where to begin!" Then he spoke capably of the impelling love which he now felt for all "poor lost souls" and the clear-cut call that his life should be a ministry to his "own people first and then to all who will listen." He entreated and implored us all to seek for that great gift which he had found. And as I looked on his earnest face and remembered that he had nothing in the world and wanted nothing in the world but this sense of God, I suddenly was more envious of him than I had ever been of Kurtz or Langley.

From the church where Joseph found God, he went to the heart of the Hungarian section with his Pentecostal message. He started an "assembly" in the basement of an old building on Milwaukee's south side. Former friends, who had been his devotees when he was the town's "best Hungarian violinist," now cursed him for giving up his music; and when they passed his "church," they spat disgustedly on the sidewalk. But Joseph was unaffected. "Praise be to God! Everything for His glory!" he would exclaim, regardless of what happened. After spending his days in prayer and visitation, he preached every night about the thing he had found, and his congregation grew. He was perpetually inflamed by a heavenly rapport that drew his listeners into his divine partnership. Always he was the "upper-room" disciple transforming his own experiences into breaths of tranquil joy for believers and into disturbing warnings for the unsaved. And when the spirit moved him, he played his violin at the services.

His preaching, his music, the man himself fascinated me so much that I gave up my job as director of the orchestra and attended his services. To me he became not only a synonym for Holy Ghost power but also the personification of perfect happiness.

Almost every day he encouraged me to seek the baptism. "It is my daily prayer that you and every other Protestant may experience the great blessing," he would say with his usual graciousness.

He came frequently to the printery and never left without calling a prayer meeting in my behalf. Kneeling beside the desk where I translated sermons, poems, and testimonies about the latter rain "spoken of by the prophet Joel," I heard Joseph and the others pray to God to give me the blessing, to prepare my heart to receive the Holy Spirit. Then we would all sing a rousing Pentecostal song which brought shouts of praise from my baptized comrades and left me puzzled and envious of the joy they had found.

Through Joseph, I began to understand the people to whom the Pentecostal faith was real and satisfying. It was in his enthusiasm and through his continual and tireless ministry that I slowly divined their utter devotion to the concept of Holy Ghost power. Most of his friends and followers would never have been happy in the traditionally institutionalized churches. Protestantism for them had grown formal and cold, and they had come to warm themselves in the flames of Pentecostal fires. It was not my way, but it was theirs. It was not my belief that noise and clangor were needed to clear the way for God to come through, but they believed it. Their prayers were not my prayers, but I felt the power of their sincerity.

Often I accompanied Joseph on a sick call and heard him summon the healing power of God into the humble homes of his parishioners. We appeared together in violin duets at large church gatherings, traveled together to Pentecostal meetings, and sometimes took a small ensemble to the prison and hospital services which were an important adjunct to the church's evangelistic program.

One Saturday night I accompanied Pastor Ulrich and Joseph and a group of singers to a busy downtown corner for a street service. Often I had wondered about the sensibilities of rescue mission teams or the Salvation Army workers or the Full Gospel squads when they planted themselves under the street lamps. What was their reaction to the indignities of passers-by and the blast of auto horns? What did they think? How did they feel when only a few morbid and questionable spectators comprised their motley congregation? Personally I felt that religion was being made vulgar and cheap. I resented the shamelessness of the testifiers, and I was uncomfortable under the blistering sermon of Pastor Ulrich and the emboldened testimonials of the "saved." Though I knew that occasionally an arrogant spectator of Saturday night appeared in church on Sunday morning and sometimes a drunk sobered up and remembered that religion had been offered to him, I questioned the value of such an approach. Though the Pentecostals were laying the robe of Christian friendliness around the shoulders of many a Protestant prodigal, my part in the street service was violent shame for myself and my friends. But always there was Joseph, and when he preached, the street was transformed into the pavement of Jerusalem, and when he testified about his baptism, it was again the morning of Pentecost.

Three months later I was testifying with the same unmitigated passion about *my* baptism. I was preaching with the same defiant earnestness. Bible in hand, I was laying down the gospel law. But not on a street corner. I had returned to Protestantism with the good news. I was standing in the pulpit of the beautiful First Reformed Church in Wichita, Kansas, where my brother was pastor. Having arrived late Saturday night, I had had no opportunity to relate the details of my experience to Roland, but my laconic responses to the usual ministerial queries had puzzled him. When he asked me for my sermon topic, I had answered, "How do I know? The Lord always selects that!" What text did I plan to use? "Who can tell, since the Lord will direct me to it?" What did I intend to preach about? "How should I know that when it is up to the Lord to put the words into my mouth!" His concern had mounted steadily, reaching its peak when he introduced me to his congregation of prominent Wichita families and leading citizens.

"My brother wrote me a short time ago that he had had a religious experience," he began hesitantly. "I was very happy to invite him here to share it with us. I am sure we are always interested in the religious experience of any young man just turning twenty-five."

He swung around to me with a courteous but somewhat distrustful nod of invitation. His giant body stiffened inside the black silk gown. Uneasily he seated himself on the velvet cushions of the mahogany sedilia.

Scorning the large gold-edged Bible on the massive pulpit, I snatched my worn Testament from my inside coat pocket and instantly found my Scripture quotation: "Ye shall receive power, after that the Holy Ghost is come upon you!"

My heroic pronouncement of this strange text was explosive. It startled the three hundred sedate church members out of their Sunday-morning complacency, and they looked up at me with astonished, unbelieving eyes. That was all I needed to lose myself in a flood of extempore sermonizing. It was my experience I was talking about—a Holy Ghost message that the Lord was putting into my mouth. "The need for the baptism is the same everywhere," I exclaimed, "whether on city streets or in prison cells or city pews. The supreme need, Christianity's only hope, the crying hunger of the church, is the baptism of the Holy Ghost!" Illustrations came to mind straight from the tracts off the printery desk. The turbines of the Lord were turning. Power swept through me straight from the dynamos of Pentecost. I was a missionary to a divided and dying Protestantism, and fearless and bold I struck at the apathy that infested the institutionalized churches of all Christendom.

"In my first pastorate," I cried, swaying under a spirit of great conviction, "I tried to unite the churches in the town. I foolishly believed that by uniformity or union or co-operative effort, religion could be revitalized! What an error, what a delusion! Power and vitality must come from God through the Holy Ghost! Praise the Lord! 'Ye shall receive power, *after* that the Holy Ghost is come upon you!' Unite the divisive Protestant denominations? How? On what basis? Develop a world Christian fellowship? Through what? Through which agency? Where is the common denominator in Protestantism? Here it is! Here in Acts 2:4! The baptism of the Holy Ghost! The joy and bliss and passion and unifying power of the Comforter which Jesus promised to send! There's the answer! Hallelujah!"

Then I told how I had received this baptism in an attic printery one summer afternoon, how the Holy Ghost endowed me with power and the desire to broadcast this message to the Protestant world. This service, I told them, was the beginning of my great mission. How wonderful to be invited first of all to my brother's church! To begin at Jerusalem! Praise the Lord!

But into this manifest victory and this preaching as the Spirit moved me came another force—abrasive, uncomfortable. And as the moments passed, I found myself groping for words and frequently stumbling against a phrase. I was dimly conscious of my brother repeatedly clearing his throat. Glances of perplexity were passed from one worshiper to another. A man touched his printed program thoughtfully against his lips; a woman tapped her fan contemplatingly against her gloved hand. Furrowed brows, glances of consternation, smiles of incredible wonder. "Be strong in the Lord—preach the word," came the retaliating inner voice of Pentecostal faith. But gradually my text was burning out. My message was cooling off, as if in a vacuum. My audience sat unmoved. For the first time since "my experience" there were no hallelujahs, no raised hands, and no amens.

When I finished after this exhausting overtime period, when I tucked my Testament into my coat and turned to sit down, the huge form of my brother rose like a mountain and enveloped me in the black shadows of his consternation and shame. With professional skill he folded his hands gently on the gold-edged Bible, rubbed his palms together deliberately and with a light, disarming laugh said, "Well, friends, I think we all agree that we heard a typical street preacher this morning. Let us rise, please, and receive the benediction."

While Roland hurried to the vestibule to shake hands with his parishioners, I sneaked into his study. I had expected my sermon to be somewhat shocking because it was not cast in the conventional Protestant mold. I knew it was not the kind I had preached for four years in Fairfield. But how could a Holy Ghost sermon be such a complete failure? How could my preacher brother and his entire congregation shut out my message from their hearts when it was the message God had given me? Protestantism's dilemma and my own suddenly became more puzzling than they had ever been in Fairfield or Milwaukee.

Roland swung open the door and looked at me in unconcealed disgust. "What in the world happened to you?" he demanded.

"You wouldn't understand," I said uneasily. "To people who close their hearts against the baptism, the baptism is foolishness."

"Foolishness is right!" he agreed, removing his pulpit gown and tossing it unceremoniously on his desk. "Anybody with strong lungs who isn't afraid to shout 'Hallelujah' can be a Pentecostal. That's for sure. What happened to you—that's what I want to know?"

I evaded him by relating the story of Joseph and his healing and of my interest in the changed lives encountered in the Assemblies of God.

"And you had this . . . baptism?" he asked incredulously.

I nodded steadfastly.

"Well, all right," he said impatiently. "Come on. Cast your pearls before swine. What is it? If the baptism's nothing more than something that makes you feel you can get up and preach to an intelligent congregation without preparation, I'm against it."

"It's a mystical experience," I said. "A Pentecostal experience that changes lives. It changed my life."

"I can *see* that!" he shouted with a wave of his hands.

"I've started tithing," I told him. "Things I once thought important don't seem so important any more. The one thing that seems worth while is to tell people about the baptism. I have never had such a real insatiable desire to preach——"

"I'm sure of *that!*" he exclaimed and impatiently stuffed tobacco into his pipe. "But I tithe, too. And I'm preaching all the time, but I certainly don't offend the sensibilities or the intelligence of my congregation."

"That's the trouble with Protestantism!" I retaliated. "Nobody offends anybody. You preach what people want to hear. You never convict anybody of sin. You never challenge your people with their need for Christ. All right, I offended the congregation. You preach to a Pentecostal congregation and you'll offend them because they aren't interested in a comfortable, easygoing sermon that tickles their ears."

"All right, all right," he complained. "Christianity is big enough for all kinds of people. But let's stay in our own yards and behind our own fences. If you want to be a Pentecostal, be a Pentecostal. But if you want to be an intelligent Protestant, that's another thing."

"Fences!" I exclaimed. "That's just the trouble. Protestantism has plenty of them all right. But what Protestantism needs is something that cuts across fences, and the power of the Holy Spirit would do that, but you think you don't need it! You think you can save the world by your own power. But just remember that the Protestant churches have been trying to do that for four hundred years and what's the result? Every man's effort is dissipated in denominationalism! No Protestant's ministry will be effective until the churches find something that will unite them. And that something is the baptism of the Holy Ghost!"

"Whoever told you that Pentecostalism is united!" he cried, swinging around in his chair and snapping out of the shelf a book on church statistics. "If you're still hepped on church union, you'd better look for another system!"

He leaned back in his chair and as he opened the book, he moaned, "Oh, heavens, it's worse than I thought!" Then he began his devastating enumeration: "The Pentecostal Assemblies of Jesus Christ; the Pentecostal Assemblies of the World; the Pentecostal Church, Incorporated; the Pentecostal Church of God of America, Incorporated; the Pentecostal Churches of

America; the Pentecostal Fire-Baptised Holiness Church; the
Pentecostal Holiness Church; the Pentecostal Bands of the
World; the Assemblies of God; General Council, Church of
God; Church of God Apostolic; Church of God and Saints of
Christ; Church of God in Christ, Pentecostal; Church of the
Full Gospel, Incorporated; Church of the Gospel; Fire-Baptised
Holiness Church of God of the Americas, and so forth and so
forth! And all of this," he concluded, snapping shut the book
with a bang, "in less than fifty years!"

He pulled at his pipe and eyed me disconsolately. "My Lord,"
he went on vehemently, "if you're interested in church union,
stick to your own faith. We just united last month with the
Evangelical Synod. You should have gone to Cleveland and been
in on that. The birth of the Evangelical and Reformed denomination, bringing together about a million Christians separated
for a hundred and fifty years. That's progress. Protestantism's
good enough for me any day. My church is crowded, too. My
people are good Christians, too. Sure. I wish they'd be better,
but you don't find perfection anywhere, not even among the
Pentecostals. Of course my members don't go around asking,
'Are you saved? Have you had the baptism? Let's kneel down
at every street corner for a word of prayer.' But most of them
reflect more of the gospel than you realize, and the majority of
them live the good life, far as I know. Certainly they're as good
as the Holy Rollers."

"Holy Rollers," I retorted, "is a nasty nickname."

"Well, they roll and jump, don't they?"

"The term Holy Roller originated with a small Pentecostal
group back in 1900. They rolled and jumped when they got the
spirit. But the larger Pentecostal denomination doesn't relate
itself to the Holy Rollers at all. It claims a spiritual succession
straight from the first Pentecost and it certainly has much of

the same power. And I met many people of perfectly good social standing in the Assemblies of God, if that's what you're worried about."

"I'm worried about you," he said. "If you want to join the Pentecostals, ask the Synod to take your name off the yearbook. And if you want to break the denominational tradition of the family, do it. Only don't move into this town with a tent and a marimba."

Vainly I struggled against the inured concepts of his contented faith. It did not seem fluid. It was formal and impersonal. Through the weeks of my Wichita visit I tried to break through with stories about healings among the Pentecostal people. I reviewed their faith, their selflessness, their ministry in prisons and hospitals, their street preaching, and rescue-mission work, their tithing programs, the unpaid clergy, their assistance to the poor during these depression years.

His answer was that Protestantism co-operated in all kinds of social agencies and that many Protestant ministers also labored untiringly among the underprivileged and down-and-outers. He himself was unusually active in reform among juvenile delin-quents and often accompanied the Wichita police in gambling raids, remaining to counsel with prisoners and bail out "poor devils" whom he considered worthy.

I suggested that Protestantism was no longer the religion of the regenerated individual life. He was just as sure that he was "saved" as I was! I maintained that Protestantism was no longer out to fight sin and oppose wars and worldliness. It was compromising too much in the affairs of the world. The churches had become social clubs, fraternal organizations. Min-isters, I argued, were being secularized. Ministers were neglect-ing their prayer life. They were divided in beliefs, in interpre-tations, in their moral and ethical codes. They were running their churches like big business corporations, and the board of directors, not God, dictated how things should be done, while money dominated the programs.

"What you need is education. A few degrees. A broader outlook," my brother harped back at me. "Pick out a university somewhere and maybe you can get a church to supply on the side to help things along. But don't preach the baptism of the Holy Spirit with manifestations! Check that off as an interlude, something that caught you at a low ebb. And don't talk about it to any of our ministers or somebody will think you're nuts."

Under his persistent badgering I was driven to reconsider my Protestant heritage. Though there was a good deal wrong with Protestantism, I was strongly moored to religious thought according to evangelical tradition. All my life I had been indoctrinated in Protestantism. Early experiences had forged the chain: baptism, confirmation, Sunday school, old Uncle August's sermons and prayers, the Christmas services, Easter communion, the midnight watch on New Year's Eve. I was saturated with Protestant thought: sermons heard and sermons preached, the worshipful, formal, traditionally severe services, parental counsel, the orthodox plan of salvation, the direct relation of myself as a creature to God as Creator. All went back before birth and out beyond death on the rugged path of faith.

But I could not easily forget or deny that one afternoon I was supposed to have had "the baptism." At least, Joseph called it that and so did I. I was alone that day when Joseph came in. We knelt to pray, he in the center of the room, I at my desk chair. Quietly and earnestly he began pouring out the deepest desire in his heart: the baptism for his good friend—the great glory for his good friend—the divine blessing for his good friend who had been led into Pentecost by the hand of God.

I listened with my head pressed into my arms as the room throbbed with Joseph's words. Monotonously his impassioned voice sent the taut supplication heavenward: "Give him the baptism, O Lord; give my good friend the baptism." Gradually through my tightly closed eyelids I felt rather than saw a patch of light filled with a pandemonium of scenes: white church steeples, violins, country prairies and city parishes, church services and employment agencies, all crazily fighting against: "the baptism!" In my mind, the words were set in the bed of type on the big press and the cylinder went round and round, and the type moved back and forth, and the big gear ground out "the baptism" and delivered it to Joseph who read it and reread it.

As I listened I was overcome by a mystical presence of something immensely good and compassionate within easy grasp of my soul. Reaching out for this, I again saw the patch of light with the steeples and violins and prairies and parishes and services and agencies. But Joseph was still praying close to me, lifting "the baptism" off the bed of type on the big press, reading and rereading it—"the baptism". . ."the baptism". . ."the baptism."

Gradually "the baptism" burned out the scenes in the patch of light, burned out the patch of light, burned out all my conscious thoughts in a sudden blinding burst of glory. Like a lightning flash, the Something I had reached out for possessed me completely and with a power that lifted my arms in exultant praise. I rose to my feet, joining Joseph in his incredible "Glory, glory!" and then fell to the floor, laughing and weeping in a sense of wonder and peace.

After that the world was different. The desire to help people and to take part in the various ministries of the assembly were real. Then, whenever I spoke at meetings, the service broke out all over with hallelujahs! Believers testified and there was something indefinable and genuine about the happiness that people felt.

But when I returned to Milwaukee from my visit in Wichita, Joseph, Mrs. Sorge, and the rest looked at me and said I had changed. They spoke with me and said I had lost something. They invited me to the prayer service, and I was ready with an excuse. Pastor Ulrich claimed that he could divine what had happened.

"The world," he said, "is too strong. It's got Protestantism all wrapped up and ready for delivery to the Devil. I told you when you left that you were making a mistake ever to try to preach Pentecostalism from a Protestant pulpit. The new revival must come from outside the churches. You can't pour this Pentecostal wine into the old Protestant bottles."

Joseph called it a plain case of backsliding. "Liberal Protestantism," he said, "is a subtle force, a blinding force that darkens the spiritual sight of men to the ultimate demands of the gospel."

"Don't talk as though you were in a special category, Joseph," I warned.

"I am nothing!" he answered with a despairing cry. "But I have one title that is better than any theological or academic degree. It is: Saved by the blood of Jesus! Praise the Lord! I have no desire but to save others and help them find what I have found."

"Many Protestants have the same zeal and enthusiasm as you," I argued weakly.

"It's you—you I am thinking of. A man dare not grieve the spirit. Can't you understand that? That is your first responsibility. But that is how Protestants are—religion all around them—religion for everyone—and only a form of religion for themselves, a form of religion which denies the power of God."

"But there are good people in traditional Protestantism, Joseph," I protested.

"Ah, how you talk! How you have changed! Yes, there are good people in Protestantism but there is no power. There can't be or the churches would be making much more of an impression on their people. Religion to the average liberal Protestant is not something vital and on fire. It doesn't change his life fully, completely, instantly, as lives are changed among us by the Holy Spirit. He joins a church just as he joins a lodge or a club. He is a member, but nothing has happened to him. He has not been changed. And the Christian religion must be the religion of changed lives."

Joseph looked at me as if a stranger stood in my place. "There is only one thing Protestantism needs—one thing you need," he said slowly; "the thing you had: the Holy Ghost. Then there will be no more hypocrisy, no more wars, no more lust for domination of one person or one nation over another. But you are going to school——" And he extended his hand. Quietly he said, "Well, that is how things go."

With this he pressed my hand and sadly said, "Good-by," which was more final and now more honest than *"Aufwiedersehen."*

CHAPTER FIVE

The Cults Are Coming

"No one church is big enough for this town. No single denomination can ever be big enough or all-inclusive enough
to minister the fullness of the gospel to the entire world."

"But the great need and the great ideal is unity. Division
among God's people is shameful."

"Competition is as necessary in religion as it is in business."

I was not back in the Evangelical manse struggling with
two dissident church boards; this time the unyielding
farmers and bankers and the cattlemen were doing as directed. Fairfield was coming to life again, but only behind the footlights of an experimental theater.

Three years at the State University of Iowa had made religion
comfortably objective. Philosophy and the sciences had balanced
the Evangelical-Pentecostal equation and had consigned my
idealistic crusading for church union to the unhurried process
of social change; English had conveniently permitted the Bible
to be interpreted as literature; courses in the fine arts had provided an excellent opportunity to interpret religion and life im-
personally. But my major field was speech and drama. The
ready-made plot of two small-town churches trying to get together was sufficiently rich in human interest and regional appeal to be a thesis play, partially fulfilling the requirements

for a graduate degree. It was more than that. It was an instrument for getting many of my prejudices against sectarianism out of my system. But for an ironic twist of fate it might have been the final abjuration of my intervention in church business. *Happy Merger,* awarded first place in the Charles Sergel National Playwriting Contest, led to a Rockefeller fellowship in creative writing and research. Then Director Mabie had an idea: "Listen, man, if you want the most exciting material in the world, stick to religion! That's what made our country great!"

His interest and enthusiasm swept me back into the wilderness of denominationalism for a hasty, frightening glance. It was not for me. Let Protestantism fight its own battles. Let churches get the Holy Spirit or reject it. Let ecumenicalism flourish or fade. Though I still clung to my youthful polemic about the trivial differences which obscure the significant common heritage of all denominations, I had relinquished the right to interfere with those who wanted to perpetuate the battles of the Reformation. I would do my research in secular fields.

But Professor Mabie was insistent. "There are religious groups in America which no one has ever sympathetically investigated. The average church member doesn't even know they exist, and they don't know that our denominations exist. They're interested in finding God in the most marvelous ways you ever saw. There's your field."

He directed me to a settlement of Old Order Amish within twenty miles of the university. No one had ever tried to understand the horse-and-buggy life of this religious folk group. For nearly a hundred years they had been written off as queer ones, the backward hook-and-eye Dutch, the bearded Mennonites. I found them devoted to extraordinarily high ideals and perpetuating a rich cultural heritage. Their music had been handed down by oral tradition for nearly three hundred years; their literature went back to Anabaptist Menno Simons.

In Iowa I found also one of the four Trappist monasteries in the United States, New Melleray Abbey at Peosta. After visiting there and observing the remarkable faith of the cloistered contemplatives who had taken a vow of perpetual silence, I made a retreat in the protoabbey, Our Lady of Gethsemani, fifty miles south of Louisville, Kentucky. For two weeks I lived with the members of this Catholic monastic order whose routine years of renunciation are untouched by wars or worldliness. Through days of fasting, prayer, and work, they rigorously keep their vows of poverty, chastity, obedience, and silence, losing themselves in the thought of God.

Professor Mabie was right—American religion furnished exciting possibilities. My research led me down the cold but ever-interesting trails of the Icarian experimenters, the Shakers, the builders of Illinois' Zion City, and Benton Harbor's House of David.

The Lenten worship of Los Hermanos Penitentes called me to New Mexico where, in the communities between Santa Fe and Taos, I found rich dramatic fare. Los Hermanos had been scandalized by the press and accused of atrocities by unsympathetic newshawks. Though loyal members of the Roman Catholic faith, they had their own ideas about how Lent should be observed, and Mother Church was wisely tolerant of this obstreperous offspring. But the Penitentes had resigned themselves to the fate of being misunderstood. The meaning of flagellation and other forms of self-torture, the essence of their worship, would forever remain hidden from the world. That I wanted to interpret for outsiders their basic tenet, "Without suffering there is no salvation," was unthinkable. But after showing their annoyance at my intrusion by a barrage of stones and gravel, they

admitted me to a *morada* to witness the sanguinary worship of
the Third Order of St. Francis. *Calvario,* the sympathetic drama
of their faith which I wrote for production at the experimental
theater, was a gratifying reward for research which was becoming more and more fascinating. But a greater reward came from
the *Hermano Mayor* of one of the Penitente settlements. "You
are one among the few who in the two hundred years of our
American history have not ridiculed us for our beliefs," he said
with a note of friendliness in his voice.

America was revealing itself as a land rich and adventurous
in undiscovered mines of spiritual treasures. From the ranges
of the Sangre de Cristos I went to southern California again seeking the unusual, trying to put myself into the orbit of the other
man's religion. But while researching among the Russian Molokans of Los Angeles, I was ruefully dragged back to my own
years of spiritual rambling. As I drove through Echo Park one
day, I heard singing and band music reminiscent of my days at
the church on Eighteenth and Brown. "When They Ring Those
Golden Bells" was being wafted to high heaven at the gates of
Angelus Temple. Excited, shouting, jubilant devotees were
jammed in a solid wall around the circular doors of the church
to welcome Aimee Semple McPherson, who had just returned
from a missionary tour. In a niche above the marquee a life-size
statue of "Sister" loomed in saintly deification. Below, roses were
being tossed in the passageway that formed as she made her way
through the crowd. Shouts of "Praise the Lord" and "God bless
you, Sister!" rose above the singing.

This, too, was Pentecost. Aimee's Church of the Foursquare
Gospel was another division of the Pentecostal division of Protes-
tantism. The ghosts of Fairfield's unhappy local merger and
Milwaukee's baptism suddenly returned to ridicule me. When
I attended services in Angelus Temple, they hovered haunting-

ly. The pulpit antics of Aimee Semple McPherson would have offended my good friends of the Assemblies of God just as their raucous shouting at first offended me. Pastor Ulrich would never have approved of Sister in football togs, "kicking a goal for Jesus," or Sister in a speed cop's outfit coming down the aisle on a motorcycle with the cutout open, shouting to the congregation, "Stop! You're speeding to hell!" At another service I saw the saint of the Foursquare faith in the role of a cabaret singer. As she swayed with the microphone, burlesquing "Roll Out the Barrel," the Devil rolled it out from the left wing of the stage.

"What's in that barrel, old Devil?" she demanded.

"Wouldn't you like to know!"

"What's in that barrel that the whole world's following?"

"Try to find out!"

Sister called for an ax. An angel brought her one, and with hefty strokes she smashed the barrel on the platform of Angelus Temple.

"Just as I thought!" she cried. "There's nothing in the barrel! Listen, people, this barrel of fun you're following is empty! There's nothing in it! Come to Jesus!"

This was Pentecost, Hollywood-style. This was Pentecost with the last and greatest of the women evangelists. Visitors to southern California used to say, "What shall we do tonight—go to a show or go to hear Aimee?" This was Pentecost with a complete and active organization: a prayer tower to keep in touch with the heavenly powerhouse, a training school to turn out leaders for the International Church of the Foursquare Gospel, a radio station, KFSG (Kall Foursquare Gospel) to give the Devil some competition on the airways, commercial bookshops, and free commissaries to attract both the rich and the poor.

I returned to the Molokans to worship with them in their

sobranies and to find in their high exultation of worship the indefinable token of a mystic presence. Their prayers and holy jumping, their ecstatical psalms and the brotherly kiss expressed a feeling of comfort and joy in the adventure of faith. For over four hundred years, ever since their secession from the Greek Orthodox Church, they had been seeking the elusive ideal of personal salvation through a social consciousness of the group.

Again I was diverted from the dramatic folkways of this ethnic group. Everywhere in southern California I encountered Christians in flight, holding common stock in a corporation called The Church, but no longer interested in even watching the market. They were homeless, churchless Protestants whose names were fading on the dusty ledger of some congregational roll. They were spiritual windfalls and they were being garnered in by a most efficient crew of high-powered cultists—necromancers, palmists, psychics, yogis, clairvoyants, Tibetans, astrologers, theosophists, biosophists, metaphysicists, mental mystics, and self-styled spiritual technicians. Their advertisements were slanted toward the market of Protestant migrants streaming out of the Bible Belt and the great Midwest. I adjudged them commercial purveyors of unholy writ. They did not represent religion as I knew it. But they offered the religion some people wanted—people who had become dissatisfied with a traditional faith and with their churches and ministers back home.

While moving into an apartment on El Cerrito Avenue in Hollywood, I met a former Protestant from Kansas, Mrs. Minnie Klein. It was not long before our conversation turned from Kansas wind to California religions, and she asked if I had ever heard of the Mighty I Am. I had. Once in Chicago a young lady who took a peculiar interest in my spiritual life told me what she considered to be the gist of the I Am doctrine: "Six feet above you," she said, "is your perfect self, made up of atoms.

This atomic self follows you wherever you go. The object of life is to put your physical self in harmony with your atomic self. Try it and see what happens."

Mrs. Klein contended that such a superficial exposure to the fathomless mystery of the I Am teaching was dangerous. "You must meet the Ballards," she said enthusiastically. "Mr. Ballard, you know, is the reincarnation of George Washington. Mrs. Ballard is the reincarnation of Joan of Arc. And Donald—that's the son—he is the reincarnation of Lafayette."

I met the incomparable trio at a service in the white chapel of the Mighty I Am. The platform was garish with lavender lights, a harp entwined with lavender flowers, a neon cross that sputtered a violet glow, and large, sensuous portraits of Saint Germain and Jesus. On the back wall hung a large American flag, flanked by huge lavender bouquets.

Guy W. Ballard, tall, ascetic, and saintly white in a Palm Beach suit, commanded the weird sanctuary. Mrs. Ballard, vying for distinction as one of America's best-dressed women, was literally covered with rhinestones; her pink-satin gown blossomed out at her left shoulder in a cluster of orchids, and two pale roses were stuck in her hair. Son Donald, boyish though in his twenties, sat pallid and transfixed with his hands crossed over his chest.

The audience of about three hundred, made up almost entirely of middle-aged women in formal gowns, sang from I Am hymnals and sported I Am pins and I Am rings. They listened believingly as Mr. Ballard spoke blandly about his frequent tête-à-têtes with the legendary Saint Germain, Prophet and Ascended Master. They were just as credulous during his incredible discourse on how he had learned to lay aside his body and take astral flights backward and forward into time and space. No one was startled when he mentioned his friendly rendezvous with a black panther and his discovery of hidden caverns in the Tetons. When he closed his eyes and mused on the mystical, miraculous power of the "Violet Flame," all eyes were fixed on the neon cross. Mrs. Ballard played the harp and Donald prayed.

Then, while the audience was vociferously chanting "decrees," which are antiphonal texts, Ballard suddenly threw up his hands. "I have just had a message from Saint Germain!" he cried. "He says he wants us to take up another offering and raise five hundred dollars more! Beloved, you have done fine tonight, but surely you can do better for the sake of Saint Germain!"

The audience agreed they could, and the collection plates came around for the third time that evening. After the service Mrs. Klein explained that the Ballards as a rule did not ask for money. It just "came to them." In fact a thousand dollars had come to them on one occasion from Mrs. Klein.

"I gave Mr. Ballard this," she elaborated, "because he has done things for me that my minister never did."

"What?"

"He is teaching me how to live so that I will never die."

"You think you will never die?"

"Not if I learn the Mighty I Am secrets. Mr. Ballard says he will never die and I believe him."

"What will happen to him if he does not die? Will he live on earth forever?"

"He may, or he may be translated bodily to heaven."

What I considered quixotic tales were rigorously accepted as gospel by Mrs. Klein and other Ballard enthusiasts. They were avidly reading I Am books written by Ballard under the name of Godfré Ray King and published by the Saint Germain Press with a post-office box in Chicago. They were accepting as a new revelation the trumped-up stories of buried cities in the Amazon, of Ballard's triumph over gravity, of intimate visits with vestal virgins in underground sanctuaries, and of bodiless flights through the stratosphere to the mysterious ruins of Oaxaca. They were chanting their decrees:

> "Turn the darkness into day;
> Kill the sins for Godfré Ray;
> Manifest, manifest, manifest,
> I AM, I AM, I AM!"

At a testimonial meeting a man got up and said, "The way our faith works is wonderful. My little five-year-old son was playing in the yard. I watched him from the window. I saw him go to our cellar doors, the kind that lie down flat to the ground and have iron rings in them. He wanted to open those doors, but he couldn't. He wasn't strong enough. He took hold of one iron ring, then he took hold of the other, then he yanked with all his might. The doors wouldn't budge. Then my little boy stepped away from those doors and shouted, 'Mighty I Am Presence, open that door!' Lo and behold, the door opened. 'Mighty I Am Presence, open that other door!' The other door swung up all by itself just like the first, and my little boy walked proudly down into the cellar."

Groping in this fog of modern mythology, I came upon Mrs. Ferber, a former Methodist, who claimed that she discerned the true philosophy of the Mighty I Am system.

"Forget that you heard about panthers and stratospheric flights," she admonished. "Every religion has things in it you can't understand or explain. The basis of I Am belief is that every person is the reservoir of the power of God. The words 'I Am' are from the Bible. 'I Am that I Am.' That means me.

That doesn't mean God. That means me. When the Bible says, 'I Am the resurrection and the life,' that means me. *I* Am the resurrection and the life. *I* Am the light of the world. *I* Am the bread of life. As Mr. Ballard so often says, '*I* Am the self-consciousness of life, the one supreme presence of the great flame of love and light.' Let me give you a few books to study. It's easy once you get onto it."

I was continually being invited to California's inner sanctums. One night an ex-Baptist asked me to accompany him to a musty little mosque on Crenshaw, just south of Wilshire Boulevard. The bulletin board identified the place as "Agabeg Temple— Violet Greener, minister—The Ghost of Hollywood!"

We were met at the door by a young man with red hair and with a blue flower in his lapel. His greeting was "Do you want to pay your fifty cents now or later?" Those who did not pay the fifty cents now or later sat in the roped-off section; we sat in the unroped-off section. The printed program carried the names of the church staff, with an additional note at the bottom of the page: GOWNS WORN BY MISS GREENER BY RAMON.

Before us on the platform was a neon cross and a fountain that spouted colored water. At the console the organist swayed rhythmically under his improvisation of "Beautiful Dreamer." The two hundred people in the audience leaned back contentedly. Through the strains of music I could hear the equerry at the door asking newcomers about the fifty cents. Then the Reverend Violet Greener ascended the platform. Her hair was dyed purple to match the sash which cut in half the long yellow gown by Ramon.

With an upward sweep of her jeweled hands she brought believers and sight-seers to their feet for an opening prayer. That was the religious introduction to a meeting which immediately turned into a fortunetelling act. Miss Greener came down from the platform and started giving intimate readings to the fifty-centers in the unroped-off section. Bending familiarly over an elderly worshiper at my side, she confided, "I get the word six. Does six mean anything to you? Someone six years old? Six or sixteen? Maybe sixty? Ah, I get it now! Sick! Ah, yes. Is there sickness in your family? I get distinct vibrations of sickness. Did you ever have trouble with your kidneys? No? I get distinct vibrations that say kidney trouble. I'd sort of watch that."

Ramon's yellow gown swished against my knees. Looking steadily into my eyes, she began, "I get the name Joe. Does Joe mean anything to you? Think hard," she sighed soulfully. "Joe. Maybe it's Josephine, Joan, or Juliet. No? You know," she interrupted with a whisper, "you have a kissable mouth." Then she went on, "I get vibrations of travel. . . . Scenes. . . . Many scenes. Do you travel much? If you don't, you will."

Whether Miss Greener was getting vibrations from a higher power or making wild guesses, the thing she predicted for me came to pass. The rest of my stay in this mecca of the marvelous was spent window-shopping up one street and down another, looking for situations, settings, and characterizations for a great religious drama. My findings were more sensational but just as much a part of America as the folk culture I had come to Los Angeles to study.

I found John Amen-Zat and his Pyrimidians at the Osiris-Coptic-Christian Brotherhood Temple. In a chapel decorated with Egyptian symbols and illuminated by the shiny eye of Horus, a congregation was being asked to forget Habakkuk, Zephaniah, Haggai, Zechariah, and Malachi of Sunday-school fame and accept Kika Yoakhim, Hehu, Merula, and Su. "I give White Magic for your protection and Black Magic to exterminate your foes," Amen-Zat promised, but not for free.

"My friends, we do not take up an offering," he explained with a broad grin. "But we do have a box at the door into which you may drop your contributions. You may drop into the box whatever you want to give to the Lord—I mean, the landlord!"

In the Embassy Auditorium I met Joe Jeffers, son of Yahweh, who collected the phone numbers of all his converts—"so I can call you as soon as the heavenly tip-off about Armageddon comes through," he explained. He collected also canned goods and automobile tires and stored them in the basement of his Kingdom Church—"so we will all have a way to get to Zion and will have food to eat during the famine which must come before the millennium begins." Eight hundred followers believed him. Many of them, acting on his advice, gave up their jobs and prayerfully awaited the destruction of "California first, then the rest of the country, and then the whole world." Brother Joe was calling together the 144,000 chosen of the Lord. I met him through the invitation of a former Protestant who had given up a three-hundred-dollar-a-month job in anticipation of the end of the world.

There were other date-setting prophets in the Music Arts Building which cut across Spring Street to Broadway. It was a religious bargain counter: cosmic practitioners, astrologers, mediums, mystics, cabalists, phrenologists, and seers.

On a third-floor door I was confronted by a startling sign: JEHOVAH'S OFFICE. The headquarters had no connection with the Son of Yahweh. It was a new and popular cult devoted to "divine unfoldment." In answer to my rap, "Jehovah" appeared—a tall, hungry-looking man, without a beard. His faded blue shirt was half in and half out of his shabby gray pants and he was barefooted. The room was a confusion of disordered bookshelves made out of orange crates and dingy walls gone berserk with crayon drawings of wheels within wheels and stars within stars. From a curtained-off area in the corner someone was restlessly turning in bed while the lean man explained the gist of his teaching: "The solar plexus is the organ of the subconscious mind. The sympathetic system of nerves presides over all subjective sensations. It is through the subconscious that we are connected with the Universal Mind. It is through the solar plexus that we are related to the world within. It is in the equalization of these two centers of our being that we find the great secret of life. Can't you see what the churches have overlooked?"

Through the open door of a small room in the Music Arts Building, I saw an elderly man reclining on a day bed idly reading a letter. By his side was a basket full of unopened mail addressed to the First Mystics World Congress.

"Yes, yes," he cried, jumping up when I knocked, "I was just having a vision. Sit down."

I seated myself on one of the folding chairs which filled the disarranged room. Papers and pamphlets were scattered on the floor and stacked on a large table in the corner. A sign on the wall explicitly stated the numerical aims of the World Congress: "Ten good men might have saved Sodom and Gomorrah. The same fraction of our population—approximately 1,000—might save this country and, through it, the world."

"Yes," said the mystic, "we're signing 'em up fast."

"Who?"

"The approximately one thousand," he said impatiently. "Got about thirty at the meeting last night. Look here." He led me over to a table on which lay a cardboard covered with zigzag marks of blue blitz and a whirl of numerals. There was a large red X in the center.

"That," he informed, "is Station X. Whenever I want answers to religious questions or world peace or ambassadorial, gubernatorial, cosmic consciousness, and stuff, I just stand here—like this, with my hands behind my back—and my eyes glued on old Station X. Vibrations start coming. Light starts breaking. I get waves. It's wonderful. And all we need to save the world is the nine hundred and ninety-nine men just like me! We're getting 'em. We are for the establishment of a trust fund of twenty-five dollars per capita for all students under the age of eighteen, with a three-years' graduation course of travel to all principal parts of the earth as a finished education before entering the fields of labor of their choice until their retirement at the ripe age of fifty years. You are cordially invited to join up just as others are doing."

Soothsayers, diviners, occultists, metaphysicists, apocalyptists, colporteurs: hawkers of patent spiritual tonics, preying upon the public with pamphlets and books which were a strange mixture of lunacy and compassion. One nameless group urged me to consider the mystery of words.

"Bible," I was informed, "actually means that a man should 'B' the 'I' which means be the I Am or God. The word 'Know' is also rich in symbolism. 'I' is Kaph or Spirit. This means we should be K-Now or Spirit now!"

My notebooks were growing heavy with warnings and promises: "It will be a great day for you when Jesus comes, especially if you are out of employment and if you are a Christian. The Lord will snatch you up for a job in His kingdom. Sinners should be careful about riding in automobiles with Christians. For when Jesus comes the Christian drivers will be snatched up and the cars will be wrecked. Oh, what a glorious day when Jesus comes! Then there will be no more need for dentists because the Bible tells us plainly there will be no more decay."

More practical purveyors of Holy Writ were issuing less-frightening bulletins. One of these men was Edwin J. Dingle, news reporter, fellow of the Royal Geographical Society, and metaphysical consultant. He had got religion on a walking trip through China when he sighted a Tibetan temple. Then he came to Los Angeles with "Dingle-ism," a remarkable brand of mind power "taught by a great teacher who probably knows more about the Inner Teachings of the Masters of the East than any man in America." I followed his familiar advertising teaser, "Everybody goes to heaven," to the headquarters of his Institute of Mentalphysics on South Hobart Boulevard. There, he promised, he would reveal to his Sunday-morning congregation a secret that had been hidden for ten thousand years, a secret that had been guarded for centuries in a monastery in Tibet.

Somehow the prayers did not mean much that Sunday morning. The hymns were superfluous. The soloist was just another obstacle in the way of the great secret. The offering and announcements left us impatient and tantalized. Then handsome Mr. Dingle picked up a small tin can from the pulpit and held it in his slender white hands. The label bore a picture of the administration office of the Institute, and in the top of the can was a slot, large enough to receive coins or bills.

"This," Dingle admitted, "doesn't look like much, but if you will get one of these little depositories and follow directions, you will never want again. You will be taking on yourself the divine privilege of becoming the custodian of the universe!"

Soon we were fighting our way back to the table where three women were handing out the tin cans. Six hundred anxious seekers, eager for a formula for riches, stretched out hungry hands for a depository.

"Follow instructions!" cried the women as they supplied us with cans and mimeographed outlines of the necessary steps in sowing the seeds of supply. "Follow instructions and sign your name and the number of the can before you leave. Don't break the spell!"

Outside, in the brilliant Sabbath sunlight, I joined the Disciples of the Depositories who moved slowly away from the Institute, reading with awed expressions the rules on the mimeographed sheets. I paused under a palm tree.

FOLLOW INSTRUCTIONS

1. Each morning when about to deposit your coin in the Bank (can) stand in silence, and declare, *"I Draw My Supply from the Source of Infinite Supply. . . . This is My Seed."*
2. As you say the words, you will feel the Power. This Power will be revealed to you in the growing unshakable conviction that for this day, your Supply will come to you.
3. Having dropped your coin, declare: *"I am Abundance as Thou the Source of All Supply in the Universe, art Absolute Abundance. . . . I am my own supply."*
4. Hold your Bank in reverence.
5. Make this a daily discipline, and never fail to add one coin a day, regularly and reverently.
6. Return your bank as soon as it is full. BUT IN NO CIRCUMSTANCES KEEP IT MORE THAN A MONTH.

The instructions were addressed to the "Dear Seeker After Higher Things" and were signed "The Order of Melchisedec." Whatever the order, Mr. Dingle remained supreme councilor and preceptor emeritus of his organization, teaching "the Faultless Philosophy of Life" to followers who fondly called him Dingli-Mei.

Always I was seeing these sensational new religionists as

leading characters in a fantastic pageant of American life. The men and women who followed them were assuming significant roles in my research. When I returned to Sister McPherson's Temple and interviewed the uniformed workers and listened to their testimonies, I realized that the great ingathering at Angelus was not merely the result of this enterprising evangelist's appealing personality, nor did the crowds follow her because of her sensational showmanship and her driving, tireless energy. These people had been waiting for her when she pulled up the FOR SALE sign in a weedy lot near Echo Park and began building her Foursquare empire. They responded when she boldly beckoned with the ancient "Follow me" because they were looking for a leader. Humanity was blindly searching for an outlet in a maze of confusion and unrest. Deliverance was welcomed whether it came via the Mighty I Am Presence or the Ghost of Hollywood or the Black and White Magic of Amen-Zat.

The mystical power of Jehovah and the Son of Jehovah, the vibrations from Station X, and the spell of the Dingle depository were one and the same thing—an answer to a search that had ended at least momentarily in southern California. Some were deluded, some were obsessed. And there were many religious racketeers. But always I found sincere believers following their pretentious guides through muck and mire; when the going was must rugged, they inevitably consoled themselves with the remembrance that "persecution" has ever been a prophet's destiny.

So the mystical power of the Violet Flame blazed on, even though the lavish and fabulous life of the Ballards was exposed. When a Federal suit was filed against their Chicago office for using the mails to defraud, the Mighty I Am Presence was sent to the nation by railway express. Charges of plagiarism from Rosicrucian H. Spencer Lewis and archaeologist Baird T. Spalding failed to dislodge I Am believers from the Ballard parishes.

When Mr. Ballard died, I expressed my sympathy to Mrs. Klein.

"What makes you think he died?" she asked.

"I read about it in the morning paper."

"Don't believe everything you read," she warned.

A photostatic copy of Ballard's death certificate only evoked the accusation that I could not understand these things because I was not a member of the movement.

Unquestioning loyalty was the rule. Members of the Foursquare Church explained the McPherson scandals as the work of the devil. When the court ruled the kidnaping story "perpetuating a hoax," when Aimee's divorces and romances were Hollywood gossip, they remembered the poor whom she fed during the lean years and the miracles she performed in the days when her indomitable faith worked wonders with the sick and suffering.

Nor did the followers of the Son of Yahweh desert him during a divorce suit when Mrs. Jeffers, thirty-nine and beautiful, stunned court spectators by affirming that her husband told her that she (Mrs. Jeffers) was now dead. "I was out in the mountains," she quoted Jeffers as saying, "and had the ceremony. You are now dead and buried."

The judge asked Jeffers about his income.

"It is anywhere from nothing up," said Brother Joe. "I live on love offerings."

"Do you own any stocks and bonds?" he was asked.

"I do," said the Son of Yahweh. "Two or three million—laid up in the kingdom of heaven."

"That's out of my jurisdiction," said the judge. "Let's come down to earth."

Many of the cultists vehemently denied the charge that they

were merely a part of California's "cradle of the crackpots." Their holdings were not confined to the headquarters they had set up or the following they had gained in the Sunshine State. At an international convention in Angelus Temple I met ministers who manned "lighthouses" around the globe. "We're now twenty thousand strong," Aimee declared as she traced the development of the International Church of the Foursquare Gospel. After Ballard's death, the Mighty I Am's announced, "In less than ten years Mr. Ballard has won millions of followers all over the world. We will prosper even more now that he is among the Ascended Masters."

To test these claims, I turned eastward and found the spiritual skies of the nation spangled with odd and mystical isms, guiding the unwise and shepherdless to the mangers of questionable messiahs. Concerned and wondering, I intensified my study, following incredible trails across the nation. Everywhere a lengthy list of satellites whirling around the Bill of Rights. Everywhere a new religious jargon playing havoc with Protestant indoctrination. To ancient creeds and to the inviolable "Our Father . . ." they were adding something new.

In Denver I heard a Pyramidian convert lead his family in a daily prayer: AMON! AMON! AMON!

The father: Hail to AMON who cometh with Su.
The family: To manifest His Will as it is in Heaven.
The father: Hail to AMON who cometh through Nut.
The family: To bring us our daily spiritual and material needs.
The father: Hail to AMON who cometh with Hathor.
The family: He cometh with the goddess of Mercy and Kindness to forgive us our trespasses as we forgive those who trespass against us.
The father: Hail to AMON who cometh with Merula.

The family: He cometh with the Guardian of the Soul to protect us from all temptation.

The father: Hail to AMON who cometh with Anubis.

The family: To deliver us from all evil.

The father: Hail to AMON, the ALMIGHTY ONE!

The family: For His is the Kingdom, and the Power, and the Glory for all eternity.

In Unison: AMON! AMON! AMON!

.

In Tipton, Iowa, the "Book of George" was broadcasting final and basic "Life Principles." It was a local movement which, according to its founder and promoter, attracted "good farmer folks from all over the state, and some from Nebraska and Missouri, all wanting healing or a better philosophy of life." In George's second-floor office on Tipton Square I observed a typical "treatment." On tables behind thin, white curtains two farmers lay "completely relaxed" while George cited quotations from the "Book of George." A favorite, oft-repeated one was "The ratio in volume of the positive to the negative condition in the soul-body of man determines whether or not it is a living or dead body. God's laws never fail."

The treatment ended, George ordered the patients to turn over and go to sleep, then looked at me with an obliging, questioning smile. I forestalled his offering me a treatment by asking skeptical questions about what he had done for his farmer clients.

"I cure 'em," he replied. "It doesn't matter what's wrong, I can cure 'em with the law o' life. The law o' life takes care of everything. It's not medicine, it's not treatments really, it's the law o' life. Cancer, t.b., debts, troubles at home—I cure 'em all with the law o' life."

"George," I said, glancing at his baldish head, "what can you do for falling hair?"

The valiant cultist gave me a startled look, covered his face with his hands and said, "Brother, you got me there!"

In Chicago I met a group of ex-Protestants who were studying Maitreya's *Secret Pyramid,* the philosophy of Mah-Atmah Amsumata. At the close of the meeting the adepts repeated an affirmation which might have come straight out of the Mighty I Am movement: "I transmute and change, through my love-will, all the forces of my three lower bodies, into divine love, and draw all into my four higher bodies and on into the aura of Lord Maitreya, to use as he sees fit in the upliftment of all mankind."

A near neighbor of the Secret Pyramidian sect was the Universal Spiritual Union whose members talked "Cosmocracy" and "natural dynamics." The Union claimed a world membership of at least five hundred thousand. Its guiding spirit was Cherenzi-Lind, a great prophet and miracle worker, who was not even in the United States.

Every city had its Ghost who, like Miss Greener of Hollywood, devised a spiritual plot with vibrations from the other world. And there were those who went a step farther and claimed actual communication with discarnate spirits. What traditional Protestantism taught, Spiritualism claimed to prove by actual demonstration: the dead live. Though this effrontery had long been condemned by major denominations, Spiritualism, according to the Census Bureau, had taken its place as a denomination.

Spiritualistic camps were maintained in Clinton, Iowa, in Lily Dale, New York, and in Chesterfield, Indiana. After attending a series of ineffectual, trumped-up séances, I was privileged to sit in on two excellent demonstrations. At Chesterfield, Clifford Bias was convincing as a trumpet medium, and Fanchion Harwood proved mystifying and highly talented in materialization. At an early evening séance, a figure appeared to me and announced that she was Paula, an only sister who had died many years before. Test questions were instantly answered. Resemblance was convincing. My skepticism was shaken, my interest aroused; I could understand why seekers in the land of the heavy footfalls accounted Mrs. Harwood one of the best of America's mediums.

Perhaps, as the Spiritualists insisted, one might find the psychic stream running through the Scriptures from cover to cover. I agreed that if the Bible were read with spiritualistic philosophy in mind, many natural deductions could be made— the handwriting on the wall, automatic writing; the voice which came to Samuel, clairaudience; the witch of Endor, a medium; the transfiguration, materialization.

Then I attended another séance conducted by a different medium, and Paula appeared again. She called me by name and I walked across the carpeted room to where she stood. Again the illusion was convincing. And the answers to my questions were more or less satisfactory until I asked, "Paula, *kannst du noch Deutsch sprechen?*"

There was an awkward pause. Then Paula said, "I'm sorry. We don't use that language over here!"

While the cultists were vying with traditional Protestantism and with one another for followers, Daddy Grace, bishop of the Church on the Rock of the Apostolic Faith, was preaching a gospel of riches and glory to his Negro followers. This corpulent, curly-haired, dynamic evangelist claimed a congregation of half a million to whom he was giving "as much of God as any man can give without being God himself." He stirred river waters from Washington, D. C., to Greenville, South Carolina, with baptized converts. He took joy rides with the Lord in his black sedans and encouraged the white folks to accept his magic doctrine of "there is no spot where God is not."

But to a spiritual competitor in New York City he lost the title of foremost Negro evangelist. Father M. J. Divine claimed two million followers who in turn acclaimed him God "absolutely, undeniably, and in the flesh." That was the only way they could explain the material wealth which this once obscure Negro now controlled as director of the Peace Mission Movement. There were a hundred Kingdom buildings in Philadelphia and New York, sixty private offices competently staffed, numerous estates along the Hudson, the Brigantine Hotel in New Jersey, Cadillacs and station wagons. Only an omniscient hand could provide such lavish fare for believers: free banquets of sixty and seventy courses, free movies, free schools, free correspondence service, free gyms, free bowling alleys, free employment service, and a respectable job in the Kingdom. And only God could speak as Father spoke:

"The churches have lost the sense of the consciousness of good and no space is vacant of the fullness thereof. I am come to make the realness of God true by making the realness of God plain so that it can be seen among the children of men. That which is invisible I make visible, that which is intangible I tangibilitate, and that which is unimaginable I make imaginable!"

To this, devoted followers were inspired to cry: "Peace, it's wonderful!" and "Thank you, Father dear!"

And to sing:

> "Father Divine is God Almighty,
>   He is now on earth to stay;
> Father Divine is God Almighty,
>   He's the Life, the Truth, the Way.

"Father Divine is God Almighty,
Jesus Christ, the selfsame one;
Father Divine is God Almighty,
To the whole world he has come!"

Among the incomprehensible cultist leaders, Father Divine
was most impelling. With rare insight into his people's spiritual,
social, and economic needs, with the ability to analyze and prescribe and counsel, he was playing the role of "De Lawd"
grandiloquently, and restoring to forgotten heirs the keys of the
kingdom.

In his office on the corner of Broad and Catherine streets in
Philadelphia, Father explained to me the basic aim of his work:

"I mean to bring an abolition to all division and to create one
big family universally. I have white people and those of the
darker complexion. I have people from the Methodist Church,
from the Presbyterian, from the Baptist. I have even had a priest
from the Catholic Church to speak in my church. We are coming to a light of understanding where we understand each other
better spiritually and as we understand each other better spiritually we can also harmonize more economically, politically,
socially, and otherwise through harmonization by the unity of
the spirit. As I often say: by the unity of the spirit, of mind, of
aim, and of purpose, we unify!"

From California to New York I had found that which was
spoken of by the oracle of Main Street, old Doc Reynolds. It
was mitotic division gone wild. And, despite the questionable
aspects of obsessed leaders and deluded followers, Old Doc
would have said, "Wonderful! That's Protestantism!" In Fairfield my reply had been, "At its worst," but since my zeal for
union had been displaced by more practical interests, I was not
so sure. Watching and listening to America's carousal of un-

believable religions, I had transferred my interest to individuals
—Protestant individuals, men and women who represented a
Fairfield congregation spread out across the nation, seeking God
as they pleased. The cultist leaders were invariably ex-Protestants, and the majority of the people who made up the cultist
laity were ex-Protestants.

In Springfield, Missouri, and in Cleveland, Tennessee, I found
Pentecostal headquarters as replete with ex-Protestants as
Angelus Temple. In Pulaski, Virginia, a town of 8,000, I counted
seven rival Pentecostal churches. Pentecostalism, either in spite
of its divisions or because of them, was growing at the rate of
two hundred per cent every ten years and always by the
Saunders-Ulrich method. Holy Ghost-filled congregations came
from Lutheranism, Anabaptist and Baptist, the Reformed faith,
the Presbyterian faith, Anglicanism, Congregationalism, the
Quakers, the Church of the Brethren, the Methodists. . . . As in
the cults, so in Pentecost: the first requirement for contentment
was discontent with the church back home. Though good or
bad, honest or dishonest, genuine or counterfeit, the daring
fishermen were doing well. Protestantism was the spawning
ground and in Protestant shoals they watched and waited, continually filling their nets with easy catches.

As a sequel to my research off the beaten Protestant path, I
turned to Protestant ministers with a question: "What do you
think of my little-known religions?"

"They're the lunatic fringe! . . . The cults of the psychopath!
. . . Rackets! . . . Catamounts! . . . Crackpots! . . . If any of
our members can be drawn away by such fraudulent trash, let
them go. I'm not trying to compete with them."

Back in California a minister spoke his piece. "The cults
don't bother me. Neither does Aimee. All the church must
do is to fight these groups with their own weapons. If sensa-

tionalism is what people want, give it to them. Jesus was
sensational for His time."

One Sunday morning this preacher demonstrated what he
meant. He was carried to the pulpit in a coffin. When the coffin
was set down, he slowly rose up and preached a sermon on the
resurrection.

"I'll tell you what I think," said a minister of the Church of
the Nazarene. "Some of those sects in southern California and
in other places, too, are the work of the Devil."

"I can tell you why they get started," asserted the editor of a
religious journal. "They get started because Protestantism is
divided, disunited, weak, and without authority."

"No, I don't think denominationalism has much to do with
it," another observed. "People are just plain restless in keeping
with the age. They want heaven right now and that's what
these cultists promise them."

"When the church broke with a belief in hell," said a fundamentalist, "hell broke loose in the church. Men no longer fear
God. When fear is gone, every godless group lays claim to
godliness."

In Wichita my brother again reprimanded me for squandering my religious birthright, for prostituting the family faith.
But I was not ready to abandon so productive a field of research.
It was a ready-made extravaganza to be observed through the
proscenium of the other fellow's quest. I was the spectator, and,
eager to see where the network of trails would lead, I resolved
to continue to go a whoring after the strange gods of a new
Americana.

CHAPTER SIX

Reformation, U.S.A.

OLLOWING the cultists for dramatic loaves and fishes, I again became involved in Protestantism's dilemma. The great problem of the Fairfield invasion was the problem of every Protestant minister. My youthful deduction was right: Fairfield mirrored the world. The renegade religions which had preyed upon my congregation were preying upon congregations everywhere. The menacing groups which had moved into my Kansas parish had moved into every parish. My hasty recording of sensational episodes had yielded a startling conclusion: the cults were but a barometer on the fringe of the Protestant world registering the cyclonic winds within. The cults might be dismissed as a questionable carnival attracting religious migrants with their colorful exhibitions, but something more cataclysmic was happening up and down Church Street. The old churches still stood on the old locations, but new groups had elbowed in and most certainly were telling Protestants to move over. Sure-footed contemporary reformers who could not be classed among the cults were demonstrating a vital and spiritualized faith which, they declared, could no longer be found within the traditional churches.

Gradually my interest in experimental drama was lost in a growing awareness of a modern reformation. The vision of myself as a watchman on the Protestant ramparts returned; the warnings which I had hesitantly voiced in an obscure Kansas town now demanded a hearing across the nation. I would rouse a slumbering Protestantism with an alarming report. I would tell my story as I had heard and seen it on Church Street, U. S. A.

More than fifty years had passed since Massachusetts churchmen had scoffed at the heterodox announcements of Mary Baker Eddy: "Evil is but an illusion. . . . The Science of Mind disposes of all evil. . . . Mind is God. . . . Life is divine Principle. . . ." Luther's salvation by faith was the trumpet blast of the old Reformation; Mary Baker Eddy's "scientific statement of being" spearheaded the new. Theologians and natural scientists alike were startled but this was only the beginning. Soon another presumptuous offer was made from Kansas City to the churches: an auxiliary faith for the rediscovery of the "Christ within." From Mackinac Island came the accusation that the institutionalized churches are incompetent: they cannot change or remake lives. A man in Moscow, Idaho, was bluntly condemning Protestantism: "The trouble with the churches is that they talk about God and preach about God and sing and pray about God, but they don't manifest the power of God!" From a Brooklyn headquarters came the stinging denunciation that organized religion had become the instrument of the Devil; from Wilmette, Illinois, a decree that a divided Christendom can never save the world and a command to accept a Persian saint as the last and greatest world messiah.

When I followed these cries, I found more than phantom voices. The potent and challenging proclamations came from stations as strong and fortressed as Castle Church. And they were breaking through walls as strong as those which crumbled when the democracy of faith broke the chains which bound the world to Rome.

In Boston I found the capital of the Christian Science empire.

The cathedral dome of The Mother Church guarded the tri-
angular-shaped plot of impressive administration buildings and
a two-block-long publishing plant. I interviewed church officials,
office and printery employees, tourists to whom this stop was a
part of seeing New England, and tourists to whom it was a
spiritual mecca. I joined the admiring crowds in the auditorium
seating five thousand where the gray-white Bedford stone, the
mahogany pews, and the hand-wrought swinging lamps typified
the meticulous attention to detail so characteristic of Christian
Science enterprises. I might have been walking a Wittenberg
street. Quotations from Mary Baker Eddy inscribed on the
walls of The Mother Church were as revolutionary for my time
as the ninety-five theses had been in 1517: "If sin makes sinners,
Truth and Love can unmake them. . . . He who perceives the
true idea of Life loses his belief in death. . . . Today the healing
power of Truth is widely demonstrated as an immanent, eternal
Science."

If Boston was Wittenberg, Kansas City was Zürich. On Tracy
Avenue a robust contemporary of Christian Science had stirred
into giant strength. The roar of the mammoth presses in the
Unity School of Christianity was Zwingli debating with Luther:
it was Charles and Myrtle Fillmore splitting theological hairs
with other divine scientists in a disputation that had been going
on since 1889. From a back-room study hall in Kansas City
Unity was growing into a thriving colony covering thirteen
hundred acres. The Fillmores were "setting up on earth the
kingdom of the heavens." Mystical Unity City with its chapel,
prayer chambers, and training school was sustained by the fertile
acres of Unity Farm. And crews of workmen were building
larger schools, printeries, homes, and dormitories for a growing
population.

I met also a Wesley in this twentieth-century reformation.

Frank N. Buchman, leader of the Oxford Group and Moral Re-Armament, maintained modest rented quarters at the Island House on Mackinac but, like Wesley, he claimed the world for his parish. He was riding his circuit in Cadillacs and airplanes, nettling the churches with his claim that he wanted to convert men, not proselytize them. But on Mackinac Island the changed ones met and tarried, as if waiting the day when their "Holy Clubs" would be formulated into a new church for changing men and changing nations.

I found Psychiana, the radical, separatist wing of the reform movement, solidly stationed in substantial buildings in Moscow, Idaho, ruthlessly bent on changing the church from without. Psychiana—coming through the mails with founder Frank B. Robinson's searing charge, "The Power of God has built Psychiana greater in two decades than the power of men has built denominations in two hundred years!" Psychiana—filling the postmen's packs across the nation with a correspondence course which promised miracles to every student.

In Wilmette, Illinois, I stood transfixed before the million-dollar Baha'i temple, an architectural wonder symbolizing a faith which had made its American debut within my lifetime. Again the East was determined to conquer a divided West. On the eve of Europe's Reformation the Mohammedan Bajazet vowed that his horse would "eat oats on the high altar of St. Peter's in Rome"; today the followers of a Persian prince, Baha'u'llah, audaciously predicted that their faith would consume the wild oats of the Christian harvest.

Undaunted by this or any other challenger, Judge Rutherford built in Brooklyn his Theocratic headquarters: a Bible college, dormitories, refectories, bookshops, and a printing plant operated by a staff of his ordained ministers, laboring without salary for Jehovah God. Day and night they worked and witnessed, fighting against time, calling out God's anointed before the dread day of Armageddon. Jehovah's Witnesses—like the Zwickau prophets who slogged through the Reformation comparing themselves to Noah, predicting the end of the world; like the Zwickau prophets, despised by Catholic and Protestant alike, condemned, denounced, ridiculed. But Jehovah's Witnesses fought back in vigorous strength with an organization that linked sixty-four countries directly to Jehovah's throne via the Brooklyn office.

When I looked into the religious chronicles of America, I found that this modern reformation had descended upon Protestantism with amazing speed. The Christian Science denomination was founded by Mrs. Eddy in 1879. In 1884 the Watch Tower Bible and Tract Society was established as the legal corporation of Jehovah's Witnesses. In 1903 Myrtle Fillmore's Truth Students became the Unity School of Practical Christianity. The Baha'i Faith became an American religion in 1912, when the son of Baha'u'llah turned the first shovelful of ground for the temple at Wilmette. Frank Buchman sent out his first missionary team from the Oxford campus in 1921. Robinson placed his first Psychiana advertisement in a national periodical in 1928.

Carried on the tide of this new reformation, other groups filled the gaps between these red-letter years. As Luther's dissenting voice inspired less courageous prophets to speak, again heresy followed on heresy. The cults had spread their epidemic through weird concoctions of faith and fancy, but more erudite groups presented qualities of permanence. Like Pentecostalism they had surged in with mighty strength, built their religious households, and provided their tenants with substantial fare. Even the lesser householders were imposing. The prolific Divine Science family, emphasizing personality and self-culture through the mind of man in harmony with the mind of God, had offices and lecturers in every important American city. The New Thought movement, with its emphasis on the individual as an absolute expression of God-consciousness, formed an alliance and made its bid for the millions who believe in heaven here and now. The Anglo-Israel Federation pioneered for the recognition of Britain and America as the lost tribe of God's chosen people. Vedanta, brought to America from India, taught the rediscovery of the inner life through paths of spiritual wisdom. The Church of the New Jerusalem, founded in the late eighteenth century by Emanuel Swedenborg, was only now, in an age of metaphysical interpretation of the Scriptures, coming into its own.

Theosophy, Rosicrucianism, Swamis and Yogis, the Church of the Absolute Center, the Church of Higher Life, Scientific Christianity, Christian Philosophy, Spiritual Science, Metaphysical Alliance, Universal Truth, Mental Science, Fellowship of Life Abundant, Church of the Healing Christ, Radiant Life Fellowship—all had arrived within the last half century. The new reformation was moving with the speed of the modern world.

While reading an account of healing in the Gospel of Matthew, Mrs. Eddy was healed almost instantly of a severe injury. Then through a gradual process which she described as "divine revelation, reason, and demonstration," she established the scientific basis of a new religious approach. "God is good—Good is Mind—God, Spirit, being all, nothing is matter." As a member of the Congregational Church she offered this discovery to Protestantism with the plea that the faith which cannot heal cannot live. She wanted to restore to the churches the ministry of healing which, she claimed, had been lost to the Christian faith since the third century. Church doors were closed against her. Ministers called the new system a mind cure and healing by suggestion and described it as a menace to the health of the nation. But Mrs. Eddy said, "Must Christian Science come through the Christian churches? This Science has come already, after the manner of God's appointing, but the churches seem not ready to receive it.... 'He came unto his own, and his own received him not.'"

A Kansas City miracle gave rise to another extraecclesia movement of healers and teachers. Myrtle Fillmore, a Methodist, healed of tuberculosis through the use of an affirmation, believed that she had made an astounding discovery. A recognition of the "Christ within" could heal and help and empower every life. While Christian Science denied the reality of sin and disease, the Unity School insisted upon the negation of these evils. The whole gamut of Christian doctrine was recast in metaphysical formulas. "God shall supply all your needs" became "Whatever man wants he can have by voicing his desire into the Universal Mind."

The Oxford Group had its origin in a conversion rather than in a healing. Frank N. Buchman had been a Lutheran pastor for many years when he bewildered Pennsylvania parishioners with the announcement that though he had prayed and preached, he had never "found God." Then he went on a pilgrimage to England, and in a little wayside chapel in Keswick his life was "changed." The miracle accomplished, his denomination suddenly became narrow and confining. He had a message bigger than any church—big enough for the world. The pulpit lost its appeal. There was a more efficient method of getting hold of a man, washing him clean, filling his soul with power. Soon from the Oxford campus where Buchman was conducting a one-man revival, teams of young men set out to change lives by substituting a daily "quiet time" for a weekly sermon, by taking prospective converts to house parties instead of church services.

The tree of Psychiana sprang up out of the eroding terrains of a human soul. After years of seeking God in Baptist and Congregational Churches and rescue missions, Robinson suddenly arrived at what he called complete consciousness of the God-Power in his own life. Like his fellow reformers, he accepted this unusual conversion as a great commission. "The Power of God is available in exactly the proportion in which you avail yourself of that Power!" was the message he had for the churches which he accused of having lost that power. But the denominations in which he had failed to find God now turned down as counterfeit the demonstration of his heavenly rapport. They would not accept the claim that his was a divine revelation. They refused to take him seriously when he spoke of "easy miracles," so he, too, found a way of propagating his power-packed gospel without the co-operation or approval of Protestantism.

When I discovered Baha'u'llah in ancient writings and in modern American disciples, I heard a direct appeal to all Protestant churches. "The oneness of mankind" was emblazoned on the banner which Baha'is had unfurled across America. They were challenging Protestantism to take the lead in unifying the religions of the world in an international tribunal. They were seeking to remedy the confusion of tongues through a universal language. The churches would not listen. They construed the Baha'i movement as a Persian cult making its bid for American prestige and American dollars. But Baha'is continued their plans at the Tabernacle of the Great Peace on Wilmette's Sheridan Road. Their faith included the followers of all the great prophets, from the most ancient to the most modern, through Moses and Jesus and Mohammed to the great new prophet, Baha'u'llah, who said, "The Lord hath ordained as the sovereign remedy and mightiest instrument for the healing of the world, the union of all its people in one universal Cause, one common Faith."

The Baha'i pleas for peace and union were often lost in the din of the dreadful warnings continually sounding from the tireless apocalyptical voice of Jehovah's Witnesses. They were not offering salvation to the world, for the world was doomed. God's great clock was fast ticking out the hours before the inevitable end. They had His timetable. They knew His plan. The name which Rutherford gave them in 1931 placed them in the prophetic tradition, linked them with Noah, Daniel, Isaiah, and John the Revelator. Organized religion they condemned; it was the Devil's tool, blinding men to the truth. Modern clergymen were not like the Master's disciples who went from house to house warning and witnessing, carrying neither scrip nor purse. But Jehovah's Witnesses perpetuated the apostolic commission. They contended that they were subjects of an invisible King, rightful heirs to a new world.

Every discovery brought me closer to an understanding of this modern reformation. Bold heretical leaders sounding forth from businesslike inner sanctums, temple guides, and typesetters doing the necessary work at headquarters, Unity students at Unity City and Psychiana students in their homes, missionary teams and race conferences on college campuses, witnesses and practitioners—all were a part of my report to Protestantism. But every discovery was but a reflection of the faith and energy of the founders. They were the whirling turbines whipping up the complacent streams of Protestantism. Having made a great spiritual discovery outside the churches, each began a frantic search for devices which would take his message quickly and efficiently to all mankind. And the result rivaled the daring

anarchism of the Reformation fathers. Further, they had translated the Bible from the meaningless garble of Latin phrases into
colloquial languages and set up catechisms to guide the priesthood of believers they had created. So modern reformers were
defining newly discovered truths in a modern idiom. The
symbolism of language which the churches inherited from the
theological disputations of the sixteenth century were not
meaningful to modern ears. Tenets of faith calibrated to the
needs and tensions of contemporary America brought religion
up to date.

Christian Science led the way in its "scientific statement of
being" proclaimed by Mrs. Eddy in her chapter on "Recapitula-
tion" in *Science and Health with Key to the Scriptures:*

There is no life, truth, intelligence, nor substance in matter.
All is infinite Mind and its infinite manifestation, for God
is All-in-all. Spirit is immortal Truth; matter is mortal
error. Spirit is the real and eternal; matter is the unreal and
temporal. Spirit is God, and man is His image and likeness.
Therefore man is not material; he is spiritual.

The Unity School of Christianity declared:

There is but one Mind in the universe. Mortal mind is false
mind, or intellect. It gathers its information from without.
Universal Mind sees and speaks from within. Our ways of
thinking make our happiness or unhappiness, our success
or nonsuccess. We can, by effort, change our ways of thinking. God is at all times, regardless of our so-called sins,
trying to pour more good into our lives to make them
larger and more successful.

The Oxford Group defined its aims:

A new social order under the dictatorship of the Spirit of God, making for better human relationships, for unselfish co-operation, for cleaner business, cleaner politics, for the elimination of political, industrial, and racial antagonism. ... Upon a foundation of changed lives permanent reconstruction is assured. Apart from changed lives no civilization can endure.

Psychiana proclaimed:

The Spirit of the Living God which created the whole universe and everything in it, lives in you. In you are all the limitless capabilities there are in the realm of God. You need not beg. You need not implore God to give you this or that. That is not the way God operates. God is here —in you. And all of God is here—in you. For it is the Spirit of God which endowed you with life in the first place.

The Baha'i faith taught its followers:

Error is lack of guidance; darkness is absence of light; ignorance is lack of knowledge; falsehood is lack of truthfulness; blindness is lack of sight; and deafness is lack of hearing. Therefore, error, blindness, deafness, and ignorance are nonexistent things. In creation there is no evil; all is good. ... Religion and science walk hand in hand and any religion contrary to science is not the truth.

Jehovah's Witnesses warned:

Only those who are diligent in studying God's revealed Word, and who keep in mind God's message, particularly relating to the kingdom, will be able to hold fast and withstand the assault of the enemy. Those who for any excuse or reason turn to the things of this world are certain to lose everything. Those who put their trust wholly in Jehovah and his King, and who with diligence press on in the fight in obedience to his Word, will continue to behold what is God's purpose and what shall be the result.

Methods employed in the propagation of these new gospels surpassed the unorthodox contrivances introduced in Europe's Reformation. Luther had led the way by printing and circulating his sermons. Zwingli had distributed his doctrines to the armed forces. Calvin had written a best seller. Anglicans had covered the British Empire with tracts. Catechisms, Testaments, Bibles, special papers, and regular publications were smuggled into forbidden areas. Classes for study met in secret. When books were burned, new books were written. Each reformer was determined to make his "damnable heresy" a worldwide religion.

Having built for themselves strong arks of faith, modern reformers proceeded to deluge the world with a flood of inspired writings. But none were marked by more dignity of form or profoundness of thought than those sent out from The Mother Church in Boston. In metropolitan newspapers the story was being told in column-long announcements:

HOW CHRISTIAN SCIENCE HEALS. A man crippled by rheumatism diagnosed as incurable, began to read the Christian Science textbook, *Science and Health with Key to the Scriptures,* by Mary Baker Eddy. "As the truth was unfolded to me," he wrote afterward in one of many similar letters now included in the book, "I realized that the mental condition was what needed correcting, and that the Spirit of truth which inspired this book was my physician. My healing is complete...."

This publicity brought to the Boston office unnumbered requests for copies of *Science and Health*. In public display racks conspicuously placed in railroad stations, hotels, lobbies of public buildings, corridors of schools and colleges, current Christian Science literature was gratuitously offered to the public. More requests for *Science and Health*. Wherever a Christian Science church was built a Christian Science reading room was authorized and competently staffed. In surroundings designed to reflect the perfect peace of mind toward which the Scientist strives, the latest Christian Science publications and bound volumes of back copies were available: quarterly, monthly, and weekly periodicals, tracts, pamphlets, and bulletins. All repeated the story of healing through the realization that the mental condition needed correcting; all induced faith in Mrs. Eddy's textbook, *Science and Health with Key to the Scriptures*. The increasing multitude of testimonials from men and women speaking from personal experience was Christian Science's most effective method for the dissemination of truth. But by far the most distinguished medium for publicizing the faith everywhere in the world was the illustrious *Christian Science Monitor,* recognized in journalistic circles as the wonder child in the family of international daily newspapers.

The Unity School of Christianity was no less ambitious. As I walked through the mailing rooms at the plant in Kansas City, I could believe what I had been told: an average of four thousand pieces of mail was leaving Unity every day. Many of these were heavily stuffed envelopes from Silent Unity, a prayer room equipped with a telephone. The attendant who answers when Victor 8720 rings relays the requests to a group of Unity believers who pray without ceasing. Someone is at the altar of Silent Unity day and night, receiving requests, tuning in on God, and stuffing envelopes with a mimeographed letter, a booklet of testimonials, and a printed affirmation, "The healing power of God, through Christ, is now doing its perfect work in me, and I am made whole." The output of Unity's efficient publicity machine is astounding: a million monthly periodicals, thousands of tracts, pamphlets, pocket-sized editions of daily devotions, and numerous books written by the Fillmores. To an amazingly varied clientele they bring a realization of the "Christ within."

In Kentucky I saw a laborer pull a Unity tract from his lunch box and read it over a noonday sandwich. I found Unity literature in an isolated Doukhobor home in Saskatchewan. I met businessmen who subscribed to Unity's *Good Business* and parents who bought *Wee Wisdom* for their children. Braille brought Unity's philosophy to the blind; Unity benevolence sent it to prisons and state institutions. In a small-town parish I uncovered the most telling evidence of the thorough dissemination of Unity literature. On the desk of a successful Protestant minister I found a copy of Unity's *Daily Word.* "A year's subscription came to me as a Christmas gift from one of my best parishioners," he explained in a puzzled voice. Perhaps the Unity School of Christianity approaches an accurate estimate in its claim that nearly nine-tenths of its publications reach Protestants.

Like a lone wolf baying at the dead moon of the church he had forsaken, Buchman sloganized his way from house parties, where public sharing of sins and "quiet time" meditations were emphasized, to the Moral Re-Armament movement. The old thesis about changed lives was planted on streetcars, busses, and outdoor billboards. Believing that a spiritual formula could stop a world war, the Oxford Group staged international conventions and circularized ten countries with the *Rising Tide,* a fifty-page graphic analysis of what their plan would do for a world threatened by self-destruction. Apparent failure did not halt the surgeon of souls. Buchman built his message into a dramatic musical revue, *You Can Defend America,* which played auditoriums across the nation. When that was no longer timely, he launched *Drugstore Revolution* with a colossal world premier. The lone wolf was still baying at the churches which lacked a spiritual dynamic.

Robinson's Psychiana, a one-man discovery in advertising genius, packed the power of an inquisition. Fifteen hundred newspapers and two hundred and fifty magazines shocked the public into attention with the advertisement, I TALKED WITH GOD—YES, I DID—ACTUALLY AND LITERALLY! Detective magazines, the romance pulps, weekly news reviews, tabloids, and slick periodicals brought the name of God where Robinson wanted it to go: "To fallen Protestants and the unchurched who may be going to Hell in some damnable saloon." The Moscow miracle was also publicized on broadsides, circulars, bulletins, folders, brochures, and match covers. Extensive mailing lists transported the announcement of the "God-Consciousness" into sixty-two countries. Railroad clerks and postmen were personally aware of the endless publicity line which was Psychiana. A rural mail carrier told me, "I was stuffing those picture-envelope-Psychiana-fliers into farmers' boxes for so long I ordered the darn set of lessons myself!" There was hypnotic appeal in Robinson's persistent claims: "THIS POWER IS FOR YOU! YES—we mean just that. We mean that YOU and YOURS can find and consciously use the GOD-POWER which with unerring accuracy whirls the limitless stars in their orbit. Just give us 15 MINUTES A DAY and we'll show you how you may secure DEFINITE, TANGIBLE RESULTS!"

With considerably more dignity and reserve Baha'i encyclicals went out from Wilmette. Colored photographs of the resplendent *Mashriqu'l-Adhkar* surpassed in eye appeal all other commercial art of the new reformation and brought to a divided Protestantism a tangible symbol of religious union. Artistic bulletins, pamphlets, and books interpreted the teachings of Baha'u'llah for the Western mind. With reverence and devotion ardent apostles distributed Baha'i literature at the Temple, from local spiritual assemblies, and at conventions in city auditoriums, and on college campuses. Baha'i relics found their way into national archives. Baha'i book exhibits traveled across America.

For volume, for complete and world-wide coverage, no group surpassed the apocalyptic Witnesses of Jehovah. The men and women I had observed on Saturday-night street corners, holding in their upraised hands *Watchtower* and *Consolation,* were cogs in a Theocratic machine which annually distributed more than fourteen million books and booklets in America and twice that number around the globe. The three thousand public meetings conducted every month were publicized by the yearly distribution of nearly a hundred million handbills. Jehovah's Witnesses were donating their time, thirty million working hours a year, pushing doorbells, teaching, witnessing, using to the final letter of the law the American franchise of religious liberty. In a single year eight million people were sufficiently interested to request private book studies. Every week of the year more than a hundred thousand Witnesses sat down in homes somewhere in the world and told the story of the Kingdom's work. Every moment of the day the Brooklyn presses were running, piling up staggering production figures: *One World, One Government,* 4,800,000 copies; *The Meek Shall Inherit the Earth,* 4,900,000; *A Commander to the Peoples,* 3,000,000. All other books bearing a dedication to "Jehovah and His Messiah" had first printings of a million copies.

The new reformation was reaching the people. But I was not ready with my report to Protestantism. Astronomical publicity figures might create false impressions and arouse false fears. The old reformers who shattered the Dark Ages with the light of faith changed men; the old Reformation changed nations. Unless such phenomena were taking place today, the rapid rise of these contemporary groups could not be called Reformation, U. S. A.

Turning to a reconsideration of the people I had met, I was skeptical. Frequently I had looked on while a Witness aroused the ire of his prospect by doggedly presenting an unwanted message. And yet he resorted, when resisted, to the cry of "Persecution!" This group was ready to enjoy America, but they would not defend it. They refused to salute the flag, but they displayed it in their kingdom halls.

My Baha'i acquaintances were all wrapped up in personal adoration of the present leader of their movement, Shoghi Effendi, the Guardian and Keeper of the Faith. Though they patiently talked of the mystical power of Baha'u'llah in which the nine living religions of the world were united, they seemed impatient with the man who could not transfer his faith from the Galilean to a Persian messiah.

I could never quite forget the conversation I overheard one day near a vegetable stall on Chicago's Market Street. A ragged man whose shaggy coat pockets were stuffed with Psychiana lessons was talking to a prosperous-looking vendor about the God-Power and riches. I was bewildered and disturbed and I wondered how valid were the boasts of those who claimed acquaintance with this Moscow mail-order method of finding God.

My friend Ned was my classical example of the Oxford Group. Ned, using Buchman's "quiet time" to get tips on the races, fitted in perfectly with the scandal and gossip about sex and sin which had followed Buchmanism wherever it went.

From a Unity Center I followed through a lead which revealed the possibility of self-delusion in the vaunted healing miracles. At the home of a woman whose hearing had been "miraculously restored," I banged the knocker on the front door without response. I walked around the house. A woman was working in a garden a short distance away. I called; I yelled. Unable to get her attention, I walked around to where she could see me. With the aid of lip reading and my patient repetition of my question, she finally perceived that I wanted to know about the "miracle." Then her face lighted. "It's wonderful," she said. "It really is. I can hear just fine!"

My early experiences with Christian Scientists had been just as questionable. A neighbor in Hollywood used to read *Science and Health* to her sick dog. Long ago in Milwaukee, when I needed money, a wealthy Scientist told me I did not need money at all. What I needed, he told me, was to know what real substance is, and he handed me literature on the subject of infinite spiritual riches! I knew a man of the Christian Science faith who refused to go to a hospital, and he died.

Throughout my early indoctrination "Eddyism" had been assailed as a pagan cult, a piece of cruel and wicked humbug, and its founder was characterized as a charlatan and a fraud. But I was always encountering men and women who defied questioning. They had dedicated themselves to the high moral codes prescribed by their organization; they were manifesting a deepened insight into the correlation of religion and life. Caught between their sincerity and my own skepticism, I finally came to admit that I had wandered into sacred precincts.

In the Beverly Hills home of an eminent engineer one day my host surprised me by turning the story of the invention of the teletype machine into a lesson in the Science of infinite Intelligence. He confided that a million dollars had been spent on research and experimentation in an attempt to perfect the instrument. Still irremediable factors persisted, thwarting the plans. But one day while riding in the subway in New York, he prayed to reflect more of the divine Intelligence. Instantly the solution of an engineering problem was revealed. In that moment the teletype became a workable reality.

"Christian Science," he explained, "taught me that the answer to every legitimate human problem exists in infinite Mind. My real task was to be at one with the divine Mind, whose infinite resources are ever available to bless man in every righteous endeavor."

After hearing this confession of faith, I was not surprised when this millionaire scientist requested a Chicago practitioner to fly to the bedside of his mother who had fallen and fractured her arm. Next day another Christian Science miracle was reported. I was beginning to understand why Mrs. Willard Duncan deserted my congregation in Fairfield.

The Christian Science churches in greater Los Angeles—then numbering thirty-two—which I had deliberately avoided as too large for the cults and too distorted for inclusion in Protestantism, now became my Sunday haunts. I learned that the philosophy of the inventor-engineer was the philosophy which had become the complete assurance of every true Scientist: the love of God, understood, penetrates every cranny of life, meets every need, whips every problem. I learned also that the Manual of The Mother Church, by Mrs. Eddy, prescribed the order and the context of the worship hour. Such authority was impressive, but the demanded uniformity was to me a deadening, totalitarian practice. And yet, I recalled, in the formative years of the first Reformation every leader was extremely vigilant over the absolute interpretation and dissemination of his views. Each insisted on the exclusive use of his catechism, the expounding of his ideology, and the faithful interpretation of his theology. I was witnessing the cautious re-enactment of a like procedure.

Two readers, reverently reciting Scripture with correlative citations from *Science and Health,* took the place of the sermon customarily heard in evangelical churches. It was a scrupulously planned service, a service which any two Christian Scientists might have conducted in home or office, or that any individual might have read for himself. When I learned that the prescribed readings had been studied by most of the worshipers during the week preceding the service, I wondered why they attended at all. Yet, while Protestantism was attracting about forty per cent of its members to the Sunday worship hour, Christian Science could boast of sixty per cent.

This devotion and loyalty I understood better when I stopped at a Christian Science church one Wednesday evening. For half an hour men and women in the congregation spoke of the wondrous healing power of Science, of success and miracles in business, of contentment through divine Mind. This enthusiastic testimonial service was the undergirding for the local work, and thousands like it throughout the world formed the unshakable foundation of The Mother Church. In a Protestant world where church night was almost a thing of the past, Christian Science strode in to demonstrate what reformers have always known: If one is to reach a workable faith and maintain a workable fellowship, the long worldly week between Sundays must be bridged. Daily readings, daily demonstrations of faith, and daily prayers also are prescribed as the personal responsibility of the Scientist.

"If you want an easy faith, stay away from Science. This means work," a leading Christian Scientist advised.

I heard the same expression from the young woman who was acting director of a Unity Center in a Midwestern city. She pointed to the picture of a smiling buxom woman which hung under a fluorescent light in the hallway. "Her life went into

this Center," she said. "She worked without salary and without
any thought of herself. No call went unanswered, and no request for her services was refused. Time meant nothing. She
spent many hours in getting God's directives and then we all
shared in what she had received. Yes, one must work at
religion in order to make religion work."

Midweek meetings, study groups, private counseling, silent
prayers were part of the working plans. The use of the *Daily
Word,* the morning meditations, and the silent hours provided
a busy program for the spiritual life of the Unity coterie. The
Sunday services, patterned after those of traditional Protestantism, are made personal and intimate for the worshiper by the
use of Unity's affirmations. In fact, the affirmation is the most
important part of the service. To stand together as believers,
to close one's eyes in silent prayer, and then to repeat over and
over a solemn declaration—this was the process designed to
rouse drowsy souls to life and to lift the spirit from the cluttered
world.

In Protestantism, where choirs take care of the singing and
only the minister prays, the spirit of worship has forsaken
many pews. But Unity brings back the mystical power of
corporate worship by oft-repeated affirmations. "The power of
God is awakened in me. . . . The power of God is awakened
in me. . . . The power of God is awakened in me. . . . The
power of God is awakened in me. . . ." Often when I left the
service and frequently through the week, I found myself saying,
"The power of God is awakened in me!"

Robinson also built on the invincible appeal of affirming
one's way step by step into the Infinite. He did not presume to
establish a church; adherence to the Psychiana technique was
all that was needed for the development of the spiritual life. To
discover the power of God as a usable force one must begin

with the affirmation of Lesson One: I BELIEVE IN THE
POWER OF THE LIVING GOD! "Go into a room," said the
instructions, "close the door, sit or stand in silence. Relax. Take
a deep breath. Close your eyes if you wish. Put your mind in
harmony with the mind of God. Now say, quietly if you wish,
loudly if you dare: I BELIEVE IN THE POWER OF THE
LIVING GOD! I BELIEVE IN THE POWER OF THE
LIVING GOD!"

I met Alfred, Robinson's son, after his graduation from Stan-
ford. When he told me he was joining his father in the Psychiana movement, I asked him if he would be using the affirmations in his own work. "I was brought up on them." He
smiled. "One of my earliest recollections is that of my father
taking me for a walk into the woods." He went on intently:
"When we reached a secluded spot Father would stop and say,
'Let's be still. Listen! You can hear the presence of the Almighty.' Often when he was alone he would shout in a loud
voice, 'I believe in the Power of the Living God!'"

Throughout the new reformation creeds were subordinated
to practical demonstrations. "Entering the silence" was the
secret of Buchman's offensive against sin and secularism. The
"quiet time" was the first essential in his program of spiritual
preparedness. "It's not so much prayer you need," he explained;
"it's giving God a chance to talk to you." What Protestantism
had left entirely to the discretion of the worshiper, the Oxford
Group made decisive. "Take fifteen minutes a day. Use the
early morning hours if you can. Put your mind at ease. Ask
God what He wants you to do." Groupers whom I met came
from their quiet times with divine directives jotted down on
clip boards, God's instructions for conduct for the day. "You
know you offended J. B. Ask his forgiveness. . . . Sex desire
is your worst enemy. You must whip this before you can realize

your ambitions. . . . Have a heart-to-heart talk with your boss
about your job. Tell him you've met God. . . . E. S. wants to
see you. E. S. needs your help. Talk to him. . . . You must pay
that bad debt to Alex."

Frequently, as in the case of my friend Ned, who got tips on
the races, it was necessary to check God's instructions. For this
Buchman set up the four absolutes: absolute honesty, absolute
purity, absolute unselfishness, absolute love. Every revelation
had to meet the requirements of these touchstones. They were
the golden mean which eliminated any suggestion which might
have been the trick of the Devil. They also represented the
ultimate goal in the Grouper's life. Through the quiet time
the way was paved for public testimonials, public confessions,
the washing out of sins by sharing them and making restitution.
And God's plan for the individual was God's plan for the world;
method and mission combined to challenge the best a man had
to give.

This great concept, this feeling that the capacity for doing
God's work was limitless in every believing and willing servant,
was the impelling force of the Baha'i cause. It was a personal
faith, summoning men to complete dedication of every faculty
of life. Followers of Baha'u'llah whom I met possessed the
conviction of martyrs and the zeal of a marching army. Mrs.
Robert Lee Moffett of Chicago, after weeks of gratuitous lectur-
ing and conferences, was enthusiastic. "If you only knew the joy
and thrill of service in a cause for which one willingly gives
every talent and all of one's time, you would surely want to be
a Baha'i! We have no ministers in our organization. We are
all ministers!"

From Casilla 3731, Santiago, Chile, a friend wrote: "It may
interest you to know what has happened to me. I went to school
in California and the East, graduating from Yale with a B.S.

degree and going to law school at the University of Southern California. It was during these years of study that I lost all faith in religion and became a rank materialist and what I thought was an atheist. It was through the Baha'i teachings that I discovered my error and learned that the goal I was really seeking was spiritual reality. Since then, I have given more and more time and effort to the Baha'i way of life until now it occupies all my life. Fortunately, my financial position allows this, for, as you know, the Baha'i does not receive pay for his services to the Cause."

But the Baha'i faith is more than a religion for the individual. Jesus brought the formula for personal salvation; Baha'u'llah came to reveal the design for the healing and saving of the nations. Temple services and the meetings of spiritual assemblies everywhere emphasized this great truth. There are no songs about the dark valleys of the Christian life or the beautiful home "over there." The recorded classical music written and played by the great musicians of every land is a universal expression of a universal God. The scholarly addresses and discussions which take the place of sermons and personal testimonies do not bypass the spiritual life but lead through it into the field of world affairs.

Following the people who followed the reformers, I discovered the great persuasive behind the Protestant exodus. The new religions demanded complete dedication of self to a cause, and that is what people wanted. They were asking for a change in the static routine of religious life; they were looking for a full-time job in the kingdom.

With devotion bordering on fanaticism Jehovah's Witnesses committed themselves to lifetime service as ambassadors of Jehovah God. Orders from the Theocratic office governed their lives. I accompanied one of the house-to-house servants through the long, cold hours of a stormy January day. Disdaining the elements, he went from door to door announcing his mission, playing Judge Rutherford's records, and attempting to leave his books and tracts. He called it a successful day. Though we had placed only three books for a total of seventy-five cents, the people had been warned that the day of the Lord was near. He had pledged himself to seven eight-hour days a week, to private book studies, and to leadership in midweek and Sunday services. For all this he received no salary; Brooklyn sent him a small monthly allowance—"enough to keep me going." The books which he distributed were not sold; they were "given" to patrons in return for a donation of twenty-five cents which he mailed to headquarters with his monthly report.

"But what will you do someday," I asked, "when you are too old to work and have saved nothing?"

"God," he said, "will take care of things."

He took no thought of the morrow, for the morrow might bring the millennium. Everywhere people were giving up jobs to go in business with the Lord, denying themselves the comforts of this life, despising the glory of American opportunity to be servants of the coming King. Witnesses whom I met belied the popular belief that such a life appealed only to the underdog, the man who could find no place in the business world, or the social misfit.

"What have you found in Jehovah's Witnesses that you did not find in Protestantism?" I asked a university professor.

"The message for our times," he promptly replied. "One need only look at the world to realize that something has been desperately wrong with nations which profess to be Christian. They have been swallowed up by Satan and his host; they have been sold out to religionists who have everywhere supported the nations' programs of wars and murders and intrigue. You simply cannot reconcile the actions of nations with the teaching of Christ Jesus who said, 'My kingdom is not of this world.' But this is our message and Christianity must relearn it. Somewhere, somehow, even though it means martyrdom, ridicule, and hatred, a remnant of mankind must honestly demonstrate Christlike principles. This the Witnesses are trying to do and I intend to do it, though I've been persecuted already. It does not matter. Finally on the last day, when the curtain rings down on this old sin-ridden drama of the Devil's world, people will know that Jehovah's Witnesses were right after all."

Everywhere I ran into solid indoctrination. The leaders in this reformation were driving their concepts deep into the minds of their followers.

"What have you found in Unity that you did not find in your church?" I asked an elderly housewife after a service in a Unity Center.

"A hopeful philosophy and people who take an interest in me," she said, then told me her story.

A few months before, on her sixty-eighth birthday, she had been confronted by the hopeless prospect of being turned out into the street. The house she was renting was being sold. Her husband was an invalid, and their savings were down to five hundred dollars. After canvassing the town for weeks looking for a place to live, she went in desperation to the local Unity Center.

The director listened to her story, then said: "There are times in life when the breaks go against us. There are moments when the world looks dark and the future seems tragic and frightening. There are occasions when we do not know which way to turn and when our thoughts are desperate and our hearts are faint. You are going through such a period now. You say that things have never been so bad, and you have never felt so forsaken. I want you always to remember this: When you feel that everything is lost, when one more disappointment seems more than you can bear, when you are ready to give up, remember that just then you are standing on bedrock. That is God. And because of that, you must begin coming up! He will not let you go any lower. He wants you to rise and trust Him and believe that you are standing on Him. Go back to your home with that assurance. Prayers will be said for you. You will see how God will help you. I'm going to give you an affirmation. 'I am a child of God and every moment His love and power flow through me.' Keep this in mind constantly and repeat it aloud whenever you need strength. 'I am a child of God and every moment His love and power flow through me.'"

The woman repeated these words to me, slowly and thoughtfully, again affirming the reality of the "Christ within."

"I did exactly as she told me," she continued after a moment, "and that evening when I was reading the paper, I found what I had been looking for. Boxcars were advertised for sale at two hundred dollars. I knew where I could buy a vacant lot also for two hundred dollars. We now have a roof over our heads."

I visited the couple in their boxcar home. As we sat in the curtained-off section on salvaged overstuffed pieces, the bedrock Christian said with enthusiasm, "Isn't it wonderful how God goes to work for you when you put your trust in Him!"

"But why," I asked, "didn't you go to your minister with your problem? I am sure he would have given you the very same help you received from Unity."

"Which minister?" She laughed. "The mister was Methodist and I was Lutheran, and we had got so we didn't go to church at all. But we did go to Unity."

Another Fairfield episode was being re-enacted. I was again

listening to Catherine Meyers' defense for turning Catholic: "I don't think it makes much difference. We all believe in the same God, don't we? We're all Christians, aren't we? I don't see much more difference between the Catholics and the Evangelicals than I do between the Baptists and the Evangelicals. The churches really don't work together or get along anyway." Again I was making a painful entry on the church ledger, "Lost to Catholicism." Here in the boxcar the compatibility of Methodism and Lutheranism had been tested, and two ministers had been compelled to write, "Lost to Unity."

Did it matter where people found the spark which fired the spiritual imagination with spiritual realities? Somehow it did. For this woman—lost to Unity—had not merely resigned herself to the inevitable. Her faith had suddenly become meaningful. Her soul had expanded under the impact of a consciousness of the presence of God. She had found a greater happiness in this boxcar than she had ever known in a comfortable bungalow. Somehow I wished that I might have had a part in her experience, that I might have been the one to adjure her to the great adventure. For a moment the youthful fervor of my pastoral years returned. I was again a hopeful shepherd, filled with a great compassion for the Protestants whom I had encountered during the years since Fairfield. Across the wide reaches of America I had found them, men and women alternating between unconcern and an intense yearning to find in the old paths this new thing. By what method could Protestantism be transposed into the personal appeal and the awareness of the living God which this woman had found outside Protestantism?

Church leaders were trying to bring Baptists and Evangelicals, Methodists and Lutherans, and all the rest of the Protestant family into closer relationship. Precursory international conferences which had directed attention to the need for a united Protestant voice in world affairs were crystallizing into a definite ecumenical movement. A meeting at Oxford and Edinburgh in 1937 sought a united Protestant Church of England and urged Protestantism to consider its position in a changing world. Out of it came a statement: "The Church is the Body of Christ and the blessed company of all faithful people, whether in heaven or in earth. . . ." A meeting at Madras, British India, in 1938 called together more than four hundred Christian leaders from sixty-five nations. Out of it came a statement: "Christ's true Church is the fellowship of those whom God has called out of darkness into His marvelous light"; out of it came recommendations on the problem of "How to wake and sustain in every Christian the spirit and purpose of evangelism." In 1939 there was a meeting of a new World Council of Churches in Geneva. Out of it came a statement about the church's place in a world threatened by war.

Oxford and Edinburgh, Madras and Geneva! As far from local parishes as Lausanne had been from Fairfield. Statements and recommendations couched in academic terms, freighted with idealism, while here in this boxcar were the problem and the challenge. Beside me sat the great reality, the human equation which Protestantism had to solve. This woman and thousands like her made up the new reformation—Christian Science . . . Unity . . . Moral Re-Armament. . . Psychiana . . . the Baha'is . . . Jehovah's Witnesses. While Protestantism's multicolored pattern was being extended, these people were finding a faith. Their personal lives were being touched and wakened by personal prayers from Silent Unity, personal book studies from Jehovah's Witnesses, personalized Psychiana aids, personal confession from individual to individual in the Oxford Group, personal missionary zeal in the Baha'i faith, personal counseling among the Christian Scientists.

More and more my interest turned to the individual, to the ex-Protestant who was following these short cuts to glory and who was paying for the privilege with unqualified and unquestioning devotion to new teachers and new teachings. Sacred concepts of the past had been recklessly tossed aside, old dogmas had been restated, old creeds had been reinterpreted. The true follower merely reflected and lived out the persistent guaranty of truth pronounced by his leader. Degrees of attainment varied in proportion to the individual's ability to transform belief into the reality of daily problems, but everywhere religious attitudes were standardized.

I asked a young woman who had become a Christian Scientist: "Would you call a doctor if you were sick?"

"No," she replied. "As Mrs. Eddy has said, 'If we understood the control of Mind over body, we should put no faith in material means.'"

I repeated the question to Arthur Todd, an eminent sociologist with a Ph.D. from Yale and a background of considerable foreign study.

"No" was again the reply. "It is foolhardy, impossible, to mix material medicine and spiritual healing. For God is All-in-all, therefore, the only cause and the only real healer."

Dr. Todd is the manager of the Washington, D.C., office of the Christian Science Committee on Publication.

"But sickness does exist," I insisted.

"The belief of sickness exists in mortal mind," he corrected.

"It is very real," I contended. "We see evidence of sickness and disease everywhere. We see the lame and blind——"

"To the corporeal senses these aspects appear very real as you say. But we must conceive them as sick, diseased beliefs of the human mind which need to be healed by the activity of the divine Mind."

"Then let us at least admit that the *idea* of sickness and the idea of evil exist. Will you admit that?"

"Where such false ideas originated is a mystery, but they must be thoroughly disavowed with the positive truth that God is absolute, omnipresent, and omnipotent good. Mrs. Eddy says, 'We must learn that evil is the awful deception and unreality of existence. . . . There is but one primal cause. Therefore there can be no effect from any other cause, and there can be no reality in aught which does not proceed from this great and only cause. Sin, sickness, disease, and death belong not to the Science of being. They are the errors, which presuppose the absence of Truth, Life, or Love.'"

"You believe that death is an unreality?"

"Death is an illusion. When the world has been rid of the belief that man must die, even the apparent experience of death will pass."

"And poison?"

"Poison is the result of a majority belief that a thing is poisonous."

"Would you go into a room alive with infectious disease? Would you put a malaria germ on your tongue?"

"I would do these things only if in the line of my duty as a Christian Scientist. I would do neither of these as a stunt. We Christian Scientists are not exhibitionists."

"And accidents?"

"Accidents do not exist. In the plan of orderly divine Intelligence all right ideas are eternally and harmoniously correlated."

"Is it not true that Christian Scientists have deified Mary Baker Eddy?"

"Emphatically it is not true. We revere and love Mrs. Eddy, and we pay our tribute to her continually for the divinely inspired Science she has given to us in keeping with the teachings of the Bible. Mrs. Eddy herself has warned us that 'There was, is, and never can be but one God, one Christ, one Jesus of Nazareth. . . .'"

Once more I stood face to face with the unalterable conviction engendered by the new reformation. Wherever I interviewed a Christian Scientist, I found an ardent disciple of a singular tenet of spiritual faith and understanding: The power of God is demonstrable here and now. "Those who cannot demonstrate, at least in part, the divine Principle of the teachings and practice of our Master have no part in God." So said Mrs. Eddy and her followers agree. Miracles do not exist. What appears as a miracle is simply the natural result of the recognition of the nothingness of matter and the clear realization of the Allness of the infinite Mind.

Staggering under the impact of thousands of published testimonies of healing through this method, I wondered whether Protestantism realized how far-reaching and thorough this movement actually was. Did Protestant churchmen know that *The Christian Science Monitor* was read by "teachers and pupils in 2,600 schools, 500 colleges . . . 4,000 editors in the United States . . . businessmen and industrialists . . . members of Congress . . . high-ranking statesmen . . . thousands of discriminating families everywhere in the world?" Had the average Protestant ever opened a copy of *The Christian Science Journal* or *Christian Science Sentinel* and read the signed testimonies which daily were doing their missionary work in many homes plagued by sickness and disease? Only authenticated healings, those verified by three impartial witnesses, were published.

Through the courtesy of a Christian Science practitioner and teacher I gained the permission of the Boston headquarters to investigate one of these authenticated healings. The testimony concerned the miraculous recovery of the son of a prominent businessman. When I met him and his wife for an interview, I recognized them as former acquaintances.

"One Friday about six years ago," the father began, "our son, who was then a high-school student, stayed away from school because he was not feeling well. The next morning he became violently ill, with extreme pain. We telephoned the practitioner about the boy's condition."

"Then, I read hymns from the Christian Science Hymnal," the mother interposed. "We needed the inspiration found in these words."

"However," the father continued, "in the afternoon our son lost consciousness and became rigid. Then my wife called me from the office. After I reached home, we both audibly and silently declared the truth as best we knew. Our fears lessened; yet, recognizing the apparent seriousness of the condition, we decided to telephone the practitioner again, for since morning the boy had grown worse. Through the earnest work of the practitioner, in the early evening hours the boy seemed to relax and soon had the appearance of being quietly asleep. A short time later he awoke as out of a dream. Even today he has no recollection whatever of the details of this experience."

"Did he speak to you?"

"He asked us to read to him from *Science and Health*. We did, and he gradually became stronger. Next day an unsightly eruption broke out on his face and over his body. A week later he was back in school, perfectly well."

I turned to the practitioner. "Am I right in assuming that you were the practitioner on this case?"

He replied with modesty, "Yes, but it is well to remember that it is always God who heals, never a person."

"And what would you say was wrong with the boy? What was your diagnosis?"

"The practitioner does not make physical diagnosis" was the

reply. "Jesus healed through the power of divine Mind, but the record does not state that He ever asked, 'What is wrong with the man?' or 'What ails the woman?' The power of God is infinitely greater than *any* disease."

"But would you hazard a guess what a physician might have said?"

"He would probably have called it a ruptured appendix."

"Would nature have healed the condition?" I ventured.

The practitioner smiled and added: "Mrs. Eddy says, 'The physical healing of Christian Science results now, as in Jesus' time, from the operation of divine Principle, before which sin and disease lose their reality in human consciousness and disappear as naturally and as necessarily as darkness gives place to light and sin to reformation."

I was adding "ruptured appendix" to the list of authenticated healings which I had procured from the Boston headquarters. That list was tabulated in alphabetical order and covered hundreds of cures as impressive to the believer as they might be absurd to the worldling. Among the formidable enemies such as heart disease, infantile paralysis, encephalitis, contagious diseases, blindness and accidents, and incurable diseases like cancer, dropsy, and tuberculosis, there were also corns, bowlegs, bunions, chapped condition, falling hair, and change of life. Behind them all stood the claim that these cures had all been subjected to rigorous investigation before they were publicized. No less an authority than Hermann S. Hering, onetime professor of physics at Johns Hopkins, said, "It is important to recognize that Christian Science, the demonstrable knowledge of the Christ-teaching is a discovery, not an invention. ... The power of God is the same yesterday, today, and forever. ... If this healing took place in the first century, it can take place now, since every divine law and order must be immutable and we have the same conditions to deal with which they had then."

Apparently all the new groups believed this implicitly. They went even farther. They claimed that the first-century power was completely sufficient to meet all the distresses of the present century. Christian Science, Unity, and Psychiana listed among the triumphs of faith victory over such contemporary rebels as drinking, gambling, and tobacco habits, frustrations, phobias, neurasthenia, domestic discord, unemployment, and modern business upsets. This was the all-inclusive service offered by the movements which dispensed the unlimited power of God. "Our only creed: for every need—God!" said the Oxford Group and proceeded to demonstrate its claim in the life of Steve Haverman.

Steve had often staggered drunkenly into my room, weeping and moaning about the agony of his lost life. Often during an alcoholic aftermath, deadened into silence by remorse, he would promise never to touch liquor again as long as he lived. But regularly, every three weeks, Steve ended up in the gutter or in jail or narrowly escaped death on the highway. What medical science and "the cure" and his preacher uncle had failed to do, I, also was unable to accomplish. No amount of reason or persuasion made even the slightest dent in Steve's armor. "It's a disease," he would say. "When I get drunk, then I've got to have liquor to make me well. When I'm not drunk, I've got to have liquor or I'll go crazy when the spell comes over me."

Then an Oxford Grouper got hold of Steve and worked the miracle. After stripping his soul down to absolute shame before his Maker, the Grouper nursed him back to self-respect through a friendship more watchful and more intimate than that offered by Alcoholics Anonymous. He took Steve to house parties and gave him the plan for self-surrender through public confession and the washing out of sins. He made Steve's life a God-controlled life, and soon Steve passed a three-week period without a drink; then six, then twelve, then twenty.

This plan for supplying all the needs and solving all the problems of the individual was soon applied to the needs and problems of nations. The saved and the savior embarked on an adventure. Moral Re-Armament was the Buchman dispensary of the limitless power of God. "We begin with me and soon there's you, then you, then YOU, and then a nation." To bring it to pass in every nation would be a global miracle.

The new reformation was vying with the old in an attempt to leave its mark on western civilization. The primary aim of the Baha'i movement was to proclaim the oneness of the world and the equality of all men. They were working the miracle of harmony among nations. In a world where Jew fought Moslem and Moslem, Jew, where Catholic was suspicious of Protestant and Protestant of Catholic, where Negro disdained white and white, Negro, where race hated race, and creed argued with creed, all sat together worshiping under the unifying injunction of Baha'u'llah. And within Protestantism the principles of the Great Peace were being taught. I found a Methodist Sunday-school teacher superimposing the Baha'i program for converting the world on Wesley's program for converting the individual.

Only Jehovah's Witnesses were pessimistic. They insisted that the world could not be saved, that it was not worth saving. God's schedule was calling for Armageddon. The dreadful hour would soon strike. Their miracle was the miracle of escape into the millennium, and anxiously they called to individuals to come out from the irreligious religions and gather under God's government.

Always out of global movements the new reformation returned to the individual. Luther's priesthood of believers had mounted to spiritual heights where miracles were commonplace. Lifted on the wings of healing, healing of soul, mind, and body, they had found a faith which met every urgent circumstance of life.

In a Mississippi River town a woman awoke one morning with the frightening realization that she was "slowly paralyzing." The feeling of "something holding me back" which had harassed her for many days was real now—too real. At a Minnesota hospital her condition was diagnosed as multiple sclerosis. In her late twenties she was adjusting herself to the role of an invalid, and her minister said it must be the will of the Lord.

One day when her husband, a civil engineer, was in a local dollar store, a salesgirl inquired about his wife's condition.

"She's in bed. We have engaged a nurse."

"I have something here that helped me," said the girl. "Maybe it will help her."

She handed him a copy of a Unity publication. He stuffed it into his pocket. Sheepishly he gave it to his wife. "I don't propose that what the doctors haven't been able to do, reading something is going to do," he said.

His wife paged through it, read portions of it, laid it aside. The next day she picked it up again. Her eyes fell on a poem. She read it thoughtfully, put it away, read it again. The following day she memorized the lines and continued to repeat them slowly over and over in quiet affirmation. A "feeling" came over her. Suddenly she realized she was moving her toes. Excitedly she called her husband and insisted that she was healed. He helped her to her feet, and she took a few steps. When I visited her she met me at the door.

"I am healed," she said.

"You give Unity credit?"

"God."

"But it was Unity teaching?"

"Yes."

"And the poem?"

"Oh, yes," she said. "I always keep it around."

It was Unity's popular "Prayer of Faith."

> God is my help in every need;
> God does my every hunger feed;
> God walks beside me, guides my way
> Through every moment of the day.
>
> I now am wise, I now am true,
> Patient, kind, and loving too.
> All things I am, can do, and be
> Through Christ, the Truth that is in me.
>
> God is my health, I can't be sick;
> God is my strength, unfailing, quick;
> God is my all, I know no fear,
> Since God and love and Truth are here.

"Don't you think it's beautiful?" she asked.

"Did you tell your minister everything that happened? What did he say?"

"He told me to 'stay away from that stuff,'" she said without resentment.

I had drawn another impressive story out of the miracle-packed ranks of the contemporary reformation. Always I had arrived too late to report how the wonders were performed; always the miracle had just happened. Then one night I was invited to a Midwestern home, where Robinson of Psychiana was being entertained. It was the usual social gathering until a woman guest surprised host, hostess, and visitors with "You know, Dr. Robinson, I'm one of your students."

Psychiana's founder was casual. "Is that so? How far have you progressed with the lessons?"

"Not far enough," confessed the woman apologetically, "for, you see, I'm a diabetic. But I'm sure that if I really understood and applied the deeper teaching of Psychiana, I should not have diabetes."

"That's absolutely right," Robinson agreed. "Do you really want to be healed of this condition?"

"Yes, of course!"

"Well, in the first place," he ruled emphatically, "you can be sure Almighty God didn't give you diabetes. He doesn't want you to have it. He can cure you of it instantly through His power. He has made you in His image. He is as close to you as the breath you have just taken into your lungs. Do you believe that?"

"Yes, surely!"

He rose from his chair. "The power of Almighty God is in you. Do you believe that? Are you sure of that?"

"Yes."

"Do you believe that His power can heal you fully, completely?"

"Yes."

"Do you believe that He can heal you instantly, right now?"

"Oh, yes, I do!"

"WELL, THEN, BE HEALED!"

These words lifted the woman from her chair. "My gracious!" she cried. "Something happened to me. I felt the strangest and most wonderful sensation . . . as if——I don't know how to explain it! I'm healed!"

"You are healed." Robinson nodded.

It looked like the power of suggestion; he called it the power of God. That a "miracle" had taken place was more than I was ready to admit. Apparently the diabetic was unwilling to admit it, too. When we went into the dining room for a midnight snack of sandwiches, cakes, cookies, candies, and tea with plenty of sugar, she said, "Oh, but these things aren't on my diet!"

Robinson stopped her with a glance. "You're healed!" he said.

"That's right," said the woman and reached for the sugar bowl. She ate heartily also of the cookies and the cake with the white frosting.

Later I said to Robinson, "Tomorrow I'll call up and find out when the funeral is going to be!"

"Call," he said seriously. "There will be no funeral. And there will be no more diabetes."

"How do you know?"

"Because," he said, "I felt a power go out of me."

I called the woman three days later. "How are you feeling?"

"Just fine!" she said cheerfully. "Just fine!"

"How did you feel on the morning after our party?"

"Just fine!"

A week passed. "How are you now?"

"Just fine!"

Three months passed. "How are you?"

"Just fine!"

"By the way, what does the doctor say?"

"I haven't been to the doctor. I'm through with doctors and I'm doctoring with the Lord!"

Again the ancient promise had been reaffirmed—signs were following those who believed. And converts were coming at a rate comparable to the apostasy from Catholicism during early Reformation days. Figures were convincingly impressive and the potential was alarming. But Protestants were tranquil in the delusion that what I called a new reformation was but an extension of southern California's ludicrous cults. They had tried to dismiss all new divisions in a divided Protestantism with a single word—bunk. They were blind to the recurrent phenomenon of Protestant procreation. They must learn what I had learned: tomorrow's great denominations spring from the despised heretical groups of today.

At the top of my list of modern reformation sectaries I had written Christian Science. Since its inception its membership had doubled every ten years. It was loath to give out statistics, so the government census was deceiving. But my estimate of a million followers in the United States and another million throughout the world brought a nod of agreement from a top-ranking Christian Scientist. The Unity School of Christianity was running a close second with potential Unity followers throughout Protestantism. All that was needed for Unity to show its strength was the acceptance of a plan to change the School into a denomination, to replace Unity Centers with Unity churches. Founder Charles Fillmore had consistently opposed prominent Unity ministers who were vigorously supporting such a transition. Though the Baha'i faith had less than six thousand members in America, it referred to hundreds of thousands around the globe and claimed a great potential within Protestantism. Moral Re-Armament and the Oxford Group spoke blithely about millions of followers; Robinson's Psychiana had enrolled nine hundred thousand students. Jehovah's Witnesses had a hundred and fifty thousand active workers in the field, attracted a hundred thousand people to their national conventions, and often spoke of "the millions who are reading and studying the millions of books."

These were figures. I could take them or leave them. Tenuous claims about millions on millions of followers could be revised and discounted. One indisputable fact remained: Many Americans were finding God outside the traditional churches. Early qualms about Lutheranism, Anabaptist and Baptist, the Reformed faith, Presbyterianism, and all the rest were pitted against the twentieth-century reformation: Christian Science, Unity, Moral Re-Armament, Psychiana, the Baha'i faith, Jehovah's Witnesses. And there were scores of others, swirling out of this vortex to form new channels of faith, swept on by a storm which would not pass. They came to appeal to those whose personal religion had been buried under shibboleths, and outmoded symbols and creeds no longer understood. They came to harass Protestantism's hundred and fifty thousand churches with the sharply pointed query, "What does the Christian religion mean to your people?"

Gradually I felt myself isolated, stranded midway between the old traditionalism which I loved and the new faiths with their abundance of spiritual ardor and their intimacy with the power of God. Anxiously I took stock of my disturbing impressions: The uneasiness over Protestantism's dreamy tranquillity, the dread that we were being destroyed by our own quiescence, the danger of further weakening ourselves by our own self-criticism, and the fear that these Lilliputian movements had already tied us down and were out to slay us in our sleep.

Protestantism must be warned and advised. If the inroad made by these new groups during the past fifty years continued for another half century, the traditional churches would be forced off the thoroughfare where men sought action and power for the self-unfoldment of their spiritual lives. Though these newcomers were adding confusion to confusion and creating more schisms than they could ever bridge, though they were opening more wounds of dissension than all their vaunted spiritual therapeutics would ever be able to heal, they were here and Protestantism would have to rise to meet their challenge!

CHAPTER SEVEN

Crossing Catholic Boundaries

MY FEARS about Protestantism's major weakness were verified when I returned to the churches with my report. The initial reaction was always the same whether I was addressing a ministerial association, a ladies' auxiliary, a men's club, or a young people's society. The incredible stories of faith healing and mystical flights into the infinite were rich in entertainment but were not thought-provoking. Making God the servant of man and creating a heaven on earth in the consciousness of the God-power was alien to Protestant ideology. But always there was sudden interest when I turned to personalities. The sincere men and women who had convinced me that their search for God outside Protestantism had had honest motivation and had received an honest reward also convinced my audiences. I summoned my witnesses one by one: The reclaimed alcoholic of the Oxford Group, Unity's bedrock Christian, the house-to-house servant of Jehovah God, Psychiana's healed diabetic, the inventor-engineer of Christian Science, and the onetime atheist whose faith was renewed in the glory of Baha'u'llah. Out of the question-and-answer periods came evidences that the personal spiritual quest which vitalized America's new religions was present also in the old. The faithful who filled the pews every Sunday morning were seeking the elusive reality which a new priesthood of believers had found.

Within Protestantism, as without, no one was reluctant to complain that there was something wrong with historic churches. But when I enumerated the ex-Protestants I had met among the Pentecostals and the cults and the new sectaries, when I warned that the new reformation was a threat to Protestantism, neither clergy nor laity was alarmed. They refused to make the problem a matter of personal concern. They were content to wait for a remedy to evolve from some point within the status quo—a big announcement from denominational headquarters or an organized crusade from a professional spiritual analyst. I was surer than ever that this apathy was Protestantism's greatest stumbling block, and it was rapidly becoming mine. But with my report clutched hopefully in my hand, I continued up Church Street, entering the doors that were open and rapping at those that were closed.

That is how I met Dr. Richard Paul Graebel, one of America's great preachers. It was he who first told me that I should add another name to my list of invaders. As pastor of the First Presbyterian Church in Springfield, Illinois, he had encountered a proselytizing Catholic priest. This convert getter had just wound up a city-wide campaign with the announcement that "the fire destroying the world is modern paganism which began with Martin Luther and his contemporary heretics." He had sent out seven hundred and fifty letters to non-Catholics inviting them to a Cathedral Inquiry Class. Three hundred responded. A hundred and forty-five were maneuvered into Mother Church.

Protestant congregations had been invaded and Protestant ministers were retaliating. In sermons and publications they warned their people against this subversive activity; in letters to the bishop of the diocese they objected to the unwise Christian strategy which the Inquiry Class employed. Battle lines were

decisively drawn. Principle was pitted against principle, conviction fought with conviction. My warning lost its significance
when sounded amid this controversial issue.

"Maybe your new reformation is a threat," Graebel allowed as
I visited with him after addressing a meeting of the city-wide
church federation, "but it's Roman clericalism that is attempting
to undermine the whole Protestant, antiauthoritarian world. It's
not just a local situation. That we could handle. But take a look
at this."

He pulled open a drawer and began tossing news clippings
across the desk.

CLARE BOOTHE LUCE JOINS CATHOLIC CHURCH

SON OF JOHN FOSTER DULLES COMES "HOME"

SENSATIONAL NAME ADDED TO LIST OF MONSIGNOR FULTON J.
   SHEEN'S FAMOUS CONVERTS

PROTESTANT FAMILY UNITES WITH ST. MARY'S

JOHN WU REPORTS ON HIS CONVERSION

LOUIS BUDENZ, MANAGING EDITOR OF COMMUNIST DAILY WORK-
   ER, BROUGHT BACK TO THE CHURCH

"If this isn't a concerted drive to break down Protestantism,
what is it? And if this isn't turning the religion of Jesus Christ
into a marathon, what shall we call it? The local bishop claims
that Catholicism is getting eighty thousand converts a year and
they are always *Protestants*. The eighty-thousand figure is the
bunk. The claim that these converts are all Protestants is also
the bunk. But most vicious of all is their idea that anyone who
is not a Catholic is a pagan. They forget that we have converts
from Catholicism. I have them in my own church. I have not
publicized them and I am not telling you about this for you to
publicize it. But I do wish people would know that when we

take in members who were Catholics, we receive them merely
on reaffirmation of faith. We certainly try to be respectful
enough to admit that anyone following Christ is a Christian.
When we take in Catholic members, we do not even rebaptize
them! And we certainly don't gloat over our converts. But
every one Catholicism gets is publicized to high heaven. Such a
practice is as unchristian and godless as these local campaigns.
It is all the result of a vast propaganda machine. Take a look
at this editorial."

Graebel handed me a clipping from the New World, and I
read:

> The number of converts entering the Catholic Church is
> astonishing. Nearly every week some prominent person em-
> braces the faith. Each day dozens of unknowns capitu-
> late. . . .

"That, of course, is far from the truth," he interrupted mili-
tantly. "Actually the Roman Catholic Church is losing out in
religious and political influence all over the world. That is why
it is engaged in this frantic convert-getting campaign and this
fanatic Hollywood type of publicity. Springfield is just an example of what is happening all over the country. If you ever
read the Catholic sheet, *Integrity,* you know that the church is
out for the conquest of urban America. And the conquest of
what it calls the 'key intellectual positions' in America. That's
the threat to Protestantism which we need to worry about first.
I don't object to a man finding God in a Catholic cathedral
rather than in my church. But I have sorted and sifted Catholic
history; I have weighed and analyzed contemporary Catholic
thought and action and I'm dead sure that Catholic laymen
have no idea how sinister and political-minded dear old Mother
Church actually is. Authoritarianism in religion is just as dis-

tasteful to the American layman as is authoritarianism in politics or philosophy or art. I'm not blaming the Catholic people. They are really unaware of the danger that exists. And most Protestants are just as ignorant of what is going on. At least, we do nothing about it until an aggression like this one puts us on the defensive. Then we are called bigots and Ku-Kluxers!"

"And what do you think should be done about it?" I ventured.

"I'm not sure," he admitted with intense earnestness. "But I believe the answer is slowly evolving. They have pushed us just about as far as they can. The churches are about ready to take a definite, united stand. I think Protestantism is being brought together through this convert-getting blackmail. It is becoming increasingly evident that a divided church will go down under a thing like this. But a *united* church can meet the challenge head on and whip it, and I believe—at least I sincerely hope—that we will see it happen—and soon."

"You mean the local churches are uniting to combat the Inquiry Classes?" I asked, remembering the reactions of two Fairfield congregations when I suggested and fostered union as the means of Christian strength.

"No, but there is a great deal of co-operation among the ministers in this local situation. As I said before, though, it is more than a local problem. Wherever the insidious power of Roman clericalism gets a foothold, the democracy of faith, the basis of all Christian doctrine, is endangered. So it is a world problem which will remain unsolved until Protestantism can present a united world front."

"But," I protested, "if the genius of Protestantism is its democratic nature——"

"You have been so infected with the glories of the cults," he interrupted, "that you don't know what is happening in historic Protestantism. But you must surely have heard of the ecumenical movement and the Amsterdam meeting, scaled to bring a hundred and thirty communions into a united front. Of course, the main purpose behind this is the need for all Christian churches to meet the threat of secularism and to co-ordinate their efforts efficiently. But you can rest assured that the meeting won't overlook the Roman Catholic problem. And if out of Amsterdam comes a constructive plan for combating clericalism, it will be a blessing. Though I don't expect it to come in the first meeting, I believe that while the Catholics say that Protestantism is dying and while your report makes the situation look gloomy for the historic churches of the Reformation, this ecumenical movement may be a big step toward our salvation."

"Perhaps you are right," I said, "but I wonder if the men who are trying to bring a hundred and thirty communions together have ever tried to unite two small-town congregations. I did— in Fairfield, Kansas, where the Baptist and Evangelical churches stood on opposite corners, separated by a dusty, gravel road. When I tried to get them together I found that they were separated by eighty years of local sentiment and four hundred years of Reformation tradition. They are still standing on those corners, separated by the gravel road, by sentiment and by tradition."

"If a common enemy from without attacked those two churches, if standing on opposite corners meant that they would be destroyed, don't you think the people would have sense enough to get together?" Graebel suggested.

"Perhaps," I assented, "but is that the basis on which churches should unite? Would the union continue after the enemy was destroyed? Sometimes I think church union of any kind is impractical, unnecessary, and impossible. An old doctor, very wise and very realistic, might have been right. Protestantism's divisions, he contended, reflect Protestantism's strength and vitality.

He called it mitosis—cells dividing and continuing to divide wherever there is life. If we try to stop this process and create our own hierarchy, there is a danger that we will also create our own clericalism."

"Impossible!" he retorted. "The parity of clergy and laity in Protestantism guarantees that there will be no hierarchy. Please note, it's not the Catholic people, not even the parish priests whom we are criticizing, except as they blindly carry out the dictates of Mother Church. You know that whenever a bishop or a priest ceases to recognize and obey the central authority, he is removed from his office and he may be removed from membership in the church. And there are plenty who have been treated that way. What about the university priest in Illinois? Wasn't it his stand on religion in Spain that caused his removal? The Spanish question is the Romanist stumbling block! All authority emanates from Rome. All aggression against Protestantism and the American way heads up in Rome.

"When I stand in my pulpit and think of that, when I preach the word of God and the democracy of Christ, when I look down from my pulpit and see the American flag—raised above the pew where Abraham Lincoln used to worship—I think of the glory of our heritage of religious freedom. I begin to understand what the reformers may have felt in their day. I believe in my church just as much as they believed in their cause, and I mean to fight Roman domination just as they did by demanding higher loyalty to Christ Himself in all Christians."

I soon discovered that Graebel's militant attitude toward Catholic aggression was widespread among Protestant clergy. In pulpits across the nation a quotation from *Christian Century's* editor had become a Sunday text: "U. S. Catholicism is working hard, fast, and efficiently to reap the bumper harvest of souls wandering between a decadent Protestantism and a sterile secularism." Ministers were referring to *The Churchman,* which exposed the role of the Vatican in world affairs. In the *Converted Catholic Magazine* they were reading the stories of ex-priests who accused the Roman Church of falsehoods and intrigue in furthering its aims and building up its power. Catholic lobbies were exerting political pressures on state and national legislatures, demanding public funds for parochial schools, breaking down the democratic tradition of a complete separation of church and state. The power of Catholic hierarchy threatened intellectual freedom. On a bulletin board in a Chicago church I read a story from the *Christian Herald,* "Shadows Over Our Schools," which described the death of free education in Dixon, New Mexico.

Clergymen were quoting the publicized statement of Albert Lévitt, former judge of the United States Court in the Virgin Islands, who said he would willingly appear before the Un-American Activities Committee and present documentary proof that the Roman Catholic Church in the United States was engaged in subversive activities which were undermining the American form of government and were designed to destroy the political and religious freedom. While *The Nation* was banned in Catholic schools because of Paul Blanshard's articles, "The Roman Catholic Church," Protestant ministers were pegging sermons on this exposé of the undemocratic extension of Catholic authority in medicine, sex, and education."

One spring morning in Iowa City, Iowa, the bulletin board at the First Methodist Church announced a sermon called "Truth and Freedom." At nine-thirty cars lined the streets, north to the English Lutheran Church, west to the Congregational-Christian, and east to St. Mary's Catholic. Nearly a thousand worshipers filled the large stone Methodist Church for the first of two regularly scheduled Sunday-morning worship services. University students and teachers, townspeople, and farm families had come to hear Dr. L. L. Dunnington, noted preacher and author, present his views on the Catholic problem.

"... The time has come for plain speaking" marked the end of a mild introduction and launched a sharp denunciation of the Roman Catholic attack on the American way of life.

"The Roman Catholic Church does not believe in freedom!" came the emphatic announcement from the slender, benign clergyman behind the pulpit microphone, as he classified Catholicism with political Fascism and totalitarian movements. He was in dead earnest and there was no doubting his conviction.

"The Roman Catholic Church does not trust its people to study both sides of a question. . . . How are we to find the truth unless we are free to read scholarly and factual articles? ... What chance does a Catholic child have of learning the truth when he is forbidden to read certain books and magazines?"

Around me Dr. Dunnington's parishioners nodded their assent. And yet, living in a town with three Catholic churches, they surely had good Catholic friends who were excluded from their prejudices. Dr. Dunnington acknowledged that he had high respect for Catholic individuals and the "Catholic people." He made it clear that his words were directed against "Roman statements." His denunciation was leveled against the power which Mother Church held over her followers.

"The Catholic Church does not believe in the public-school system" was the next accusation. "Through a pamphlet by Father Paul L. Blakely, S. J., it has announced, 'Our first duty to the public school is not to pay taxes for its maintenance. We pay that tax under protest, not because we admit an obligation in justice; justice cannot oblige the support of a system which we are forbidden in conscience to use or a system which we conscientiously hold to be bad in its ultimate consequence. . . . The first duty of every Catholic is to keep his children out of it.' "

Dunnington's warnings were emphatic and battened down with quotations from Catholic law and with the facts and figures behind Catholic policy. The congregation was seeing Catholicism as a totalitarian instrument of destruction aimed at the freedom and democracy which we cherish and hold dear. Under the forceful pulpit art of this Methodist leader we saw the urgent necessity for the national organization recently established to maintain constitutional separation of church and state. Protestants and Other Americans United had been called into existence by such men as John A. Mackay, president of Princeton Theological Seminary; Edwin McNeil Proteat, president, Rochester-Colgate Divinity School; G. Bromley Oxnam, bishop of the Methodist Church; Louis D. Newton, president, Southern Baptist Convention; and Charles Clayton Morrison, former editor of *The Christian Century*.

Dunnington read the manifesto of this organization: "Our single and only purpose is to assure the maintenance of the American principle of separation of church and state upon which the federal constitution guarantees religious liberty to all people and all churches of this Republic." This we were told was another Protestant contribution to the democratic system, a part of the vigilance to sustain the democratic institutions Protestantism had created. Patriotism sprang into our hearts as we heard how the cherished Bill of Rights was being assailed, how the Constitution was being tampered with, and how legislation was yielding to Catholic political pressure.

"The Federal Supreme Court," the sermon continued, "in two decisions has confirmed state legislation which sanctions the use of public-school funds to provide free textbooks for parochial schools [1930], and to transport pupils to such schools [1947]. The four dissenting justices in the bus-transportation case solemnly warned the nation that these two breaches in the wall separating church and state are only the beginning. Other breaches in this wall will follow unless we keep guard. . . . On a bolder and more ambitious scale this same church now demands aid for its schools from the Federal Government. . . . Thus far, Congress has withstood this demand. But two bills [on Federal aid to education] have been introduced . . . one of which completely yields to the church's maximum demand while the other plays directly into the policy of the church by providing that the funds may be distributed by each state in accordance with its own statutes. The latter . . . is a disguised evasion of the issue. . . . [The Church] has already secured legislation in eighteen states, permitting financial aid to parochial schools. . . . In effect the latter bill invites the states to violate the mandate of the first amendment. . . . The Catholic Church shall have the freedom to teach their people as it wishes to teach them—but never the right to use public tax money for that purpose!

"We believe," Dr. Dunnington concluded, "that friendly but frank speaking along the lines indulged in this sermon will prove to be the best safeguard for future friendly relations between all religious groups in America and that the basic cause of truth and freedom can thus be best served."

We stood under the familiar "May the Lord bless thee and keep thee . . ." but I was mindful only of the charges and countercharges resounding across the Protestant and Catholic divisions of American Christendom. Stacks of printed sermons near the door provided eager and anxious hands with copies of "Truth and Freedom." Dr. Dunnington stood at the door, shaking hands with the departing congregation. "Well, Doc," I heard an elderly man exclaim happily, "you certainly hit the nail on the head this morning. The things you said about the Catholic Church are things that caused me to renounce that faith and become a Protestant. I just wish every Catholic could have heard that sermon!"

Outside the morning was warm with spring. The streets were jammed with cars; the second congregation was already gathering. Other worshipers were making their way to the many other churches in the neighborhood. Crowds were coming out of St. Mary's Catholic Church where Mass had been celebrated. When we all mingled on the city streets, it was impossible to tell who was Methodist or Catholic or Lutheran or Congregational-Christian or Presbyterian or Baptist or Disciple of Christ or Evangelical-Reformed. This, too, was Church Street, U. S. A.

Protestantism was rising against the outspoken claims of Catholic officials. It was taking issue with Cardinal Spellman who charged that Protestants daring to criticize the Roman Catholic system were bigots. It was calling for an end to Catholic slander which condemned Protestants as neopagan and heretical. It challenged the descriptions of Potestantism as "a vanishing culture" and "a decaying sect." It vowed that Protestant churches must ever retain the American policy of religious liberty. It suggested that Roman Catholic leaders sit down with Protestant leaders and discuss interreligious relations.

In California the Council of Bishops of the Methodist Church made their position bluntly clear: "We wish the fullest of co-operation and offer it gladly as Christian brothers. But we can no longer tolerate bigotry and discrimination in Roman Catholic-controlled lands, particularly in view of the Roman Catholic ability to act as one and to stand for religious liberty and brotherly co-operation if it so desires."

I heard a sermon on Reformation Sunday: "Catholicism has never recovered from the sting of defeat inflicted by Luther and the reformers. It is out now to have its revenge and it will stop at nothing which will advance its purpose."

I heard an aged Protestant layman: "Before I die I hope to see the nefarious Roman clericalism exposed and destroyed."

The challenge of the new reformation regaled no one. My anxious cries that new groups were making a bid for power continued to wane, were reduced to a whisper. The dominant undercurrent swiftly rising among the clergy was the "Catholic threat." In California I addressed an interdenominational ministerial alliance. Once more I preached preparedness against the encroachments of Christian Science, Unity, Jehovah's Witnesses, Psychiana, the Oxford Group, the Baha'i Faith, Pentecostalism, and the cults, but my warnings aroused no one. My report was a swan song, lost in the cacophony of Protestant confusion: Orthodoxy, liberalism, modernism, the social gospel, humanism, pacifism, rationalism, and neo-orthodoxy. And throughout this group of Protestant clergymen I sensed a superior and ever-prevalent opinion: Catholic imperialism is the enemy; Catholic clericalism is the evil genius to be feared.

At the end of the meeting a minister presented me with three sermons which he had preached on Catholic-Protestant relations and in which he denounced the "unparalleled depredations of the anti-Christ."

An elderly, intensely sincere minister who had spoken fervently and frequently during the question-and-answer period invited me to accompany him to his church. As we walked through the sheltered church patio, he spoke of his long ministry and his affection for Protestant ideals. As we stood in the tranquil surroundings of the worshipful, high-vaulted church auditorium, he told me that this was his cathedral, his diocese, his bishopric, that it was as sacrosanct as any where altar and votive light hinted of some special Presence. And in his church study he said to me with utmost sincerity:

"A minister's greatest service to Protestantism lies in bringing the evil threat of the Catholic Church to Protestants in the pew. We are faced today by a satanic force masquerading in the cloak of religion. It is dictatorial and proposes to be theocratic. It is superstitious and pagan. It deludes and deceives its people and it is bent on destroying Protestantism through a modern inquisition. The awful situation in Mexico, Spain, Italy, Yugoslavia, and in South American countries should be our warning."

"And the answer?" I asked.

"Protestant unity!" he replied emphatically. "In this crucial hour we must unite! Nothing less than a world church will halt this Catholic aggression. Nothing but the ecumenical movement will put an end to Catholic usurpation. Think what a world population of two hundred million united Protestants will accomplish when spurred to action by One Lord, One Faith, One Gospel. Only in union can Protestantism emerge as a transcendant world power rightly to be reckoned with!"

I looked at him. There was a moment of powerfully restrained eagerness in his expression. He was my ecumenical prophet of the Kansas City meeting, breaking through a tremendous vision into prophetic paths and leading me backward and forward across the years, through my own forgotten hope of a completely united church into the universal presence of ecumenicalism. Out of Amsterdam, he decreed, would come this mighty force, this powerful church of a united Christendom with its inspiration and spirit and its awakened zeal. The slumbering giant Protestantism, the leviathan Protestantism, the champion Protestantism coming like a warrior girded with union and bearing on its armor the fearless, fearful saying, "For Christ and Church!" ·

"Here," he said, "is my sermon for next Sunday—'Why I Am a Protestant.'"

I took the printed folder from him and read:

"Roman Catholicism claims that outside the church there is no salvation. . . . The pope is the vicar of Christ on earth. . . . The church is the instrument of God's will. . . . The church is infallible. . . . She teaches all there is to be known about the gospel. . . . She administers all the divine means of salvation. . . ."

"I'm calling upon every member of my congregation to rededicate himself to the democracy of faith." The old man's words were fired with holy fervor. "Sometimes I think modern Catholicism is more subversive than it has ever been before. From Pope to parish priest it is trying to convince the world that Protestant churches are dying, that we are impotent to save the world. Why, do you know what an old Catholic cleric told me the other day? He said he was glad that Protestantism is coming back to an emphasis on the liturgy. 'It will just be so much easier when we take over,' he said. But we're answering back. We're getting ready to meet this enemy with a united front."

The impassioned oration of this aged disciple of Protestantism took me back to an old stone church in a Wisconsin village. I was again hearing the anti-Catholic warnings of ardent, faithful Uncle August as he stood in his church *Kanzel* high above his congregation. I heard him as he sat impressively at the head of the table at a family Sunday dinner, dominating the conversation with volcanic blasts about Catholic power in local affairs and assuring us that the struggle with Rome was a long battle. It might last straight through till the end of time. The Reformation had been a valiant beginning, but eternal vigilance was the price of Protestant freedom. Did we know that the bloodiest wars ever fought had been religious wars? Were we aware that the most murderous of all massacres had been the Inquisition? The colonization of America was sulphurous with religious intolerances. American Protestants learned at an early date that clerical domination must be met with anticlerical organization.

As Uncle August talked, I saw the American frontiers opened up by two irreconcilable forces: Catholic and Protestant. I saw American expansion as a race between the Catholic cross and the Protestant Bible. The victor was always the one who first planted his symbol on the untilled acres of Indian land. I saw Rome beat us on the Western seaboard, but our faith had won out in conquering the great American Midwest. Even here we were plagued with staked-off areas, Catholic-Protestant, a division which continued after death in fenced-off cemeteries, Protestant-Catholic. There were two kinds of people: My people and Catholic people. There were two churches: The good church and the Catholic Church. There were two worlds: Our world and the Catholic world.

Those early years of my life had been crisscrossed with Catholic experiences. My first romance, my sophomore affair of the heart, had revolved around Theresa the Catholic; my first violent revolt against parental counsel, over Theresa; my first clandestine visit to midnight Mass on Christmas Eve, with Theresa; the first girl I ever kissed, Theresa the Catholic. And when I tried to kiss her again a few nights later, she said emphatically, "No. It's Ash Wednesday. I'm making a Lenten sacrifice." Theresa had given up kissing for forty days! After that I always thought of Theresa as the helpless victim of the ever-ominous Roman Catholic Church. Old Sabina was another. I used to watch as she hobbled to church every morning with pebbles in her shoes, doing self-inflicted penance for having been divorced.

Every year on the first day of Lent my brother and I counted the boys and girls who came to school with ashes on their foreheads. My mother always condemned the pre-Lenten dances and the after-Easter festivals, as well as the bingo games and roulette wheels at the Catholic parish carnivals. The Catholic vote in school-board and town elections was always a matter of more concern than the issues of a national referendum. The local Protestant-Catholic struggle was extended round the world when I first leafed through a copy of *The Menace* with its cartoons and headlines about the evil strategy of Rome. But through these fearful memories came the pleasant picture of my father and the jolly Catholic priest cheerfully playing skat over their beers. Often as I watched them I wished for courage to ask the black-clad *Priester* all about the mysteries of his faith—the confessions, the holy water, the medals of St. Christopher, the rosaries, the prayer books, and the images of the Bleeding Heart of Jesus.

Fears and prejudices engendered by childhood concepts of Catholicism were bolstered when I visited Mexico as a young man. The celestial splendor of the rich churches with their gold-encrusted altars and alabaster saints was blighted by the shocking sight of beggars leaning their shriveled bodies against cathedral walls, begging centavos in the name of the Mother of God. In the Capilla del Pocito, I watched the black-veiled worshipers crawl down the aisles on their knees, clutching lighted candles in their dark hands and whispering prayers to the Virgin of Guadalupe. Guards stood in the shadows. The women kissed their beads. The men made the sign of the cross over their unshaved faces. Just as a chant was begun, an attendant leaned over to me and whispered, "In this place, señor, better you watch your pocketbook!" During Holy Week life-sized statues of Jesus, draped in a cheap velvet robe, were set up in booths in the market places. A crown of thorns was thrust on the head and the cheeks were garish with red paint. Near by sat a trinket vendor with a box of tin gadgets which could be bought for whatever one wished to give. The trinkets were legs, arms, eyes, and animals with a ribbon and pin attached. If a believer had a sore leg, he bought a leg and fastened it on the robe of Jesus; or an arm, or eyes, as the case might be. Or if his cow was not giving sufficient milk, he bought a tin cow and pinned that on the royal garment.   .

In Cuernavaca I stood before the murals in Cortez' palace; the counterpart of Diego Rivera's portrayal could still be found throughout Old Mexico. He had depicted Indian slaves kissing the soft, fat hands of priestly conquistadors; I had seen Mexicans bow to clerics who stood regal and secure in lavishly emblazoned vestures. And the bewildered eyes which the impoverished peons of the murals raised to the branding irons and the whips I had seen in dirty village streets, in unkempt adobe homes, and within the sacred walls of historic *catedrals*.

But fending against this dark backdrop of early indoctrination and youthful prejudices were later experiences. My research had led me out of an alien relationship with Catholicism into an intimate knowledge of Catholic culture and into cordial acquaintances with Catholic personalities. Two little-known Catholic orders had helped to set the pattern for my years of research and had been instrumental in establishing a sympathetic approach to peoples of all faiths.

Los Hermanos Penitentes was known to Protestants as the bloody order of the flagelants, and to Catholics as the problem child of Mother Church. But when I met in Denver, Colorado, a young Mexican-American who told me that he had grown up among these New Mexico "self-crucifiers," I was interested. After two years of college, Carlos spoke thoughtfully of his spiritual heritage, but I was sure he would never again identify himself with the Penitentes. He would never again pull the black *Carreta del Muerta* until the ropes bruised his breast, or drag a heavy wooden cross through the cactus-covered desert. Los Hermanos would never have the privilege of selecting him as the young man to be strapped to a huge crosspiece on Good Friday to suffer for *El Cristo's* sake.

But when I stood with Carlos in a *morada* the sudden change in him was puzzling. As he spoke about the meaning of the liturgy, I realized that early faith sends deep roots into the soul. He turned a blacksnake thoughtfully in his hands and said, "It is easy for a man to say he is sorry for his sins, but the true penitent shows he is sorry by suffering." It was evident that he regretted having helped an outsider penetrate the crude adobe sanctuary of the barren chapel. Penitente history was sacred to him. It went back to beloved St. Francis of Assisi who, seven hundred years ago, established his Third Order for the laity, confusing the Holy Orders of Mother Church.

Carlos seemed particularly guilty when he reluctantly led me along the trail up which the procession of black-clad and half-naked men wound their way to a desert *Calvario* before the daybreak on Good Friday. Through long dark hours we had waited outside a *morada* where the entire village was assembled for their strange macabre worship. Then the procession moved out into the night, following the eerie sound of the flute, chanting their songs, murmuring their prayers, flailing their bare backs with the blacksnakes. The whirl of the whips was their testimony of abject devotion and supreme loyalty.

Suddenly Carlos was overcome by the demands of his faith. Without a word he left me in the shadows of the scrub oak which lined the *Calvario* trail. He threw himself to his knees in front of the marching worshipers, tore off his shirt and begged for the whip. As the vicious lashes struck his naked body, he piteously entreated the *Hermano Mayor* to hear his confession. Though his intellect could not justify the sadistic practices of his people, he could not reject the faith of his youth and the church which had given him the right to believe that the greater the suffering, the greater the glory.

My retreat among the Trappist monks furnished another memorable example of Catholic fidelity. At Our Lady of Gethsemani I found a community of religious undeniably devoted to the purpose of their self-imposed slavery. Through ceaseless intercession they were wooing God's good favor back to an errant world. Within the rigor of the ancient order they were finding a secret mystic glory which had eluded modern man. The outpouring of their souls formed an unbroken cycle of prayers from Matins to Complin. At two-thirty in the morning, the hallowed hour when communion with their Lord began, I followed them from the bare cubicles, where they sleep on hard straw cots, to the beautiful chapel, where the Mother of God waited to hear their supplications. I ate with them during the great fast when there was only a bowl of barley soup and a slice of black bread for each lowly guest. I walked in the fields where the lay brothers work during the long hours of the day. I read the scholarly texts in the library where the choir religious study and meditate. I visited with the monastery officials who were men of extraordinary learning, men who could have held responsible and highly remunerative positions in the world.

The wise and saintly countenance of the Father Confessor and the reverence of his counsel reflected an awareness of God toward which every ardent disciple of any faith aspires. The Father Guest Master, who had been in the monastery for thirty years, spoke intimately of sacred things. He was an impressively

large man with a jovial heart, and he laughed at my surprise
when he confided that he had never heard a radio. He assured
me that the sweetest music and the loveliest voices came only
in the Great Silences. I met also a postulant, a boy of twenty-one,
a college graduate, who arrived at the abbey to join the order
during my retreat. He had studied toward a business career, but
the church had called. His explanation of his vocation was not
difficult to understand: "I have looked for peace and an ideal in
the world and have found only wounds. Maybe through prayer
I can help to change things."

The postulant became the main character of *Within These
Walls,* my play written for the experimental theater at the State
University of Iowa. Through his unquestioning belief in the
relentless rule of Mother Church, through his youthful eagerness to embrace the exacting vows, and through his struggle to
adjust himself to the monastic life, my doubts and my questioning followed him. The play was his conflict, his attempt to
justify intellectually and spiritually the extreme demands of the
order. The anachronism of a twentieth-century youth in a
twelfth-century monastic setting provided an intensely interest-
ing and dramatic situation. My Protestant fears and Protestant
queries were superimposed on what I considered blind Catholic
devotion. My resentment toward the excruciating Trappist life
was eventually lost in a sincere attempt to appreciate the monks'
weary abasement of body and soul. And always in the men who
had been granted permission to speak to me and those who were
always silent, I sensed behind self-invited degradation a hidden
majesty, an inescapable sense of peace and promise.

A few days after a seminar reading of my play, Professor
Mabie informed me that the director of drama at a Catholic
college was interested in seeing the script. With characteristic
enthusiasm Mabie said, "Shoot it in and see what they say." I

did, but I was fearful. Though I felt I had caught the spirit of the monastery life, I wondered what would happen when Catholic professors and Catholic critics put the script under the powerful microscope of Catholic criticism. What would be their reaction to a Protestant's interpretation of the Trappist life?

Then a letter came, my passport through the Catholic-Protestant battle lines. Eager and unscathed, I headed straight into the Rome of the American Midwest. Loras College, planted firmly atop one of the hills of Dubuque, Iowa, had adjudged the play stageworthy, and I moved in to live with fifty Catholic clerics and six hundred Catholic students. The director of drama, a young priest, had been described to me as "a real guy." But I was wary, knowing how fifty ministers of my denomination would have received a Catholic who had presumed to write a Protestant play. No doubt the Catholics would ply me with questions about my faith and more particularly about my presumption that I could adequately depict the passions and purposes of the cloistered cenobites of Our Lady of Gethsemani. Yet here I was, pleasantly bidden by a captious circumstance to unpack my bags for six or eight weeks in this active area of the united Catholic kingdom.

When I met Father George, my fears were allayed. As he came into my room, an overcoat slung over his clericals, I was sure his friendly charm would have beguiled even my old preacher uncle. He extended a hand.

"Welcome to Loras. You'll be thrilled with the boy who's playing the lead. Edward is one of our best students, a fine clean-cut chap, wonderful stage presence; takes direction, sensitive; just the kind of fellow who'd go into a monastery with lots of ambition and then suddenly wonder whether the business of continual silence and seclusion is really what the good Lord ordered. You'll like Edward. Then there's the fellow for the part of the Father Guest Master. A jolly, good-natured boy with a heart big as the world. Wait till you see him in a white habit and a tonsure wig. Now, about the Father Confessor——"

We were already in production. Father George was director, designer, stage manager, and comptroller, directing the cast, the crew, and me. To him there was no criticism or questioning of the Protestant faith or any faith. He knew only that his religion was totally, unquestioningly satisfying and that it completely ruled his days.

His attitude was reflected in all the priests on the staff. The basis of their belief had been settled once and for all by Mother Church; thought and action moved within that framework. It was difficult for me to forget that their idea of the fellowship of believers was limited to the visible Holy Catholic Church. And yet I never felt like an intruder at Loras College. As I associated with the priests at their work and during their leisure, I wished for every Protestant such an experience as mine. I wished for every priest the opportunity to meet our ministers in the same circumstances. Soon the wall between Protestantism and Catholicism was only a wall of doctrine. Soon I was as close to the knowledge and religious convictions of these men as I had been to Langley or Kurtz or Saunders or Pastor Ulrich. I spoke of my feelings to Father George.

"I've been expecting to hear this," he said. "You're really a good Catholic at heart."

"But what about your belief that outside the Church there is no salvation?"

"Who knows how great the Mystical Body is in the sight of God? We believe also that many are united with the Church in desire, though they are not united with her in fact."

So the Catholic-Protestant fellowship at Loras was not heretical. The fifty priests had been brought up in their faith and I in mine. My devotion to Protestant religious obligations and convictions grew stronger as I observed their ardent loyalty to what they considered truth and divine direction.

When I ate with these men at the dormitory tables, I often joined in the hasty, sincere, "Bless us, O Lord, and these Thy gifts which we are about to receive through Christ our Lord. Amen. In the name of the Father and of the Son and of the Holy Ghost." Sometimes during the chapel services I participated with reverence and humility in acts of worship which I had once considered meaningless. The monotonous drone of Latin intonations became the music of a universal litany, and the vestments of the celebrants proclaimed a people's desire to render to the Lord the best for beauty and the loveliest for adoration.

But, of course, there were times when I interpreted these reactions as the romanticizing of a young Protestant caught in the enthusiasm of the drama of worship. Though my priestly associates seemed perfectly secure and perfectly sincere, I often wondered if they were ever tempted to flee from their religion. Did they ever weary of the celibate life? Did they ever long to throw aside their clericals and renounce their vows? Did they ever have their doubts and disagreements with Rome over matters of dogma and doctrine? They argued freely in the field of speculative theology and frequently differed sharply in historic interpretations, but always they came back submissively to the final authority of the Church.

When I turned from teachers to students, I found the same reactions and responses to the Catholic faith. The prayers before rehearsals were sincere, though formal. The often casual and familiar "Hail Mary" reached back through tradition and anchored those who believed to the indestructible rock on which the Christ had founded Mother Church. Tradition and unquestioning faith were perpetuated in the lives of the members of the cast. Of this I was assured during the early readings. Father George had been right about Edward. He made a convincing postulant. He was the young man I had watched enter the monastery grounds when the gatekeeper opened the black door at Our Lady of Gethsemani. He was the boy who had looked for "peace and an ideal" in the world and was now trying to share with us his conviction that he had found them in monasticism.

One night after rehearsal he said, "If a Broadway audience saw this play, they'd probably say the Catholic Church is pretty barbaric, but gradually they'd understand that religion needs men like the Trappists and that it was the monasteries which kept the light of faith burning during the Dark Ages. And maybe they'd even understand that these men aren't so crazy after all, that by their prayers and their devotion they influence our lives more than we realize. That is, if Broadway audiences believe in prayer."

Once, during a break in rehearsals, while we were discussing a scene in which the postulant is visited by the Father Confessor, I asked Edward about the true merit of confession.

"The priest can say, *'Ego te absolvo a pecatis,'*" he explained, "but the sins aren't really forgiven unless something happens in the heart of the penitent. There must be sincere repentance on the part of the individual or there is no real redemption."

"How about that, Father George?" I asked. "Would you say that when you grant absolution, you don't know whether sins are really forgiven or not?"

"The priest isn't a magician" was the reply. "In the Sacrament of Penance, the penitent must always do his part by contrition and by a firm purpose of amendment avoid the sin and the occasion of it. Only God forgives sin."

"Does the Catholic laity know that?" I inquired. "Don't most

Catholics think of confession as just a form and an easy way out
by way of an external religious exercise?"

"I think Catholics know pretty well what the Church teaches
and what the Church requires," he said. "If they don't they
ought to. Many Protestants probably think that the Catholic
rule is 'Do this and you're in; do that and you're out,' but actually what matters is a change of heart and a new devotion. After
all, external ceremonies are simply signs of an internal regenera-
tion."

"But since confession is required—in fact, demanded by the
Church—isn't there some basis for the belief that the Church
has too much power over the individual?"

"The only power is the power delegated by Christ," Father
George replied. "And that extends to faith and morals. What's
the good of a church if it hasn't any power? Every religion exercises influence over the life and conduct of its believers. And
heaven help us, man needs it."

"Still I wonder if fear isn't the motivation that keeps the con-
fessional going."

Edward disagreed. "The fellows I know go to Confession
because it's good for the soul. They aren't afraid. And the
postulant in this play did not join the order because of fear. The
Trappist life is his vocation, a call of faith. And that's the way
I want to play the part. So I go to Confession because it is good
for my soul."

"But if absolution is dependent on contrition," I concluded,
"then you must show more sorrow for sin before your scene
with the Father Confessor."

"Before and after," said Father George. "Men often suffer
for sin even after the sin has been forgiven. That's Catholic
teaching, too."

Every line and every action in the play were always being

weighed and checked against the inescapable rules and standards of Mother Church, against the rules of the Trappist order, against church councils and papal decrees. Every reference to tradition, every symbol, every saying was fraught with veneration.

But Father George often laughed good-naturedly at the players' sincere effort to copy the shuffling step of the Trappist monks and to imitate their totally abject characteristics.

"Yes, yes!" he would exclaim. "Try to copy them if you can. And let's thank God we have men in the Church who are dedicating body and soul to the life of a religious. Heaven help us if we would all be secular priests. Bow your heads. Make the sign of the cross. Recite the Angelus prayer. The Angelus, boys—it's been ringing in the Church for nearly a thousand years."

Watching the players, I was taken back to the inspiring daily offices at Our Lady of Gethsemani. The sign of the cross and the genuflexions, the casual nod of the head, the eyes lifted in celestial contemplation seemed the result of well-directed characterizations. But when I attended the Mass and the vesper services at Loras, I realized that the changeless and timeless acts of Catholic worship are performed with meticulous devotion whether in Trappist abbey or college chapel. The signs and seals introduced wherever the One True and Living Church of Christ was founded are evidences of the perpetuity of the faith. Some of the students seemed to take the services and religious exercises for granted. Their acts were perfunctory; their comments, superficial. But even though they were without special sensitivity or intellectual awareness, they too seemed caught in the dominant spell of an impelling faith.

My days at Loras convinced me that Mother Church holds an activating personal appeal for the individual. As the Trappist had betrayed his awe for the Blessed Sacrament, so the student showed holy esteem for the Body of Christ; as perpetual respect was accorded the Father Abbot in the monastery walls, so respect for the priest as God's apostle was demonstrated by the most wayward son of Mother Church.

"In the Mass the Father really takes the place of Christ," a Loras student informed me reverently. Then he added thoughtfully, "Wonder what he thinks and feels when he officiates at the altar?"

A Loras priest assured me that the Mass never lost its significance for the celebrant. "The priest in the Mass is Christ," he explained. "The Mass and the Cross are synonymous. The Victim in both is Christ, and the priest in both is Christ. The Church is hallowed by that Presence."

"Something would bother me in Catholicism," I told him. "Statues and prayers to the saints."

"Something would bother me in Protestantism." He laughed. "No statues, no prayers to the saints. It's kind of nice to show appreciation to those who have shown us the way to God."

The play went into dress rehearsals. The boys playing the part of the lay monks donned their long, brown habits; the choir religious, their white. The tonsure wigs left only a small fringe of hair encircling the head like a halo. With the magic of setting and make-up the monastery of Our Lady of Gethsemani came to life. But it was more than that. It was the tradition of monasticism traveling the superhighway of the Catholic faith: from Benedict in the early sixth century, through St. Francis of the thirteenth, through the partial destruction of the monasteries during the European Reformation, through Gethsemani, Kentucky, straight to the Loras College stage and into the lives of young actors who believed and felt that these men and these places were ordained of God.

It was while I watched the first complete run-through that I became entirely aware of the meaning of Trappist life. The monastery wall was a protection against the world. Mother Church, like a guardian angel, has built a sheltered haven where, undisturbed, the soul can commune with God. The Church has provided for the welfare of the Trappist and in return they bend their affection, their prayers, and their lives toward Rome. For them there is no other faith, no other way. This conviction was not far removed from the devotion which filled the hearts of the students who had become Trappists under the stage lights. The silence vows of the Trappists reminded them of the need for meditation; the monks' Great Fast condemned the intemperate; monastic discipline spoke of church authority; seclusion from the world was a command to oppose secularism; the total abnegation of self was a warning that the Christian life demanded everlasting vigilance.

The spiritual exercises which the priests at Loras faithfully observed would have seemed like cold externalities had I not been seeing Catholicism in closer perspective than ever before. One night, shortly before midnight, when everyone was worn out from a dress rehearsal that had been in progress since early afternoon, I discovered Father George backstage. He was walking to and fro, reading his office aloud.

"Time sort of ran out on me today," he explained.

I laughed. "Wouldn't the Pope understand if you missed a day?"

"The Pope might, but how about me?" He smiled back, then hurriedly continued his reading.

Finally an evening came when prayers were said with special feeling, and God was invoked to crown with success the "world première" of a Protestant's Catholic play. The stories I had heard about Catholics praying for a Notre Dame victory or to get more milk out of a Mexican cow suddenly seemed less absurd. We had great things to pray about. There was an archbishop in the audience. A movie scout had come to town. I had my eye on Broadway. So we prayed, and those who believed made the sign of the cross. The house lights went down and the curtain went up; Protestant and Catholic lived the Trappist life for two hours and a half.

After the curtain calls Archbishop Beckman came to the stage to thank the author, the director, the cast, and the crew for bringing the play to the people of his archdiocese. He was generous and sincere in his approval. I had always thought that an archbishop, like any other celebrity, would have his say and then vanish through a back door to his limousine. But he stayed to shake hands with the cast and to give them his blessing. He stayed to say that if there was anything he could do, he would be happy to co-operate. And before he left, he drew a rosary from his pocket and pressed it into my hand.

But the appreciation of Catholicism which had warmed my heart was soon threatened by all the old-time prejudices. After the Loras College production of *Within These Walls* the power of Mother Church struck me at a very vulnerable spot. I had seen the play produced commercially at the Blackstone Theatre in Chicago. I had been thrilled with the reviews and with the evidences of Catholic patronage. My hopes soared when a producer took an option on the play and set it up for New York production. The cast was chosen; rehearsals were under way. And then the Church stepped in. The Carleton Hayes Committee, invited to watch a run-through, said, "The Trappist life is not typical of the Catholic faith, and it is not our intention to give Broadway audiences that impression. The Trappists are a relatively small religious order within the bosom of Mother Church. If people see only this phase of our devotional life, they will say, 'That's Catholicism for you. The Church imposes vows of perpetual silence, seclusion from the world, and all the other rigors which the play depicts.'"

The producer said, "Without the support of the Catholics it's useless to do the show."

My hope for a Broadway play went up in a flame of religious disapproval. Mother Church was showing the strength of her defense. Authority was her ready weapon; fear and discipline were her bludgeons. The long fingers had again crept out from the "witch house" just as they had in Fairfield. My ambitions had been strangled in the unyielding dictatorship of the Catholic hierarchy; my play had been condemned by the committee that selects and recommends the Catholics' theatrical fare. My faded Broadway dream awakened sleeping dogs of wrath and sicked them all on Rome. What right to power did this church have, this mysterious messenger of doctrines established by councils which met a few hundred years after Christ and a thousand years before my time? It was an organization which prided itself on its resistance to change and still offered its people the magical external rites of the Dark Ages. All authority emanated from Rome. The priest governed his parish by authority of his bishop, the bishop received his jurisdiction from Rome, and if priests or bishops failed to obey this authority they would be removed from their offices and could be ousted from the Church. Potentially the Church held within its intricate machinery a complete domination over life and death.

But though I believed all this, there was something more. At Loras College there were Father George and the other priests and the students I had admired and respected. There was Edward who might have done anything he wished with his life and been tremendously successful, but who chose priestly orders as his vocation. There were always the silent ones, the Trappists, who believed and trusted and loved God more because they loved the Church.

There was the man with whom I sat one day in the monastery garden and who said to me, "A man ought to meditate more. The world gets one away from God. You know what I think—I think I'll join the order."

"How can you?" I laughed. "You're married."

"We've talked it over," he said seriously. "We love each other very much. But we've raised our family and the children are all married. My wife might go into a convent and I—I might come here, if they'll take me. A man ought to spend some years of his life getting close to God."

"What really brought you to this conclusion?" I asked.

"Have you ever heard Fulton Sheen?"

"No."

"Maybe you wouldn't understand then. Something happened to my way of thinking after I heard him. He's close to God. And the reason he's close to God is because he spends so much time in meditation and prayer. Maybe you wouldn't understand that since you aren't Catholic."

There would always be things I could not understand about the Catholic life and the Catholic temperament. But like the gentle touch of a Greater Presence, there came to me a longing which despised the barriers of creed and set me in terrible desperation against whatever it was that kept kindred spirits of any faith from seeking their eternal goal by whatever road they wished to seek it and by whatever path they believed it could be found.

This was the reply I made to the ministers who saw Roman clericalism as a threat to their democratic heritage of faith and they agreed. The individual Catholic had a right to his faith and the right to practice and pursue that faith. And even the most outspoken among the Protestant castigators of Roman Catholic design admitted that they had many friends among the Catholics. But there was no armistice in Catholic-Protestant relations. Catholic officials accused Protestantism of waging a "crusade of bigotry" against their church; Catholic editorials denounced the "fanatical plot undertaken by a frantic Protestantism" to destroy Christ's Church. Meanwhile the anticlerical movement gained momentum as the suspicions of Protestant ministers increased. Catholic journals publicized Canon 1258, the divine law which prohibits Catholics taking active part in non-Catholic religious services. "This law permits of no exception and no dispensation by any authority for any reason." Canons 1398 and 1399 were also thoroughly publicized: "Catholics are forbidden to read or keep books which deny or make light of any point of Catholic belief or practice. . . ."

Protestants contended that these warnings were being reprinted because there was also a stream of conversion running toward Protestantism. The publicity given big-name converts to Catholicism was only a smoke screen to hide the many lesser-name apostates from Catholicism's one Church to Protestantism's many. Though I made no attempt to check the Catholic claim of eighty thousand converts annually or to verify the fifty-to-seventy-thousand claim of Protestantism from Catholicism, I encountered many Christians who had undergone a reversal of faith. I found clerical footprints running both ways in this animated contest for truth. Two Lutheran ministers and an Anglican who were joining in the Protestant offensive against Rome had once been Catholic priests. But then I met a priest who had been a Presbyterian and one who had been an Anglican.

Reasons given were as varied as the personalities who had made the change. While dissatisfied Protestants found spiritual security in the uniformity of Catholic faith and practice, rebellious children of Mother Church looked toward Protestantism as an escape from the "petrification of formal worship" and the "thwarting of intellectual pursuits."

I heard the Catholic stand against birth control denounced by Catholics as primitive and immoral. A woman writer left the Church because she was convinced that Catholicism had and was distorting historical facts deliberately to build up its case as the true and infallible church. I talked with a scholar who embraced the Catholic faith because he was "sick and tired of hearing that Protestantism was the author of religious liberty when, in reality, the Jesuits Bellarmine and Suárez worked out a pattern for freedom and independence two hundred years before 1776." I met a clothing-store manager who said that after he learned of the host of notables who had joined Mother Church he could no longer resist; Gilbert Chesterton, Fritz Kreisler, Henry Ford II, Heywood Broun, and Hollywood's Jo Mielziner had convinced him. But a Catholic came over to Protestantism for the same reason. Her husband, "a bad Protestant but a good man," had shown her the absurdity of claiming greatness for any church just because it had a smoothly running publicity machine. I spoke to an Iowa farmer who left Catholicism because the parish demanded too many contributions. At an AA meeting I met a redeemed alcoholic who now attended Catholic services because "one time when I was desperate with remorse, a priest put his arms around me and said, 'You're still good enough for God to love you!'" A mother, fearful of the immoral influence of secular schools, joined the Catholic Church and placed her four children in a parochial school. Mixed marriages sometimes resulted in a Catholic gain and sometimes in a gain for a Protestant church. The decision seemed to derive from personal inclinations, not from the balance of Protestant-Catholic power.

"I'm marrying Ruth," a friend of mine announced one day, "and for her mother's sake she wants to be married by a Catholic priest. Ruth was a Catholic once, you know, but she isn't any more."

"And now you're worried about signing the Catholic marriage promises?" I asked.

"We won't sign anything," he assured me. "All we want is a priest to perform the ceremony."

"There are five in town," I said. "You shouldn't have any trouble."

"We've already been to three," he confessed wryly, "and we are having trouble. Each one said he couldn't marry us until Ruth has been reinstated in the Church. Confession, Mass, and all that stuff. But you have a good friend who's a priest. Ask him to do it for us. On the q.t., or any way. Just so we can honestly report to Ruth's mother that dear old Mother Church did perform the ceremony."

I told the story to my friend the priest. He shook his head, and with a quiet laugh said, "I'd like to do it, but the Church has a law, you know. And I'm bound by that law. It states pretty clearly that Ruth must first be readmitted to the church. You could go anywhere in the world, and you'd run into the same law and the same jury. That's the way it is."

When I reported this to my friend, he cursed. He denounced the Catholic hierarchy. Then he said, "That's only their damn scheme to make us promise to bring up our children in the Catholic faith. That I'll never do. Ruth's mother will have to be satisfied with a Protestant preacher or with a justice of the peace."

A few days later he returned to my office, but not to level further accusations against Rome. "We went to the other local priest," he said quietly.

"Same answer?"

"Same answer. Then we called on the priests in two other towns. Same answer. You know what I've decided? The Catholics have something which we Protestants have never had! Think of finding seven ministers in this town who would all agree on a single religious question. That's why I've always been so confused about religion: one preacher always contradicting another, even in the same denomination. But now I'm getting straightened out. Ruth is being reinstated and I'm taking instruction. The uniformity of doctrine and the authority of the Catholic Church are enough to convince anybody!"

My friend the priest was strangely unimpressed by this confession from a Protestant. He showed no eagerness to publicize the fact that a convert was being added to the Roman Catholic scroll.

"A man can join a church without finding God," he said quietly. "A man can accept authority easily if he is not interested in historical criticism. He must have been a very poor Protestant to begin with and, since he had nothing to sacrifice, he probably will have little to gain. There is no moral fidelity in uniting with the Church just because it is authoritarian."

"But I think I understand how he probably feels," I ventured. "The democracy of faith is a grand phrase, but giving every man the right to interpret the Bible for himself has brought a thousand interpretations. The priesthood of believers is a great ideal, but I wonder if we haven't gone farther than the reformers ever intended us to go. When you have questions, they are answered by the authority of your church. But a Protestant doesn't know what he should believe about many things that seem important to him. Where can he find clerical argreement on the deity of Jesus, the preparation of the soul for eternal life, the means of grace, divine revelation——"

"And you think Catholicism would answer all your questions for you?" he interrupted sharply.

"Well . . ." I faltered, completely astonished by such a retort from a priest.

"Oh, it would," he quickly assured me with a touch of bitterness in his well-modulated voice. "Our people believe that the Church is infallible, that the Church offers to the world the only true religion and that all other churches are founded on heresy." He paused for a long moment. "But don't you think your church and mine have much in common? Aren't you and I very close together in many of our beliefs? There should be a meeting point somewhere. At least we worship the same Christ!"

"But Protestants aren't even ready for union among themselves. That I learned rather painfully when I once tried to unite a Baptist and an Evangelical church, and you certainly know that the Catholic Church will never 'union' with anyone because——"

"I suppose, I suppose," he interrupted impatiently. "The Catholic Church is a visible church. All churches must seek union in her. She is the true Church—in existence since the time of Christ." Then, raising his voice in what seemed to me an attempt to convince himself, he said, "We can prove the apostolate from the Scriptures, and we can prove the Scriptures from the apostolate. We 'declare faith an intellectual act guided by an upright will and aided by God's grace!' Yes, yes! What more shall we say?"

Catholicism was his heritage, and I had never suspected that he questioned the validity of his faith. Even after this revealing conversation I did not doubt for a moment that he loved and respected Mother Church. From a Catholic home he had gone to a Catholic school, and then into a Catholic parish. The

Church was his visa to a good land. If at times he questioned the authority of its teachings—papal infallibility, divine revelation, the efficacy of indulgences—it was only to effect that intellectual compromise demanded by his type of mind. And if sometimes the dread monster called modernism struck at his heart while worldliness struck at his flesh, it was only because he was both scholarly and human.

Our friendship deepened during the ensuing weeks and our visits together became more frequent. Gradually I realized that he lacked the irrepressible sense of an affluency of faith which I had set down as a common characteristic of Catholic priests. More and more he subjected the old dogmas to debate. Desperately he re-examined the beliefs which had been fixed as compelling lifetime convictions when he took the inviolable oaths of the priesthood.

Out of his mental distress he would say, "A man must believe for himself and have intellectual convictions—for himself. Some people can believe without effort. Others have tremendous difficulty. It boils down to this: Revelation is given through the Church and no one can reject it without sinning." Then, after a moment: "But clothes must fit the man. At least, that is easier than trying to find a man to fit the clothes. And what a preposterous thought to think of the same garment for everyone!"

I was witnessing the agonizing progression toward a spiritual crisis. Religious truths and intellectual convictions had suddenly become incompatible. At times he felt the struggle was too personal for conversation. He took long rides into the countryside. He wrote out the details of the divided state of his nature. It was evident that the authority of mind was becoming more and more formidable, but the authority of his soul would not be loosened from the rich experiences of his vocation. There was nothing I could do. I was a poor proselytizer and a bad logician. In the field of scholarship he was my superior. He had the wisdom and he could argue both sides of his case magnificently.

"I'm no Luther," he would say. "I'm just trying to come to terms with myself. I don't want to reform anything; I don't want to destroy anything the Church professes or that I have professed. I suppose you could find some priests who would say that there is need for reform today just as some admit that the Church needed reform in the sixteenth century. But Luther was a bad man. Luther was a heretic. He would have done better staying in the household of faith."

"Could he have reformed the Church from within?" I asked. "Is that possible? What if you should decide to post your ninety-five theses——"

"I'd go to my bishop."

"And what would the bishop say?"

"You mean," he asked hesitantly, "what *did* the bishop say?"

His face was serious and set. It was bloodless and his clericals suddenly seemed of the blackest black. He walked around the room, laboring with his thoughts.

"Perhaps this is a Wittenberg experience," he said as his long strides took him back and forth across the floor. "The bishop said, 'Pray. The thing any man needs in a spiritual struggle is prayer.'" He smiled grimly. "Bishops are so very wise. And sometimes so very right. But there were many things I wanted to say before I resorted to prayer. Does he think I haven't prayed—almost constantly—ever since the first doubt about the rightness of my vocation entered my mind." There was resentment in his voice, bordering on bitter accusation.

"The bishop does not understand. He has believed for so long. He has no questions. He has already won the necessary intellectual battle. He has brought himself to say, 'This is the end of the search. It is all here, black on white, the beginning and the end. There is nothing else.' If I could do this, I could be a Catholic." His words were drawn out of his inner struggle. They were sincere and satirical; they were formidable with the past and weak with a sense of present questioning.

"I tell you the Church is great. Sometimes its perpetuity, its persistence through thick and thin, through everything the world has thrown at it, through hell and high water, almost persuade any man that it must be founded on the rock of Christ. You have no idea how men love that Church. You cannot imagine how much the Church means in the lives of some of its people. It is the bride of Christ and there is no other. It was begun as the object of God's creation and shall be dissolved only at the end of God's eternal plan. Since it began, men have prayed for it and fought for it, have lived for it and died for it, have killed and been killed because they believed it to be the Mystical Body of Christ. It is the imitation of Christ and the mirror of God. You will never know, no Protestant will ever know, where its strength lies. It is not in the Pope, the vicar of Christ on earth, nor even in the primacy of St. Peter, not in Vatican councils or canon laws, not even in the claims or government of the Church—its strength is in the hearts and lives of believing men and women for whom the Church represents the living fellowship with Almighty God!"

His voice had risen to a cry. He stopped sharply.

"But every man must believe for himself! A man must have intellectual convictions—for himself!"

He went away. Sick and confused, he left the city. He was running from the Church and from himself. Three months later when I saw him again, when he came through a crowded hotel lobby to keep our appointment, no friendly, reverent glances followed him. I stood still and silent. There was no black frock and no "Roman collar." The sacrament of holy orders was completely hidden by a casual street outfit. His sport shirt was open at the neck. He was free.

"It's nothing," he said with a catch in his voice. "Other men have done it. Perhaps many more than anyone realizes."

I felt not the slightest sense of triumph over his apostasy. He had the Protestant freedom which he so long had envied; he had a top position in a leading American industry. He was on his own, answering the questions about the mysteries of life and death and God and the Church through the genius of his own dialectics. But time brought an unexpected denouement and wrote a surprising ending to the ex-priest's story.

Several years following his emancipation from clerical robes and duties, the report reached me that he was planning to return to Mother Church. His escape into non-Catholic religions had not been an escape from his struggle. He was seeking something, but delving into Protestantism's rich and diversified fields of faith had not yet yielded a satisfying reward. The roots of his religious life were deeper than he knew; tradition had moored him more securely than he realized; Mother Church still represented his liaison with God. He was going back. His reasons may have been many and complex and perhaps I would never know the truth. Perhaps the vows, fear, hell, favor in God's sight, a hundred reasons— Who could tell? It may have been that he was learning how unfitted and destitute an ex-priest feels in the current of secular life and how there is no escape. Or did he return to Mother Church from his nomadism because of the strong appeal which Catholicism exercises over the individual life?

After having crossed the boundaries of the Catholic world, having met devout Catholics, having lived as they lived within the confines of the Catholic Church, I knew that Catholicism's greatest strength is its emphasis on man's direct encounter with God. Stronger than papal infallibility or canons or claims of apostolic succession is this impulse to the personal quest. This was the Church's secret, its most powerful dynamic. It puts a rosary into the hands of the worshiper that he may feel the aristocracy of prayer. Candles and incense burn that he may smell the sweet scent of purification. Images and altars are built for him and when he kneels before them he meets God on equal terms with any man. The Angelus rings for him. The Sacrament of Communion is for him, placed on his tongue so that he can taste for himself Christ's sacrifice. The confession washes his soul. Miracles, no respecters of persons, are for him if he seeks them. The Mass, prayers, genuflexions and the sign of the cross— through all of these he is made aware that he has dignity and importance in the sight of God. Through long and systematic indoctrination he is assured that the Church is the divine channel of grace *for him*.

Despite the indisputable evidences of Roman aggression, despite the heightening clamor for the anticlerical movement, despite the fact that Catholics frequently turned Protestant, my experiences within Catholicism had led me to the same conclusion as that with which my research among contemporary religious groups had ended. Their organizations and their techniques were scaled to the believer's personal life. So I added Catholicism to my list of invaders.

CHAPTER EIGHT

The Present Challenge

IFTEEN years had passed since Fairfield, fifteen years since my fledgling call to be the Lord's watchman, signaling distress from Protestant ramparts. For fifteen years I had followed men and women in their odyssey of faith off the beaten Protestant path. Now I was reporting to the churches of my own faith. Reporting to pulpit and pew: Protestantism is being challenged from the right and from the left! Reporting: Many Americans are seeking God outside historic churches! Reporting: Many Protestants are seeking the self-unfoldment of their spiritual lives outside Protestantism! Reporting: Twenty million people have identified themselves with non-Protestant movements since the turn of the century! Reporting: Denominationalism is caught in a pincers movement; we are being challenged by right-wing Roman Catholicism and left-wing Reformation, U.S.A.!

Somewhere along the old Reformation road the traveler, Protestantism, had fallen among thieves who stripped him of his raiment of personal faith and left him half dead. The rightists and the leftists, like a certain Samaritan, had come upon him where he lay and insisted on taking him to their own shelters of faith. But I contended that the wounded traveler had enough vitality to reclaim his lost possessions and challenge the thieves themselves. I could not agree with his complaining wails of self-defeat and self-criticism; I shuddered at his constant lamentation, "Protestantism is dying!"

Yet, my journey up Church Street had yielded evidence to support the distressing claims I had often heard: "During the last fifty years Protestantism has been steadily losing ground." ..."The church is no longer a strong institution, pulsing with life and vigor." Many men and women were hopelessly floundering in confusing, ill-defined beliefs, listening hopefully for an authoritarian voice from Protestant pulpits. Many ministers looked down over congregations spotted with empty pews; loss of personal devotion characterized the laity. Everywhere the church program was carrying on, but personal faith had grown sluggish and phlegmatic. There were no plans or techniques for digging into the deep mines of the spiritual life. Church attendance records were not accurate indicators of religious loyalties because they also charted the effect of the seasons on churchgoing Protestants and measured the strength of a people's religious habits.

But even as I joined in the recurring plaint on Protestant faults and weaknesses, I proudly acknowledged the sustaining merits of the Protestant way. The imperial boasts and emblazoned testimonials of the contemporary groups and the Church of Rome had not overawed me into a delusion that my own faith was impotent. Though many Protestants had deserted the historic landmarks, turning to the right and to the left for a more meaningful faith, eighty million American believers had remained passively secure in the denominational homes that had sheltered their childhood and youth. For them there was no abandonment to defeat at the hands of either an ancient or a modern religious movement. To them the twenty-million loss was irrelevant.

Across the nation I had heard a confident pronouncement:

Historic Protestantism will continue to dominate Church Street just as it has since the birth of American freedom. In this confidence I saw a potential force as powerful and pervading as the discoveries I had made among new reformation groups and within Roman Catholicism.

This realization was shaped into a final conviction about Protestantism when my itinerary took me back to the fertile acres of my long-abandoned country parish. Depression, war, prosperity, and a disrupted postwar world had failed to alter the religious pattern of Fairfield. The two churches I had tried to unite still stood on their old corners, separated by the dusty gravel road. The two congregations gathered for the Sunday services just as they had for nearly a century. Baptist cars and Evangelical cars stuck their noses snugly up against their sectarian Sunday homes just as horse-drawn surreys and wagons had in earlier years. North of town the church-with-the-cross-on-the-top stood solid and unshaken, looking out across the Catholic acres. Behind the sheltering windbreak and the picket fence, the Lutherans clung jealously to unchanging Lutheran teachings.

At the edge of the meadow where Brother Saunders' tent once stood, the Church of God had built a small assembly hall, a brown brick-veneer structure that had a sense of "belonging." The old notion that the Pentecostals were religious fanatics had mellowed. Their loud amens and hallelujahs had calmed; the gusts of revival came in only with out-of-town evangelists. Mrs. Willard Duncan still drove her car to Christian Science services out of town. "She goes on Wednesdays, too," I was informed, "and often she takes some friends along." And whenever she had finished reading her *Christian Science Monitor,* she passed it around among the neighbors. It always found its way to the home of the high-school principal, who had not joined a Fairfield church though he had been in town for nearly two years. Every Saturday afternoon a Jehovah's Witness parked his trailer at the edge of the village. Then he and his wife and a thirteen-year-old girl took their places on the three street corners. With canvas bags flung over their shoulders and copies of the *Watchtower* and *Consolation* in their hands, they warned Saturday shoppers and farmers and heckling Kansas blades: "The Kingdom is at hand!"

This was the divided world I had fled because it refused to respond to my visionary efforts toward church union. But religion in Fairfield had gone on under its own credentials just as it did everywhere. After adventuring among America's religious zealots, I knew that merging the Evangelical and Baptist churches was as unimportant as it was impractical. I could no longer justify my escape from denominational toil by recalling my loyalty to a martyred ideal. Fleeing the invaded ranks of my divided parish had been an admission of failure. I had actually fled from the tired, unsatisfied quest of my people. Though Fairfield's Evangelicals did not manifest cultlike zeal and enthusiasm, though they did not boast of mighty miracles through contact with the power of God, they were loyally perpetuating the spiritual succession of the Protestant faith. Quietly within the human heart, religion was giving stability and direction to their daily lives. Though there were no spectacular conversions, no street-corner witnesses, no prescribed affirmations, no designated quiet times, no God-intoxicated devotees in this congregation, there were unquestionable faith and devotion.

These people had been without leadership for many months after I had deserted them. Then their loyalty had been tested by a year of uncertain supply preaching, followed by two two-year pastorates before they found "just the right man." Ministers had continued to come and go out of Fairfield. Through leadership good or bad and without leadership, the old church had survived, though I had chanted my threnody over it when I drove away bitter and confused. I had sung my dirge for the Baptists, too. But fifteen years later both churches still stood defiant and confident on their corners. They would never be great churches, but they had an endowment of life which I in my youthful ministry had never properly assayed.

As I visited again with my parishioners and worshiped with them in the little white-steepled church, I realized that Fairfield was still mirroring the world. Ever since my return to Protestantism with my report, I had been finding undeniable traces of dynamic spiritual life within the churches. The vital personal quest which was the essence of the movements I had investigated was also present among the people of my religion.

Small isolated islands of vital, usable faith jutted up out of the complacent waters of the divided Protestant streams. In a large city church a business executive was addressing laymen about the application of Christian principles in corporation affairs. He was a Presbyterian who had never read Unity prosperity thoughts in *Good Business*. A minister in Chicago made regular visits to the city hospitals, leaving with each patient a handwritten affirmation about the therapeutic power of faith. He was not inspired by Mrs. Eddy's *Key to the Scriptures* or Robinson's lessons on the God-Power; he was a member of the Congregational-Christian fellowship. A Lutheran pastor announced that members of his congregation had requested him to institute a daily noontime prayer circle, like Buchman's quiet time for tuning in on God.

Major denominations were planning laymen movements designed to provide the individual with a working program for the religious life. A Methodist minister in a university town had built up church attendance from four hundred to over two thousand in four years. He used affirmations in his services and urged his people to come to him for spiritual counsel. A country church boasted a congregation of eight hundred at regularly scheduled morning and evening services. Within the democratic Protestant tradition, man was free to seek the highest experience possible of attainment or ιo fashion his religion into as mundane an adventure as he wished.

Looking farther, I discovered other manifestations of inherent Protestant strength; men and women were making religion a personal adventure. From Protestant precincts came the scattered votes for the creed that launched the new reformation: the prayer that saves the sinner heals the sick. The president of a Sunday-school class told his story: "One of our teachers, a grocery-store clerk, was stricken with paralysis. The members of our class decided we would begin systematic prayer for his recovery. Few of us had ever really prayed earnestly, I suppose, at least not together as a group. Now we began putting aside special times for praying. We prayed for him in our class periods, too. Out of this came a feeling of real power and compassion, and we knew that our prayers would be answered. They were, and there is no doubt in my mind that God does heal if we really earnestly seek His help."

The testimony of this member of the Baptist Church was corroborated by a girl of the Evangelical-Reformed denomination. With the enthusiasm of a cultist she said, "God is as near to me as any friend. And when I run up against a problem that I can't whip, I always go to Him. I needed Him a few weeks ago. My boy friend was taken to the sanitarium, and the doctors said that they would have to remove a rib to collapse the lung. My roommate and I started praying. We got down on our knees and we prayed our hearts out. It's not just saying words; it's a feeling and a something you can't explain. Anyway, we prayed. The very next morning when the doctors came in to examine John, they said, 'It's wonderful what's happened to this fellow. No surgery will be needed in this case.' "

When I visited John in the sanitarium, he said, "Well, that's the way it is. Who knows about these things?"

My list of "authenticated" Protestant healings was becoming impressive. In a Methodist home the father's critical heart condition disappeared when prayers of faith were prayed. In another Methodist family prayer was helping a boy recover from a gunshot wound. In a Lutheran home the young wife was recovering from poliomyelitis through prayer treatments. The sick calls of a progressive city pastor were "more than pastoral visits." He was bringing his parishioners "the healing power of God through a well-developed spiritual therapy."

From scattered Protestant pulpits I heard a new definition of salvation: "deliverance from cross-bearing—heaven here and now—through personality adjustments."

A sallow-faced boy of fourteen presented his evidence: "I am a stutterer, but I have learned that if I pray real hard according to a plan I have developed, when I get up to speak, I don't stutter!" This young Presbyterian had never met a Christian Science practitioner.

The story of Ivan the barber was just as provocative. He and his wife had lived for four years in a little boxcarlike house near the river flats. Their garden plot was flooded out every spring, and their cow and pigs were lean and hungry-looking. Ivan was often seen at the local taverns. Then he got religion and started "making good." Beer money went for home improvements. Soon he owned the barber shop. Chairs were added as his business grew. Then came the chance to buy an auto-supply store.

"Doggonit!" he exclaimed during our interview. "I wish I'd started working with the Lord as my partner twenty years ago instead of five. Do you know, last month I cleared over a thousand dollars!"

"You give the Lord all the credit?" I asked.

"Why not?" He laughed. "Though I've done my part. The minute I got religion I started tithing. A penny out of every dime and a dime out of every dollar went into the heavenly treasury. If you ever know any place where I can put a little money to help the religious life along, let me know. But it's more than just making money. Giving God a tenth puts your whole life in tune."

"What's your denomination?"

"Methodist."

I interviewed other Protestants who were tithing their way to prosperity, happily doing business in partnership with God. A Methodist car dealer signed his religious contribution checks: "Treasurer of the Lord's money." A tenth of his income went into a special bank account which he referred to as the "Lord's side of the ledger." A member of the Disciples of Christ spoke proudly about getting three raises in salary since he started tithing two years before. The manager of a gift shop reported: "The windows of heaven have been opened upon me since I started bringing my tenth to the Lord's storehouse."

Protestants experimenting with spiritual techniques had restored a tremendous vitality to their faith. Religion had become the corrective measure for life's manifold ills. Healing, social and economic adjustment were becoming a part of a modern redemptive plan. But the question of eternal salvation remained the heartbeat of the Christian faith.

"How can I be saved?" Alvin Kramer, a university student, asked.

"Believe on the Lord Jesus Christ," he was advised.

"But how can I know I am saved?"

He was instructed to pray. He was urged to make it a daily practice to pray. He did, and a time came when he could say, "By the testimony of personal experience I know that I belong to God and God to me."

Alvin was not a Catholic student. His conversion did not take place in a Catholic church. He had no rosary, but he had his prayers. He had no priest, but his pastor joined him in his daily hour of seeking. He was not required to make confession to the minister, but he made it. He was a Baptist and he found what he wanted without going a single step out of his own denominational path.

Someone should mount the citadel of Church Street and cry out to all weary, wandering Protestants: "Don't go away! It's happening here, too!" Though lost among two hundred thousand congregations and eighty million church members, these "miracles" supported my contention that an indomitable force lay dormant in Protestant life. No single denomination or group had a monopoly on the spirit of God. No one held an exclusive franchise on the highway that led to all-there-is-to-know about the spiritual quest. There was nothing in the new religious groups nor in old Catholicism, there was nothing in any religious movement anywhere which could not be found in Protestantism if a man would but look for it and work to attain it. He could find God on church corners old and new, in cathedral and adobe *morada,* in gospel hall and tabernacle, in revival tent and in the church-with-the-cross-on-the-top. He could find God in Protestantism's multiplicity.

Wherever the slightest adventure was undertaken, static religion was converted into spiritual self-realization. Every true faith was the hub of the everlasting truth, poignantly phrased by the One who said, "The kingdom of God is within you." This was the big idea behind the priesthood of believers and the infallible Book. The individual was more important than the Church or the priest, more important than the denominational creed or the preacher. Out of this concept Protestantism was born. It had always specialized in man's right to find God in his own way.

But somewhere along the old Reformation road the traveler, Protestantism, *had* fallen among thieves who stripped him of his raiment of personal faith and left him half dead. Evidences of vitality were far too infrequent. "Miracles" and "changed lives" were too isolated. Less than half of the eighty million church members were found at Sunday-morning worship hours. The divine imperative of the democratic faith had defeated its own purpose by assuming that its followers would take complete advantage of the privilege of finding God for themselves. No totalitarian edicts, no authoritarian commands, no dictatorial compulsion—this was the strength and the weakness of the Protestant democracy. The unhindered pursuit of truth had gone remiss. Too often freedom to search had become license to give up searching.

The challenge confronting the pulpit was obvious: to provide personal spiritual directives for the people in the pew. The individual had been lost in Protestantism's exemplary world outlook. The far horizons of the social gospel had thrown him out of perspective. The unending cycle of institutionalized religion, conferences, councils, and movements had overlooked the spiritual worth of the average churchgoer. He was waiting for organizational activity to be scaled to his personal needs.

Into this dilemma came the challenge of Roman Catholicism and Reformation, U.S.A. Their big machinery did not devour the individual. Their leaders did not forget him. Their plans for global salvation did not rob him of the certainty that his salvation was their first concern. The individual Catholic everywhere believed that Mother Church had been established for him and that in the process of salvation he had to participate in prescribed acts with a contrite heart. The faith of the contemporary groups had also come to life in a brilliance of personalized glory: "God is your God. God answers your prayer if you but learn how to pray. Come into a complete consciousness of that truth and your life will be transformed now. Here is security. Here are health, freedom, wealth, adjustment to all of life's exigencies, rules for life's games, answers for life's questions, power for life's problems, peace for life's unrest, hope for life's despair."

My years of research had engraved a conviction immutably upon my heart. Though isolated Protestants were finding spiritual power, though churches here and there were completely serving their people, though laymen's movements were stressing a "new evangelism," though Protestantism had unlimited possibilities within the framework of its democratic nature, one great truth needed to be re-emphasized and restated: The strength of the Christian faith is in the individual, and faith demands personal work.

Overlooking and ignoring this ideal had been the fatal error of my Fairfield pastorate. In my anxiety about church union, I had by-passed the spiritual quest of my people. Vividly I recalled the night when Larry Tyler and I had enthusiastically called together the members of our two church boards. We had planned and prayed. We had typed out proposals that would revolutionize Fairfield's Protestantism. I set seventeen chairs in a single circle in the parsonage room—eight for the Evangelicals and nine for the Baptists. Larry Tyler and I were pioneering ecumenicalists, sure that church union was the new religious order for Fairfield. Larry's prayer resounded across the years: "Behold how good and how pleasant it is for brethren to dwell together in unity—thou knowest the spiritual needs of our community, O Lord——" I was Ezekiel, feeling the hot breath of Jehovah, gathering together the broken sticks, binding into one that which was divided. "There are three ways in which our churches can get together, gentlemen." Shuffling feet and uneasy movements, nervous glances, and a moment of intense waiting. Then the Baptist banker was on his feet, stamping into my dream, shattering my hopes with a cry: "Why shouldn't there be denominations? Lots of them." Then the long, lean figure of the cattleman, holding back the everlasting Kansas wind, stopping the hopeful march toward one church for Fairfield: "Maybe when we are the best Evangelicals we can be and the Baptists are the best Baptists they can be, when every man is the best Christian he can be according to the light he has, union will come about automatically."

Fifteen years had passed and the chairs were being set again but not in a country manse. Once more Protestant delegates were meeting, but not from two churches separated by a narrow gravel road. Representatives of the entire non-Roman Christian world were gathering at Amsterdam, Holland. The call for world-wide Christian union was being answered by more than a hundred and twenty church bodies. Four hundred and fifty laymen and clergymen were the official delegates to a World Assembly, which was the consummation of a long line of ecumenical conferences: Edinburgh in 1910, Stockholm in 1925, Lausanne in 1927, Jerusalem in 1928, Oxford and Edinburgh in 1937, Madras in 1938. The visionary ideal of a united Protestantism which I had pursued in Fairfield was assuming reality. The Amsterdam Assembly was an organizational meeting, setting up a permanent World Council of Churches. The scattered Christian flock was gathering under the messianic prayer, "That they may all be one." The divided families—Lutheranism, the Baptist faith, the Reformed, the Presbyterian faith, Anglicanism, Congregationalism, the Quakers, the Church of the Brethren, the Moravians, the Methodists—were coming home.

Hopes ran high for extraordinary success. From the delegates came the announcement that the barriers separating denominations were breaking, differences were being resolved, elements of division were being recognized as delusions. Protestantism was entering the ecumenical century. The gospel of fellowship was rapidly writing the text for a new era of faith. The enthusiasm of preview pronouncements took me back to my premature hopes for a local miracle of merger: "This is one of the greatest steps forward that the churches have ever taken.". . ."It is the logical way to meet the mighty strength of evil and to show that God is far greater than these terrible forces.". . ."Help remake this shattered earth by sponsoring an unknown delegate to one of the greatest Assizes of our God."

My Fairfield evangel returned in the prophetic voice of the world-famous missionary, E. Stanley Jones: "When the representatives of one hundred and twenty churches come together in Holland to form the First World Assembly, the stage is set for another possible Pentecost. At the first Pentecost, the number was one hundred and twenty individuals; here there will be one hundred and twenty churches. If the Spirit of unity and power falls upon that assembly, we can expect a new burst of regenerating and quickening power throughout the world. This gathering in Holland has untold possibilities if, like the first gathering of the Disciples in the Upper Room, they will wait for God's power and God's leading."

This should be Fairfield's hour. The World Assembly was soliciting the wholehearted interest and the vigorous participation of local congregations. But somehow, for the Protestant in the pew, ecumenicalism was a difficult and a foreign word. The eager haste of regimentation against a rising secularism did not arouse the average churchgoer. The ancient banner of one Lord, one Faith, one Baptism did not bring him to his feet in cheers. He wanted to know how far Amsterdam was from Fairfield. How far was Amsterdam from the heart of the Christian who walked to worship on his church corner everywhere in the world?

Anxiously I reviewed the World Assembly literature and communicated with the leaders. The task confronting the Amsterdam meeting was fourfold: to complete the formation of the World Council of Churches; to assess Christianity's resources, handicaps, and problems; to establish basic principles for Christion community; to submit to the churches "a message both centrally Christian and immediately relevant to the needs, the questions, and the burdens of men today." Amsterdam was building upon the urgency of a challenging theme: Man's Disorder and God's Design. Study Commissions had been created to break this theme down into workable units. Commission number one had pledged itself to define the Church in terms of its genius as a divine and human institution. Commission number two was designed to point the way to better methods of reaching "the vast un-Christian majority which surrounds the Christian community." The third commission was making a study of the relationship of Church and Government. Commission number four was tackling the international problems of a de-Christianized world.

Where was Amsterdam's interest in the people of Fairfield? Where was the message for the cattleman and the banker and the farmer and the businessman? Was this Assembly ashamed of the utmost simplicity of the Christian faith? Had the Commissions not discovered that Protestant power lay dormant in the hearts of Protestant believers? The real Protestantism is the individual. The real Protestant leader is the local minister who has become the spiritual good neighbor to the people of his parish. Fairfield's problem was the problem of Protestantism and Fairfield's answer was Protestantism's answer. The cattle-man again took the floor. "Maybe when we are the best Evangelicals we can be and the Baptists are the best Baptists they can be, when every man is the best Christian he can be according to the light he has, union will come about automatically."

I had traveled fifteen years only to agree that the personal religious life must come first in any Protestant plan to fathom the inexhaustible power of faith. If the leaders of the World Assembly failed to challenge the individual to demonstrate the great potential within himself, they would declare unity with their lips but retain plurality in their mission. The essential attribute, the heart, the core of ecumenicalism, rested within the man and woman in the pew.

Then on the Amsterdam roster I spied the name of a long-time friend. Elmer G. Homrighausen, noted interpreter of Protestantism, able theologian, and member of the Princeton staff, was Secretary for Evangelism of the Department of Reconstruction and Inter-Church Aid. For information on the Assembly's "personal program" he was the man to consult.

Long distance gave me the overseas operator and I called the European headquarters of the World Council of Churches. Quickly the magic of communication facilities spanned the distance that separated Fairfield from Amsterdam. The geographical boundaries melted away. The great breaches between a small-town parish and a world assembly dissolved.

"Hello . . . hello," said the voice. "Who is calling?"

When I told him, he laughed and asked, "Where have you been all these years?"

"I've been researching in religion, but right now I'm wondering about Amsterdam."

"Amsterdam!" he repeated, and there was a thrill in his voice and great expectation in his words. "It's the thing we've been waiting for and working for. It is a progressive step ahead. The Christian world uniting—taking counsel together—pooling our spiritual resources——"

"I know," I answered impatiently. "But while the challenge at Amsterdam is union, the challenge here at home is a personal spiritualized faith. While ecumenicalism is winning the miracle of a united church, isn't there a danger that we may lose the battle for powerful religion in the Protestant rank and file?"

"Yes, we recognize that," he assured me. "The great emphasis, the real, driving force must come from the grass roots. Can you hear me? From the grass roots. The ecumenical movement is inextricably bound up with the individual worshiper. The degree to which we succeed depends on the vigorous spiritual co-operation of every Christian everywhere in the world."

"That's right," I agreed. "But there's something more. I'm sending you the report of my research. Please find a place for this among the many reports that will be flooding the assembly from all over the world. I think it is tremendously important. More important than the material and political conditions affecting religious life. There should be a Commission on techniques and directives for Christian living. Individual Protestants need this desperately."

"The churches have their own programs——" he began.

"I know," I interrupted, "but the need for tapping the power within the individual is so great that it must be included in the Assembly's program. The true ecumenicalism must be undergirded by the ecumenicity of spirit——"

He was agreeing and suddenly a vision of Protestantism's greatness was woven into our conversation. Amsterdam and Fairfield stood together on the heights of a mighty awareness.

The confused denominational streams were flowing into the mighty ocean of a united faith, and the powerful tributaries of individual lives were feeding those streams with vitality.

But as I hung up the receiver, I knew there was no hope for an easy miracle. The reality of Protestantism with its weakness, its need, its vision, and its great potential lay within the eighty million men and women who had not been listening in. Very few leaders and even fewer churchgoers knew what was happening to religion in their time. At the top ecumenical leaders must plan the strategy to conquer a growing secularism and to bring God's design into a disordered universe; on the parish level the individual Protestant must embark on the high adventure of an unlimited personal faith. This was the final challenge, and with it I continued up Church Street, taking my report to the preacher in the pulpit and the people in the pew.

THE END